Sarah Pat O'Brien was born in Dublin in 1942. She moved to England at the age of 14 and married at 18. She pursued an interest in politics, managing a small housing and community team and becoming Chair of Nalgo Housing Stewards and Assistant Branch Secretary. Writing in her spare time, in 1992 she won the Irish Post Award for Journalism. Sarah Pat O'Brien has three sons and two grandchildren and lives in Kent.

Rooms of Dust

The Search for My Father

SARAH PAT O'BRIEN

POCKET
BOOKS

LONDON · NEW YORK · SYDNEY · TORONTO

First published in Great Britain and Ireland by Pocket Books, 2005
An imprint of Simon & Schuster UK Ltd
A Viacom company

1 3 5 7 9 10 8 6 4 2

Simon & Schuster UK Ltd
Africa House
64–78 Kingsway
London WC2B 6AH

www.simonsays.co.uk

Simon & Schuster Australia
Sydney

A CIP catalogue record for this book is available from the British Library

ISBN 1-4165-0255-6
EAN 9781416502555

Typeset by SX Composing DTP, Rayleigh, Essex
Printed and bound in Great Britain by
Bookmarque Ltd, Croydon, Surrey

In memory of Mary and James Colgan,
my dear Granny and Grandilla

Introduction

This story began to write itself twenty years ago, when people from my youthful life insisted on visiting me. In dreams they came, not as ghosts, but as they were, that time, in those Dublin houses, fifty years ago. On waking, I scribbled down lines to hold the immediacy of their nocturnal visits. Shiny Grandilla. Granny with her troubled feet and generous heart. Droopy Mr Grogan in his left-hand parlour. Moll in her jet-studded hat. Uncle Paddy, the Sun God. Auntie May and picnics in the Up and Up Park. These lines, written from a place between this world and that, in the half-light of early mornings, grew, effortlessly it seemed, into stories for my own delight.

As they grew, striding through the pages, came the central character, insistent, belligerent, demanding his mention. He never came with the others. Always alone: a cold draught in an empty room. A wraith. And so, I could not write him out, but I could not write him in. How could I? I knew so little about him, my absent father, Patrick Francis O'Brien, dead too, though I did not know it then.

He left us in Dublin when I was not yet three and Joan was five. I made do with second-hand memories of him, some offered without asking, most grudgingly given, nearly all bad. He became a blot obscuring everything, looking over my shoulder, or waiting on some distant corner only to vanish when I reached him.

I was unaware that he had been laying a paper trail for me, beginning with the poems he left in the vaults of a Dublin church. This trail led me across the country and across the water, backward and forward in time, until I had enough pieces of paper to open a file. It grew fat with his fecklessness and lies. The more the file filled with facts enough to hang him, were he still alive, the more elusive he became. Facts could not compensate for the sound of his voice, or the tilt of his head. I wanted to hold a pen of his or read a favourite book. I wanted more than anything to discover the essence of the man who was my father, so that I might be the writer I was meant to be as well as the person. Most of all, I realise, I wanted to exorcise the anger his desertion implanted in me, deep. So deep, I did not know, until the exorcism began.

Part 1

Ten Green Bottles

One

Morning sunshine wakes me early. I lie still, watching dust dancing in the light, recalling another room long ago and a day full of shifting, shimmering, dancing dust. People, my mother and my father, kept walking through the particles, disturbing them, making them dance in a different way. When the dust finally settled and my father had gone, we became no more than dust: drifting, rising, falling, blowing in and out of rooms, other people's lives, other people's houses. Other people's country.

I rise, aware that the day ahead is part of my own dust settling at last. I have been floating in it for over half a century. Downstairs, I open the door and let the summer in. They are coming at noon. High noon.

'We'll come to lunch, if that's all right?' Gerry, Sean's partner, had said.

I walk into the garden with my coffee to reflect on my long and laborious search for my father. I am a small girl again searching the faces of dark-haired men on the streets of Dublin. I am a young immigrant looking for him at railway

5

stations and along the lonely winding roads of London. I am forty-five, sitting in a bar in Limerick, talking of him with old men, buying them pints to listen to their lies. I am looking through records, running up and down blind alleys, making small discoveries, piecing them together with long-remembered crumbs swept from the tables of other people's recollections. I am making pilgrimages.

One pilgrimage takes me to Hull, in the summer of 1989 and, at last, I stand outside my father's house. It adjoins the house where the poet Philip Larkin once lived in his high-windowed flat near the university. The house is large with the ugliness of the self-important merchant classes. What it lacks in elegance, it makes up for in size. I imagine my father living in the house, taking strolls around the park and crossing to the seat near the duck pond on fine days. He was a poet too, my father, and he is no longer in the house. He is dead. He died eight years before I found him.

And so my second search begins, not for the man any more, but for relics of his existence, so that I may verify my own. I start next door, with the man in Philip Larkin's house.

'Yes, I remember your father,' he says, all the while inspecting my face. 'He was a bit aloof. Kind of quiet, though his wife was friendly enough. There was a son too. They gave him his own flat there in the house. A student. A clever fellow.'

In the main library in Hull, my father's extinction and his son's existence are confirmed in the death notices in the local paper, placed by a woman describing herself as 'wife of the deceased'. She paid tribute to a dearest husband and beloved and devoted father of Sean. I am drowning in my father's stated devotion, suffocating with rage at how hollow it is for me. And as I am drowning, my past swims into my heightened awareness, causing me to feel the pain of abandonment again, dragging me down to those old familiar depths of darkness.

In another library, in the archive of a Dublin church, a few years later, I sit at an ancient table and read my father's poems. He is speaking to me at last, adult to adult. We are not equal, because he is my prisoner and I am his judge. Each word I read is a length of the noose I am using to hang him with. His words deceive and weave the suggestion of a heart that never existed. The room I am in smells of stale lavender cloying on slow-decaying flesh. I shiver as I feel his dead man's fingers prodding me from the grave, pushing me onward with my search for the truth of him that I do not find in his words.

There are thirteen poems in all, his only legacy to me, the one who found them. In 'The School Bell', written in the year I was born, I read:

> Truth must nurse
> The seed of learning
> As sapling
> Grown with tender care
> Make bulwark
> From life's rough fare.

I laugh aloud. His own actions and consequent events denounce him as a hypocrite and a liar.

7

A few years later, his finger prods me again, causing my heart to miss a beat. I am reading the *Sunday Times*, a review by a poet called Sean O'Brien. As well as the poetry he reviews, he mentions his own publication of essays on contemporary British and Irish poetry. I read the review again, searching for clues. Could he possibly be the beloved son as he had become in my mind – the son of the 'beloved father'?

'It is more than possible,' I say, as if echoing someone else's affirmation.

Browsing in a bookshop weeks later, I pick Sean O'Brien's book of essays from a shelf. I remember the *Sunday Times* review and turn the pages, feeling faint, trying to remain in control.

As I read, my half-brother speaks to me, just as my father had spoken to me in his poems. There are no clues to tell me so, apart from the name and my absolute conviction that he is my father's son. I am alone with my miracle. There is just a presence unseen and a finger placed firmly on my spine.

Eventually, I wrote the letter, apologising for any offence. Almost apologising for my own existence, for being a blot on his personal landscape, telling him small things, mere scraps to prove the truth.

And that is how, this morning, I sit in my garden, sipping cold coffee and wait for Sean O'Brien, poet and beloved son, to arrive for a very special lunch. The lunch of a lifetime, with the life and times of Patrick Francis O'Brien, poet, soldier, boxer, father, to discuss. Are Sean and I alike in any way? Is there a common thread connecting us to our ancestors? Are their traits surviving in us, shining through our differences of location and upbringing? Sean, an 'only' son, well-loved and brought up in middle-class comfort in London and Hull. Joan and I, abandoned daughters, brought up by aged and impoverished grandparents, aunts and a distracted mother in Dublin, a beautiful and gracious city, dominated by religion and recovery from occupation.

Is he remembering his childhood as he travels to meet me, sifting his recollections for the experiences that shaped him, as I am doing now? Is he examining his reality and separating it from truth? Will he be warm and open with me, or closed and defensive? What will I tell him? Will I tell him a fairy story to make him comfortable, full of romantic half-truths, or will I tell him the unadulterated reality of our loss, forsaken as we were by our mutual father? Will I tell him all this?

Dublin, 1949

The Meanest Cat watches me, keeping me prisoner by the fire. Turf sparks hiss at the kittens in the hearth. At the long table, three women huddle like witches casting spells. Keeping my face straight in case they see that I am ear-wigging, I strain to hear them – my mother, Sally, Mrs Purcell and her sister Bella. These are the times, in Mrs Purcell's underworld, that I learn about my father. From the rooms upstairs, hushes and whisperings drift downwards, filtering through door gaps. Chairs scrape on linoleum and wirelesses play different music for different lives. Where the stairs curve to the top of the house and the room I was born in seven years before, I like to sit and watch the front door. I know that one day my father will walk back through it. In a minute, when the Meanest Cat takes a nap, I will sneak past the women, along the flagged basement, under the pufterings of light from gas mantles and take up my vigil. For now, though, I listen, but the talk is of Billy Monty and not 'that bowsie, Paddy O'Brien', my father.

'I tell you, Sally,' Mrs Purcell complains to Mam, 'the mattress was alive with everything that creeps and crawls. It nearly stood up on its own and walked downstairs itself when he left. I'm telling you!'

'More's the pity it didn't,' the outraged Bella says, her plump bosom pigeoning out under her black velvet frock. 'I had to drag it downstairs myself and right through to the back to throw it on the nettles.'

I want to giggle at the thought of the regal Bella dragging a festering mattress through the house, but I know I must respect my elders and betters, so I laugh down the back of my throat.

Mam makes suitable tuts and tsks, hoping to get on to her own woes, which inevitably are caused by my father, but Mrs Purcell still has more to say about Billy Monty.

'As God is my judge, Sally, I'll never let a room to a man on his own again, after my experiences, apart from Mr Grogan, of course. He's a lamb, a sweetheart. It's women on their own from now on. Single women. Though they'll have to be older. I want no strange men coming and going. And couples. God knows, as you do, Sally, I don't mind couples. Or children.' As she speaks, Mrs Purcell's face rises and falls like a drum beat. Her tiny head nodding and shaking, then resting again on the faded moquette, earrings still shaking as they dangle.

'Indeed I do know, Mrs P. I'll never forget how good you were to me when I was going through my troubles. I don't know how I'd have managed if it hadn't been for your kindnesses. Right up till the day we left. I'll never forget it.' Mam has a different voice when she speaks of her troubles. It is a trick only she can do. It goes higher, but is low and soft at the same time. It's an amazing trick, because people have to listen to her without interrupting.

'Aw, sure I only did what any woman would do for another, Sally. I couldn't stand aside and listen to him and his antics.'

'You saved me from many a beating all the same.' Mam's voice begins to break and she bends her head, her dark hair hiding her face.

I get up quickly. I don't want to hear any more. I hate it when she talks about the beatings. About the leather buckled belt. And the raised voices in the dust.

As I pass the front door on my way to my watchtower, it opens, making me jump. In comes Mr Grogan. He turns and shakes the rain off his black umbrella out onto the steps.

'Is that Patty O'Brien I spy behind me?'

'Yes, Mr Grogan. I'm just waiting for Mam.'

He supports me in my lie. He knows it is my father whom I wait for on the stairs.

'Now, what I need at this minute is a cup of tea, a ginger biscuit and some kind girl to share it with me. Do you think you could manage that?'

I have no doubt at all that I can.

I follow him into his left-hand parlour. Heaven on earth. I sit on a stuffed armchair amongst his piles of dusty books and watch him while he moves about, hanging his wet coat on a hanger, changing his shoes for old slippers, lighting his pipe. He draws his green velvet curtains against the four o'clock dank clinging to Mountpleasant Square. He is a droopy man, in back and in moustache, and he is slow moving. If he were a woman he'd be called Patience. It seems such a waste that he has no children and Joan and me have no dad. Well, not here with us.

It is difficult when you don't know where your father is. If you tell a lie about it, you have to remember exactly what you've said. It's no good telling one girl that your dad is Ray Milland and he's busy making films at the moment, then telling another one that he's down on his farm in Limerick and just can't get up to Dublin until the rush is over.

'So where's Joan today?' Mr Grogan is doing his usual while he talks: moving, clearing clutter, banking up the fire with turf stacks.

'She's in hospital. The fever hospital. She has scarlet fever.'

'This bloody country. Its children are either sick, dying or emigrating. I suppose you'll be sick next. Or gone. Gone with the rest of them to America or England.'

His chair finally cleared, he sits opposite me and hands me a mug. I keep my eyes cast down in case I am invited to say

12

something to start him off again. All the grown-ups I know do that. They ask a question and whatever the answer, they get angry and talk about things I never did, making me feel I did them. In silence, we sip our tea and dip our biscuits in the mugs politely. Mr Grogan and my Grandilla like politeness.

The clock ticks. At five o'clock it chimes notes wrapped in cushioned velvet and they are late to leave the room, unlike the harsh clang of the clock on Rathmines Town Hall. Everything in Mr Grogan's room seems cushioned in velvet. There are no rough edges in it. I imagine all the rooms in heaven are the same. 'In my father's house there are many mansions.' I do not know how many mansions there are in my father's house, because I do not know where it is, but I know it is full of rooms like this one. Maybe Mr Grogan knows where it is and what it is like.

'Do you think my dad has a clock like that?'

'I'm certain he has. He used to come in here and sit just where you're sitting when you lived in the room opposite.' He indicates towards the right-hand parlour.

For some reason, I want to cry. I won't, of course. I hate cry babies. Or women who cry. Like Mam. I can't ask her about anything. Especially not clocks or my dad. His name is forbidden, a sin she has invented just for Joan and me. An extra burden on top of all the sins we commit from the second we open our eyes in the mornings. Whatever bad things he did, and he did plenty, in his absence, we are responsible for them. 'The sins of the fathers shall be visited upon the children.'

13

'He had to get out of Ireland quick.' I heard Mam say that at different times. Auntie May, Mam's older sister, once said, 'Whatever he did, it must have been bloody serious. Why else would a man sell every stick of furniture, leaving his small family with nothing, not even a roof over their heads?'

Mr Grogan might know.

'Was my dad a crook?'

He starts to laugh. Then he can't stop. I laugh too, feeling great.

'God bless us and save us, Patty O'Brien, but you're a card. Your dad was no better nor worse than any of us. He was hemmed in. That's what he was. Hemmed in. He had to get away.'

I like the sound of 'hemmed in'. It means that my dad has such a lot to do and the world itself is not big enough for him to do it in.

'Do you think when he's done all he has to do, he'll come home?'

'He might. He might not. Who can say? Sure you'll have things to do yourself before long. Things that will take you away from home. You might go too and never come back. We Irish have a habit of doing that, you know.'

'Well, I always come back here to this house, even though we live up in Grandilla's now. I'll always come back.'

I know we will never live here again. Mam would never be able to find the rent of a room from Mrs Purcell. I heard her say once that she offered to do the cleaning in part payment, but then that would have done Bella out of a job. And her room down in the basement. And, of course, Mrs Purcell

14

could not be expected to mind Joan and me while Mam is at work. She never had children of her own. 'No,' Mrs Purcell told Mam, 'the best plan all round is with the grandparents. The granny is there in the house all day to mind them and what little you get in the laundry goes on the girls, not on rent and electricity. That's the best plan.'

The best plan, as I see it, is to have a dad. The second best plan is to have a dead dad. A dead dad has no choice. God would have taken him away from us. People would still pity us, but in a respectful way. Nice things would be said about him and about us. People would say to Mam, 'God bless her, hasn't Patty got her father's eyes?' And Mam would smile. 'Yes, she's the image of her father. He was a lovely man.'

Instead, she only tells us we are like him when she is cross with us. 'You're just like your bloody father. He didn't want you and I'm stuck with you. When he left, the priest told me to put you into Goldenbridge Convent. I wish I had. I'm sick and tired working my fingers to the bone morning, noon and night. And for what? Tell me that, if you can? For what? For nothing else but worry and trouble.'

There is a third plan. Mam could give us away to a nice mother and father in the country. She might part with me, I realise, but not with Joan, and as long as she keeps Joan, I suppose she may as well keep me. Anyway, it's her mother and father, Granny and Grandilla, who are really keeping us. They wouldn't give us away. Would they?

'Penny for them, Patty,' Mr Grogan asks.

'I was just thinking what it would be like to have a real house and a real mother and father. That's all.' I shrug.

Suddenly, Mr Grogan stands and moves to the window, nodding to me to join him. He places an arm around my shoulder and raises his other arm to draw back the curtains. Rain washes the long window. He points beyond it to where the trees are swaying behind the railings of the tennis court gardens. Pale lights from the lamps cast beams along the curving path and a man with a small dog passes by. He is holding an umbrella in one hand and the dog lead in the other, in no hurry, despite the rain. Nothing to do and all day to do it in.

'Wherever you go, always remember this.' Mr Grogan's voice is a whisper. 'All this. This is the place your father and mother gave you. If they give you nothing else, they have given you more than most of us dream of.'

'I don't know what you mean.'

'They gave you a good place to be born in.' He grasps both my shoulders and leans close to my ear. 'What do you see out there?'

'The Square. And the old houses. The trees. And the tennis court gardens.'

'Do you see a river?'

'No.'

'Just because you can't see one, doesn't mean there isn't one there. Out there, an ancient river used to flow. The Swan River. Its course shaped the roads of Ranelagh and Rathmines and all the battles and happenings around it helped shape the history of Dublin. Of Ireland. It still flows there, though secretly. It flows in the small gullies and channels underground, like the blood flows in the veins beneath your skin. It makes its own course still. It is built upon: tennis courts, roads, houses, gardens, railings, churches.'

He pauses, and I gaze at the beautifully curving Square, where everything seems perfectly placed to please. I marvel at what I cannot see.

'But it is there,' he continues, 'the oul' Swan River, just like all who went before you are there in you. You are connected to them. You are connected to your dad, even though he is not here. His blood flows in you. Some of his dreams are in your head. And when you leave this place and you feel lost, just remember that you are Paddy O'Brien's girl from Swan River, and be thankful.'

'Are you from Swan River too, Mr Grogan?'

'Indeed I'm not. I'm from the back of beyond. Even if you knew where it was, you'd never want to go there.'

Poor Mr Grogan. He has so little and I have so much and neither of us can change anything.

We stand looking out until Mam knocks softly on the door. She opens it and peeps through the gap: 'Come on now, Patty, it's time we went home.'

Later, I will tell her that I was already home.

'Is that the time?' Mr Grogan checks his clock in amazement and beckons Mam into the room.

She is anxious to go, but spares him a few minutes while I run down to the basement for my coat. The Meanest Cat is sitting on it, eyeing me narrowly. He hisses as I try to retrieve it without too much fuss.

Bella comes to my assistance, shooing him off into a dark corner and shaking his hairs off my crumpled coat into the hearth. 'Here you are, dear, you'd better put it on before you go out. It's raining cats and dogs.'

We stand on the time-dipped steps to say our goodbyes to Bella and Mr Grogan. Mrs Purcell never comes to the door. It would mean disturbing the cat lying in her lap. Mam ties her scarf under her chin and pulls her collar up. They wave us to the end of the Square. They are still in the doorway when we turn the corner, as if they always have been and always will be. Waving. Desperately waving us out of sight.

'It's always the same when we visit the Purcell Rooms,' Mam says as we hurry along the Ranelagh Road. 'They'd keep us talking all night if they could. They've nothing better to do with their time, but talk. If they had to work for a living and bring children up, they'd know all about it. They wouldn't keep me beyond what's reasonable.'

'I though you liked them, Mam.'

'I do like them. It's just that it's a one-way street. I always have to make the effort to go there. I can never invite them up the Hill to see me. That's all.'

I know what Mam means. Granny and Grandilla don't like callers. Possibly because they have enough people living in their little house already.

'When I grow up, Mam, I'll buy a house with velvet curtains and chiming clocks on the banks of the Swan River and talk all day.'

'Where the hell is the bloody Swan River?'

'Just here. Under our feet.'

I wait for an answer or another question, but she has already stopped listening.

Two

Mam and I hurry along, heads bent, in the steadily
falling rain, up the Hill into the gloom of Mountpleasant Buildings, across the vast dirt concourse, past the
tenement hallways, each housing nine families. In several,
the street children shelter from the weather, shouting abuse
to each other or singing their lungs out. This part of
Ranelagh, hidden away from the big houses where long
gardens sweep down to elegant roads, is small and mean and
teeming with children – no room for them in their over-
crowded tenement homes. Some families have as many as
fifteen children living in two and three rooms, their only
amenities a cold-water sink, a gas stove and a lavatory.
Winter and summer, morning, noon and night, the younger
inhabitants roam the streets. I love to roam with them.

In the ball alley, a game of handball is nearing an end and
the men crowd around to cheer on their man. I want to
watch.

'Please, Mam.'

But it is not for little girls. Not when they are with their
mother, at least. Turning into Rugby Villas, where it tries
and fails to catch the light, existing always in the shadows of

19

the Buildings, we stop hurrying, though Mam's heels are clip-clipping smartly and I am still running to keep up with her. We pass Kelly's window. Frisco, their mangey cat lies stretched on the sill.

I wave to it. 'Howaya?' I say, thinking it's as well to keep in with it. It's a miserable oul' gouger, who thinks he's still a street fighter. I might not like him – I'm not particular about cats like my sister is, because of the way they stalk freely around Mrs Purcell's house – but the odd wave won't hurt.

'Don't touch that bloody cat. It's lousy, so it is.'

Mam drags me past Maguire's and pushes me in through Granny and Grandilla's front door.

We came here on the day my dad left, when I was three and Joan was five. On that day, the day they think I don't remember, I watched them from the big iron bed where we all slept together, Mam, Dad, Joan and me. That day, Mrs Purcell, wrinkled and bony and smelling of cats, picked me up and took me out of the room so I could not hear them shouting. But I heard them. They woke me up. They woke Joan up too. Sleep was in my eyes with the morning sun. When I rubbed them, the room was full of golden light. The sun was shining in an empty room. Empty except for the bed. And the dust that might have drifted onto the tops of things, like wardrobes and presses and tables, the dust that might have clung to mirrors and pictures, floated like a million starry dots around the room. I tried to catch some, but they floated away.

So did my dad. He floated away on a boat to England. We live here now, the three of us. We have no home any more.

Mam always says so. This is Grandilla's house. He moved here with Granny in 1917, before the Buildings were all built. They moved from the Liberties, with her children and his, some from her first marriage and some from her second one to him. In all, Granny had seventeen children. Mam is the youngest of the living. Granny never speaks about the dead. There was also Gussie, her eldest daughter's illegitimate child, brought up as her own.

When they had all moved into lives of their own making, Auntie May returned to live with Granny and Grandilla, with her four sons, Noel, John, Paddy and Garry. Then Mam returned with Joan and me. I am the twenty-fourth and last child of the household. Last and least. There is nothing I can do that is new.

'I want no arguments from you tonight,' Mam says as we throw our coats on the hall table under the gaze of Cleopatra and her handmaidens, ever watchful, behind the glass. Mam straightens her dark hair and inspects her flushed cheeks in the mirror. 'I want you to get yourself up to bed. And no reading. Do you hear me?'

'Why have I to go to bed early? It's not fair.'

'Because,' she says walking ahead of me into the kitchen, 'I've to go to see Joan in the hospital and I don't want you getting into any trouble while I'm out.'

Auntie May overhears her. 'God help her, Sally, she'll only be lying up there on her own. I'll keep an eye on her and I'll make sure she gets a wash for school in the morning before she goes to bed.'

Garry, her youngest son, is reading his comic. 'Ah, Ma,

that's not fair, I'm older than her. I'm nearly nine. I want to stay up to hear *Perry Mason* on the wireless. You said I could. She'll ruin it, so she will. She'll keep on talking.'

'Well, she can hear it too. And talk at the same time.' Auntie May winks at me.

Grandilla sits at his usual place, reading the *Evening Herald*. He must not be disturbed on any account until he finishes, so we all wait, mice-quiet, for the shaking of the pages and the folding of the paper, before we can sit down to our tea.

The table is set with the long-stemmed sugar bowl and the tin of condensed milk. On the breadboard, a turnover waits to be attacked with the saw knife. A large platter of brawn, scallions and tomatoes is placed near Grandilla, so that he can help himself to the best of it first.

'There,' Granny says, putting his plate before him.

He does not thank her. His 'slavey', that is what she is, or so she says when he's not here. In turn, we are Granny's slaveys, running for her messages all day long. She has been housebound for fifteen years with her bad feet. She is bent, her head hanging forward onto her chest and she is as wide as she is tall, about five foot. 'C'mere for a minute and get me purse. Run over to Priestley's for a bag of sugar. Garry, run down to Lawlor's for half a dozen eggs. Get your hoop. Sure, you won't know you're gone before you're back.'

Once, on a trip back from Lawlor's in Charlemont Street, Garry was running along with the messages bag in one hand, bowling his hoop with the other, when he tripped over a drain. The hoop went one way, he went the other, and the shilling change rolled down the drain hole. 'Bad cess to you, you little cur,' Granny shouted, though we all knew she did not mean it. We knew it was the loss of the money for the next day's dinner that troubled her. She works miracles every day with whatever vegetables and meat or fish she can manage to buy. Nothing is wasted. She somehow makes enough to go round. She bakes brown and white bread every Saturday for the week ahead, but we have devoured it all by Monday. 'A thankless task,' she says.

Grandilla does his own messages on his way home from work in the dispensary in Rathmines. At seventy-four, he needs to work to keep a roof over all our heads. 'A disciplinarian,' Mam says, but only when he's not here. 'An old soldier.'

My dad was a soldier too, but in a different army. I know they were different, but I don't know what the difference is. Grandilla has the idea that his army was better. 'Sure what battles did the Free Staters ever fight, except against their own?'

I stand accused every time he sneers the words, 'Free Stater'. Another word I am mortified by is 'culchie'. That's my dad, a culchie Free Stater. Grandilla never looks at me when he spits his rage. He does not have to.

We eat our tea slowly, Paddy, Garry and me, chewing every mouthful, keeping our mouths closed. We cannot rush, or appear to rush, even if a great game of Relievio* is going on in the Buildings. Bad manners make Grandilla our

* A game of catch-chase with two sides of limitless numbers.

gaoler. We cannot speak either, unless Grandilla asks us a question. We cannot put our elbows on the table, or leave it without asking his permission. And permission is not given until everyone is finished. Usually, Grandilla is last. Mam says it is to spite us. Another thing she only says when he is not here.

After tea, Mam goes out to see Joan in the fever hospital. I hope she doesn't bring her home. Not tonight. There is more room in the bed without her.

The kitchen is steaming and murmuring its noises. The black kettle sings on the hob. Joan was in the bed when I woke this morning and there was blue paper around the light. Mam whispered to me to be quiet and let Joan sleep. She indicated that I should get dressed in the greyness.

'Why is there paper round the light, Mam?'

'Because Joan's eyes have been affected by her illness. You're to be a good girl and you're not to put the light on to read in bed until she's better.'

'What about the lights down here. And outside?'

'They'll be OK. She'll be wearing dark glasses for a while.'

I'm raging. First she gets sick – she's always sick, 'delicate', Mam calls it – then she gets to wear dark glasses. All the kids will think she's great. There are so many of us on the streets with so little to set us apart, any small impediment or handicap is considered a gift. Ann Eccles has a rheumatic heart. We can't see it but she lets us feel it beating. It's brilliant. Another young-one from the Buildings has an iron caliper on her leg. She runs about dragging it behind her and we all stand to watch. She makes out she doesn't notice, but she keeps running past us all the time. And out on Oxford Road there's a boy who's a walking saint. He went to Lourdes on a stretcher and came back upright, swinging his case as he walked off the boat as if it was a paper bag. I can't get as much as a stitch. Half the kids in Dublin have TB and I can't even catch a cold. Health is a terrible thing. You have to go to school.

Mam is getting ready to go to work in the Kelso Laundry. She is already late on account of Joan and if she is more than fifteen minutes late, they will dock her half a crown. If she's later still, she'll be sent home for the day. I can't understand it. If I turn up late at St Louis's Convent in Rathmines, they keep me in. It's no wonder I keep running away from it. I ran away on the day I started and they couldn't get me to go back for six months. There was no one to take me, only Joan and she wasn't even six. I was terrified of the nuns. They swung their rosary beads, or swished them as they walked. Loads of little children were crying and they were being taken out of the line and made to sit on the floor. 'For boiling later,' Grandilla said. I didn't cry but waited my opportunity and when the class marched off one way, I ran the other, out of the front door.

They tried to get me to go back, but I used to scream all the way through Gulistan, so they gave up in the end. It was Grandilla who finally got me through the gates. It would have been impossible to make a holy show of him. He is the smartest grandfather in Dublin, with his long, black, tailored coat over his dark striped suit. His shiny boots, his white hair, perfectly cut to the shape of his head, his clipped moustache. So I went.

I'm going now too. It's the day for polishing the Halla. We polished the corridor and front hall yesterday. Sister Norbert gives us rags to put under our feet and Sister Agony, my teacher, splotches soft white polish from a tin with the end of a ruler. A long line of girls hold hands and wait for the music to start.

'Now!' nods Sister Norbert, and Sister Bernadette bangs on the piano.

'Laavenderrr blue, dilly dilly, laavenderrr green . . . I'll be your kinggg dilly dilly, if you'll beee my qqqueen . . .'

The lines of girls go backwards and forwards, one long line behind the other, singing our heads off. It's great when we polish the floors.

There are over sixty children in the class. We must be silent. There are real rules and unwritten rules. We must not speak unless it is to answer a question. Some of us can have our hand up until it drops off and still not get picked. Most of the questions are aimed at the posh girls in the front rows. The ones with uniforms – white shirts and ties and gymslips with blue sashes. At the back, we watch the education of others. It is almost like going to the pictures and watching a performance. Posh voices singsong answers that even if we know, we know enough not to interrupt. It is pointless putting our hands up. To keep us on our toes, Sister Agony will ramble in a lazy way between the rows, looking over shoulders as she passes, rapping the odd set of knuckles with her ruler. Now and then she will shout the name of one of us at the back. She only does it if she thinks we don't know the answer. She makes no allowances for catching us unawares. If we get it wrong, she slaps us. If we get it right, she mocks us.

'Is that a fact now? Are you sure about that? Well now, isn't that wonderful!'

It is my turn now.

'Patty O'Brien, stand up and tell the class which province Dublin is in.'

'Leinster, Sister.'

'And Belfast?'

'Ulster.'

'And Galway?'

'Connaught.'

'And Cork?'

'Munster.'

'Now, aren't you the clever girl! There'll be no stopping you, so there won't.'

My face is burning. I wish I'd got them wrong.

'I suppose you'd like a prize for being so clever, wouldn't you?'

'No, Sister.'

'Aw, now, you would. I can see it. Can we see it, girls?'

'Yes, Sister,' they shout together.

I want to go home.

'Well, now, we'll need another little test before we give you a prize.' She is holding up a bar of Fry's chocolate. 'You know your counties and your provinces, but can you tell me where your father is?'

'He's in England.'

'England is a big place. Bigger than Ireland. Is he in London?'

'Yes. I think so.'

'You *think* so. "Think" is not the right answer. You don't *think* that Dublin is in the province of Leinster. You *know* it is. Am I right?'

'He is. He's in London.'

'Is he in Buckingham Palace then?'

All the girls are sniggering into their hands. I am feeling sick. She will not stop now. She never does when she questions me about my dad. Last week it was about him being a soldier. Before that, it was whether I had a father at all. A stubborn spark flicks in my belly.

'Yes. He is in Buckingham Palace. He's a guard there.'

I might cry in a minute. My throat is being squeezed tear tight and aching.

She is madder than she's ever been now. She races between the desks and pulls me after her to the top of the class. Her eyes are bulging as she shakes me and slaps my face hard. I still don't cry, though I know that more than anything she wants to make me. I won't. Now I will never cry. She tells me to stand in the corner for the rest of the day. I stand for two hours plotting her murder or my escape, while the imprint of her hand grows redder on my face.

There is a letter on the table and silence between Mam and Auntie May. Someone has died. Someone has to be dead.

They were like this when Uncle Alec died. I know I can't ask. I'll have to wait until they forget all about me. I'll get under the table in a minute and listen.

Sitting on the rungs underneath the table is the place for the children of the house. Our separate world. It becomes whatever we want it be, a ship or a covered wagon or even a country. The best country is Czechoslovakia, but we can only play that when the table top is clear. One of us has to sit there with a rolled up newspaper, while the kids underneath poke their heads out, trying to shout 'Czechoslovakia', before they get clouted with the paper. I mostly get clouted because I'm the smallest. Sometimes, like now, I sit on the rungs on my own and people forget I'm here. They think I've gone out to play.

'What do they say in the letter, Sally?' Auntie May sounds cross.

'Here, read it for yourself.'

'Feck,' I murmur to myself. How will I know what it's all about? The silence almost swallows me. I hardly dare to breathe.

'Ah no, Sally,' Auntie May says. 'No. They can't get away with that.'

'That's what you think, May. Signed, sealed and settled it is now. That's the end of him. Gone for good after tomorrow. Free as a bird. The bastard. Free as a bird.'

I am trembling. It's my dad. They never discuss anybody else in these tones. What does she mean, gone for good?

'I've to take the girls into the Green tomorrow to say goodbye to him. He was very clever in the court. I love my children, he said. Cool as you like. I've offered her a home here or in England. What more can I do? Nothing, Mr O'Brien, you've done your best. And him never paying a penny for their keep since the day he abandoned them. Waifs and strays he's made of them. And me. I'm no more than a feckin' pauper, living on me da's charity, while their father swans about London spending his money on them he wants to impress. I wonder if his fine friends realise that while he's treating them, they're taking food out of his children's mouths? If it wasn't for me da, we'd be up in the bloody Union.'

Am I hearing right? We'll be seeing our dad in the Green tomorrow? It must be right, that's what she said. I knew it, I knew he'd come back for Joan and me. Maybe he's moved back to Dublin but hasn't got round to see us, because he's been busy getting himself settled. He'd have come to see us if he'd had the time. Last time he came to see us, about a year ago, I'd been sitting under the table with Joan and Garry. He'd come banging at the hall door.

'Where are they, where's my children? Let me see them.'

Mam and Auntie May jumped up and Granny sat down. Grandilla was upstairs having a nap. He shouted down, wondering what the hell was happening. Garry, Joan and me were under the table, thank God, because suddenly Dad burst into the kitchen. He had climbed in through the parlour window, then he ran down the hall past Grandilla.

'Jesus, May, don't let him in!' Mam was screaming. 'Shut the door.'

Auntie May tried to push the kitchen door shut, but he

was in past her. We sat crying, huddled together, powerless. Most of the time, I had my eyes tightly shut. In the uproar, all we could hear was clonking and Dad shouting.

'Ah, you bitches, stop! Stop hitting me!'

I peeped from under the table. Mam and Auntie May were bashing him with saucepans, anywhere they could lay into him. They backed him out of the kitchen and down the hall. The three of us followed, terrified. And terrified of missing anything. They gave him one last shove into the street, slamming the door. Someone had called the *gardaí*. It must have been Alfie Heffernan because the Heffernans are the only ones in the villas with a phone. From the parlour window, we watched him being escorted away between two determined officers.

I suppose that's why there was a letter. He couldn't possibly just knock on the door on the off-chance again. My dad is here in Dublin. My dad! I'm going to see my dad.

Even saying 'dad' makes me feel guilty. It's like I have no rights to a dad at all. I know I'm bad. I really wish I could be good. I want to be good. Truly. Yet somehow, I can never escape my badness. Only this morning, when Granny sent me round to Coffey's shop for a bag of sugar, as soon as Jimmy went out the back for a blue bag, I opened the glass lid of the broken-biscuit tin and stuffed a handful into the pocket in my school knickers. As soon as I'd done it, I asked God to forgive me.

While I sat on the steps of Dunne's hallway, licking the scrapings out of half a custard cream, I had visions of the fires of hell licking the scrapings off my tethered ankles. I don't know how many times I've broken the seventh commandment ('Thou shalt not steal'). And as for the fourth ('Honour thy father and thy mother'), my constant breaking of it will guarantee me a seat on the hob of hell forever. If I were to honour Mam's wishes, I wouldn't mention Dad at all. I try hard not to think about him, but just trying to put him out of my mind puts him right into it. If I get a thought about him, I try to hide my face in case Mam sees through me. But I can't hide my face from God. He is everywhere. Even in the lav, which is another worry.

Joan and I lie whispering about Dad in bed. Mam has still not told us that we are going to see him. We can't ask her about it, she'll go mad.

'He knows me better than you,' Joan says. 'Before you were born there was only me. He used to take me out with him. We'd go up to the canal to feed the ducks, or we'd go out to Sandymount for a paddle.'

'Was it great gas, then?' I ask her.

I know she isn't lying. I know all the nice things she remembers by heart. I hear them often when we are on our own. I want memories of nice things too. Even one, but I have to make do with Joan's.

'Great gas,' she says, smiling at the pictures in her head.

'Tell me about the magic pocket.' I love that story.

'Well, when he came home from the army, he used to put his best suit on. Before he went out, when he was all smart and everything, he used sit me on his lap and tell me there was something for me in his magic pocket. It was his top pocket, where he put his hanky. I'd have to pull the hanky out and say, "There's nothing there." Then he'd put his hand over his mouth and say, "Oh, Janey Mac, what have I done with it?" He'd pat his pocket and feel something. Then he'd let me push my fingers down to find a bar of toffee. He never did that with you, did he?'

Joan thinks he's more her dad than mine. I think so too. Just like Mam is more her mam.

'No, he didn't, but Mam had the baby then.'

'You don't remember him, do you? The baby. He was like a doll. John, they called him, after Dad's dad.'

They always tell me I don't remember him like I don't remember the room and the dust, because I was too young, but I see clearly the baby with the spiky black hair lying at the other end of the pram. He used to cry. So did I. I was sixteen months old. The spiky baby was dead before the day of the dancing dust. I see the baby and the dust, but separately.

'No,' I tell Joan. 'I don't remember.'

I put on my green coat and sit to the table to wait for Mam. Joan has her wine-coloured coat on and her black shoes with the ankle straps. I'm not allowed shoes like that yet and I am not too happy with my brown buckled ones. Still, he'll be a long way above my feet. He might not notice. I want him to think I look nice. I suppose he'll think Joan looks nicer than me. On the number twelve bus into the city, Mam tells us we're going to meet him. Maybe she didn't want to frighten us by telling us earlier, because of last time. I can't wait to see him, even if I won't be able to speak to him. I never know what to say to him. I don't think he knows what to say to me either.

'We've to be in the Green at three o'clock. He wants to say goodbye to you. I have no choice but to take you.'

We know better than to ask questions. I wonder if Joan is beginning to feel scared too. Why is Mam taking us to say goodbye? When they bashed him out of the house, nobody asked us to say goodbye then. They didn't even ask us to say hello.

And the time before that, when he sent a young fella over to knock on the door for us, she didn't ask us if we wanted to go to the pictures with him. She sent us out and he just took us. He held our hands walking through Gulistan. I didn't answer one of his questions. Joan did. She never shut up. In the Stella cinema, he bought us sweets and took us upstairs to the balcony. It was pitch black and the steps were steep. He didn't stop for me to catch up. We went, up near the sky and the sky was black with twinkling lights. I fell asleep and he woke me when the picture ended.

Afterwards, he took us into the ice-cream parlour. He bought us a glass of milk and a cake, and he told me off for dropping crumbs on the floor. I kept looking at him. He'd look at me, catching me out, and I'd go red. The only thing I can remember him saying to me was, 'Does your mother never cut your fingernails?'

'No,' I said and sat on my hands, pretending I didn't want to finish my milk.

At Roddy's toy shop window, he let us decide what we wanted. We spent ages making our minds up, we only usually get jigsaws and comics. He had to pick me up so I could see the toys at the back of the window. I fell in love with a pig in a green cloak holding a wand. Joan wanted a walkie-talkie doll with pursed red lips and golden hair. He tried to get me to change from the pig to a doll, but I wouldn't. He said we had taken so long to make our minds up that Mr Roddy had locked the shop to go home for his tea.

'Don't worry, though,' he said. 'I'll send them over to you from England. Just watch out for two big parcels.'

They never came.

Joan and I walk through the gates of St Stephen's Green with Mam, keeping off the grass like the sign says, past flowers lying tidily in their beds and people with umbrellas up. It is raining again and my legs are splashed.

'I told you to keep out of them bloody puddles. Look at the state of you.'

Mam's mood is getting worse. I want to tell her that she splashed me herself, but I know it won't make any difference. The buses flashing past the railings already have their lights on. The afternoon becomes night under low charcoal clouds. It is the end of the world. The Day of Judgment the nuns talk about, where all our sins are read out by one of God's disciples and we go to heaven or hell. We could go to purgatory, though. Joan will probably go to purgatory until she's paid for her sins. She's no angel. Just delicate. 'Atoned,' the nuns say.

'Atoned' seems as heavy as the clouds. I think I committed one sin too many when I pinched the pennies out of the sugar bags in the parlour. They were left there by the emergency gas man, when Granny called him in to empty the meter. It was full up to the slot and she couldn't get another penny in it to save her life.

'You'll have to mind them yourself, Missus, until the regular collector calls.'

'Bloody get, with his peaked cap, if he owned the park, he'd let nobody in.'

Granny didn't like temptation being put in our way. She'd wanted the bags taken away with him. I know I'm on the road to hell.

Mam's face is set. Her lips just a line drawn across her face. I feel sick. Joan looks as if she is going to be sick. I sense it. I know she feels like I do. The feeling is leaving her body and banging into mine, right where my heart is. My heart feels as if it is rheumatic, like Ann Eccles's. A man is walking towards us. He's wearing a long raincoat and it's flapping wildly in the wind. His hair is blowing across his forehead. Suddenly, in the middle of the path, he drops on one knee and holds his arms out wide. Is he an eejit or what?

Joan recognises him first. 'It's me daddy,' she screams, and starts to run.

Mam pulls her back. 'Don't you dare,' she says, and the words strap us to her.

The three of us walk slowly up to him and face him in silence.

'What have you done to them, to turn them against me?' he says, and I realise at last that he is not Jesus coming amongst us, but my dad.

Uncle Paddy is lovely, Mr Grogan is a lamb and Grandilla

is the smartest grandfather in Dublin, but Dad is a spot-knocker. Pure and simple. If Sister Agnes of the Torments could see me now.

'It's not what I've done,' Mam says. 'If you'd been a proper father to them, they wouldn't be frightened of you.'

He grabs her elbow, marching her away to the trees and the trees weep on them. The rain falls softly, seeping into their coats, running down their faces with their tears. We watch them as they shout at each other, but their words are whisked away by the traffic noises and the swishing of buses through endless puddles. We stand on the pathway, ashamed of the pair of them, hating them both. When the people passing by look at them and then at us, I close my eyes to make myself disappear.

When they have said all they have to say, they walk back to us. For several moments they are as silent as Joan and me.

'Well?' Mam asks him, but he doesn't answer.

They gaze at each other for a long time and I gaze up at him. All I can see is his chin, stuck out and stubbled. He is so far above me, he can't see me at all. My old brown shoes don't matter now. My neck aches from looking up and I drop my head forward, wishing he would go away. Wishing for one of the miracles they tell us about in school. As I think this wicked thought, he bends down to Joan and me, holding us both for too long a time. I don't remember him ever holding me before. Except at Roddy's window, but that was only so I could see, not because he wanted to hold me. He looks straight into my eyes. Even though I want to look away, I don't. Somehow, I know it is most important that I look right back. I stare at him without blinking. He has to turn away first.

'Be good girls,' he says, then straightens, leaving us, Mam's trophies.

We watch him as he strides out of the Green, through the arch, towards Grafton Street. A man who won't be hemmed in. I would be hemming him in if he stayed at home. I am a tyrant, because I want to hem him now and keep him here. My guilt and shame stop me screaming his name. Mam will kill me if I do. He might too, because, like a bird, he must fly free. So I let him go. I don't shout at all. The three of us stay silent and watch him until the going-home workers and their umbrellas shield him from us, making him disappear.

Back in the warm kitchen, our wet coats and mittens are steaming by the fire. I sit under the table drawing pictures of the flowers in the Green, colouring in each one carefully without going over the lines. Granny makes us mugs of hot cocoa.

When I go upstairs to bed at last, I draw a box train all along the green distempered wall. The open carriages are empty, except for one man. The smoke is blowing backwards over the tops of the carriages and over the man's face.

'You'll get into terrible trouble,' Joan says, as she snuggles under the blankets.

'I know,' I tell her.

When Mam finally comes up and gets into bed between us, all she says is, 'I'll have to get some fresh distemper and brighten up that oul' wall as soon as I have the money. Good night now, and God bless.'

''Night, Mam,' we say together.

Three

In Christy Bird's pawn office, I stand patiently with Auntie May and a host of other redeemers against the back wall. 'Hail, Redeemer, King divine . . . Hail, Redemption's happy dawn . . .'

We have to wait until the clerk calls out our name and docket number. The clerks see to the queue of private pledgers first. In small booths along the counter, shy people sit and whisper to the clerks confessionally – Bless me, Christy, for I am poor – creating more interest than if they'd stayed in the queue winding its way out of the shop and along Richmond Street. Dubliners have a liking for going in on themselves and closing doors. There's snugs in pubs and confession boxes, not to mention these in the pawn office. 'The new poor and the proud', Auntie May calls the private pledgers.

The shop is dark and musty, the shelves behind the counter packed with parcels and objects too big for wrapping. There's a stuffed parrot in a cage and the skull of a moose nailed to a lump of wood. I wonder how much we'd get if we had such great stuff. We only pawn Grandilla's suit or the good blankets, made from the wool of a hundred merino sheep, according to the labels. They are kept in the press at home like an insurance policy or on the shelves in Christy's. In and out they go like a fiddler's elbow. We only throw them over the beds when someone is coming home from England, like Uncle Paddy O'Toole is tomorrow.

'Kelly, Kelly,' a clerk calls, shouting for all to hear.

'Yes.' Auntie May moves forward, miraculously parting the crowd at the counter, waving her docket high in the air.

Kelly is the name Mam and Auntie May use for the pawn office. O'Keefe is the name for St Vincent de Paul on the Ranelagh Road, and whatever name comes into their heads for debt collectors and enquiring priests. It's only lately I've come to realise that I'm an O'Brien. Granny and Grandilla are called Colgan and Auntie May and the boys are called O'Toole. I've been using all names freely and nobody seemed to mind, until I asked Grandilla to sign for a ticket from Rathmines library.

I have just discovered the library. I rambled in out of the rain on my way home from school. I couldn't get over the amount of books in the place. Everywhere, they were, on big open shelves, not locked in the wardrobe at the top of the stairs like Grandilla's. People, even kids, were coming and going with as many as three or four books, as if they owned them. On the form, I put Patty Colgan.

'Get you daddy to sign it,' a woman with her glasses hanging on her chest said. 'Then you can come and pick your book up tomorrow.'

I'd taken ages to decide which book to have. All I ever read are comics. I finally picked Andersen's fairy tales. She took it from me and placed it on a shelf. Still out of reach, still another hurdle.

'You're an O'Brien,' Grandilla said, when he read the form. 'I wish you weren't, but the be all and end all of it is that your mother married your father when she'd taken leave of her senses, and for official forms you have to put your official surname down. That's a fact.'

I ask Auntie May about it as we carry the blankets home across Portobello Bridge and along the avenue, a hundred sheep apiece.

She just laughs. 'If you're with me in Christy Bird's, you're Kelly, whatever your Grandilla tells you.'

Uncle Paddy is so handsome. When he first walked in, he lit the room up. A Sun God in me granny's kitchen, looking like he'd had a rub of the Brasso. Once the blankets were on his bed, the waiting was terrible until we heard the knock, then we all went a bit shy, even Paddy and Garry, but then I suppose I was shy on the few times my own dad came home. It's like you know them in your head and in your heart until you see them, then you know them not at all. Uncle Paddy hugged us as if we were very important, including me and Joan and he isn't even our dad, or da, as Paddy and Garry call him. He smells of England. I only get that smell when people come back from England. Noel and John, already gone over, had it when they came home. My dad had it too. It is the sweet smell of plenty and just-unwrapped soap.

We sit around the fire all night long and listen to Uncle Paddy telling stories with his new words. He talks of working on the railway with his mates and how great the blokes are, of his digs out in Leytonstone and his grub.

'Cor blimey, I was knackered altogether lugging them sodding sleepers around when I first went over there.'

'Do they not speak English over there, Uncle Paddy?' I ask, because I have never heard such words.

The Killiney bus is waiting on the other side of O'Connell Bridge. We clamber on, Joan, me and Garry and his ma and da. Paddy can't come out with us any more, because he's fourteen, in his first pair of longers and in his first job as a messenger boy, in the College of Surgeons on the Green. The conductor clips our tickets and tells us that he'll clip our ears if we keep ringing the bell or shouting. I think he must remember us from last year, when Mam took us out. I hope Uncle Paddy hasn't heard the conductor telling us off.

As the bus leaves the city it is shimmering in the tar-melting heat like a mirage. I know about mirages since I saw that picture about men in a desert dying for want of water. They see a tented city hovering in the air. I've been thinking since that my dad was a mirage in the Green the last time we saw him.

We play I Spy all along the country roads. I know I will never be so happy again. Even if I make this journey every day for the rest of my life, I will not feel like this and we're not even at Killiney yet. There is no more space in my heart for such joy, I think. There is, though, and the feeling grows as we alight from the bus at the terminus. I pretend to myself that Uncle Paddy is my dad and Auntie May is my mam, standing apart from them like I'm fed up, the way I do when I'm out with Mam. I think, I'm only borrowing them and it's not a lie if I don't say it out loud.

Uncle Paddy carries all the bags, except for Auntie May's handbag, liberating us to run ahead of them into the Up and Up Park. The three of us scramble like mountain goats over the rocks, hiding ourselves flat on wild grasses and picking our way through spreading gorse. We whoop and roar, drunk on freedom, lost in space. Where the road curves and winds above the deep dipping bay, I stand on a rock, spreading my arms wide enough to catch the breezes and fly over Dalkey Island, or swoop to trace my fingers along the slopes of the Sugar Loaf Mountain.

They are all at the top of the Head when I finally get there. Uncle Paddy is trying to get a glimmer on the Primus. I fling myself on the grass beside Auntie May and she holds me to her.

'Do you want a tomato sandwich, love?'

She knows they're my favourite. I'm starving and the smell of the tomato sinking into the soggy bread waters my tongue. I eat it quickly. Then another. And another.

When everyone has eaten, Joan and Garry run off to carve their names on a spindly tree. Twin cousins of ten and twin torturers of me most of the time, they usually leave me straggling behind, except when they capture me and make me their prisoner. I watch them and don't want to follow at all, satisfied where I am. I lie quietly on the bee-buzzing grass, watching small puffy clouds grazing lazily, misshapen sheep, world turned upside down.

Uncle Paddy forgets all about me and changes from his banter and teasing to a sterner voice. 'I told you, May, things are hard over there. I've tried to get a place for all of us. You. Me. The boys, or at least Paddy and Garry anyway, now that the other two are fending for themselves. I've gone from one end of London to the other, following up advertisements for flats, but it's always the same. If they don't have a notice in the window saying "No Blacks, No Irish, No Dogs", as soon as you open your mouth, they close the feckin' door in your face. I try to save, but by the time I pay for my digs and send money home for the boys, I can hardly scrape enough together to get home for the holidays.'

He waits for an answer. So do I, but Auntie May concentrates on making the tea, taking the leaves from a screw of newspaper and tipping them into the water boiling in the old dented teapot balanced on the Primus. He gets up and begins to pace. The smile he's been wearing since he arrived last night is gone. Something is changing. Something always changes. You no sooner get a special thing, like an oozing tomato sandwich or a sunny day, but it changes. Crusts go stale or the sun goes in.

Auntie May seems to know what to say at last. 'If you can do no more, then I'll have to do something. I'm sick and tired of living under me father's roof. They're old, Paddy. Worn out. The way we'll be before we have a home together. I'm sick and tired watching me mother shuffling to her grave without ever having one year of her life to call her own. She's seventy-four, for God's sake. It's about bloody time she was free of children.'

I'm mixed up. I thought me granny liked us. She never says much, but she cooks for us and makes sure we go to bed and things like that. And she never shouts at us. Only when she wants us to get her messages and we don't want to go. But Auntie May means us. Granny wants to be free of us. Where will she go?

'She doesn't want us all there, Paddy. Our boys and Sally's girls. Things have to change, that's all I'm trying to tell you.'

Uncle Paddy sits back down beside her and takes her hand. 'I'll just have to try a little harder then, won't I, love?'

I'm after being punched. Who will try harder in England for Joan and Mam and me? What will become of us when the changes come? After we get back on the bus and Uncle Paddy is gone back to England and the blankets are folded back into the press. What? What then? I have no answers at all in my head. When the changes come, I'll know.

I wish now I had followed Joan and Garry to the spindly tree and carved my name, instead of listening to Auntie May and Uncle Paddy talking up a world of change in quiet voices. If I had, would I be singing my way back to Dublin on the bus, like Joan and Garry? I can never know now, because 'if' is only an empty bag. The bag I carry from Killiney Head and the Up and Up Park is a bag heavy with goodbyes. Past ones, like Dad and the baby and Noel and John, as well as ones I have yet to pack.

Joan has TB in her right lung. Her thinness scares me. It is the first time I have seen TB close up. She coughs and coughs all night long and cries in her sleep. The man in the box train sits, impassive. Never moving or blinking or reaching out a hand. Sammy Dempster, only six, died of TB last week. A small white coffin was carried out of the Buildings by his weeping father, who kept cursing God for letting him die. Who will carry Joan's coffin? I wonder now, as I hunch over the fire for warmth. Grandilla might, but he has carried so many coffins that he might not rage as magnificently as Mr Dempster had. I stood with a gang of boys and girls and watched Sammy's coffin going into the hearse. We could have followed it, because children are never excluded from the rituals of death. We go to wakes and weddings in equal measure.

Just a few weeks before Sammy's funeral, I had knocked on Mrs Daniels's door to see the corpse of her old father lying on the parlour table, candles at his snowy head. She had smiled and let me in, telling me to say a little prayer for the repose of his soul. I hadn't prayed at all, of course, just inspected him closely when she left me with him for a minute. I tried to lift his eyelids up and couldn't. He wasn't a cold solid mass, more as I imagined a lizard or a snake to be. Ugh.

'Isn't he a beautiful corpse?' Mrs Daniels asked, her head tipped round the door.

'It's not the dead you have to worry about, but the living,' Grandilla always tells us.

Instead of following Sammy's hearse, even a part of the way, we all just ran and ran, not screaming and shouting as we usually do, but in silence. I don't know why we were silent or what we were running away from. Eventually, we ran into the drying yards and hid from each other between the blowing sheets, winding them about us like shrouds, until the women in the tenements shouted at us to feck off. We never spoke of Sammy again.

I hunch forward to ease the pain in my shoulder. The fire is hot on my face, making me cough.

'That child is not well, Sally,' Granny tells Mam.

'It's not surprising, Mother, she's always out streeling the streets. If I make her wear a coat, she's no sooner out the door than she takes it off and hides it. If she gets the flu she might learn a lesson and do as she's told next time.'

I want to have the flu. I say a prayer to St Jude, saint of lost causes, that I will be running a temperature in the morning, which will gain me a special dispensation from school. No matter how hard I act the invalid, Mam always doubts me. She does so now and my cough is real. Grandilla makes me small sugar-coated rolls of butter to soothe the tickling irritation.

'You were well enough to sit out on the step with that crew from the Buildings till all hours last night. I didn't hear you coughing then.'

I don't say anything, because Mam can't understand that we have to sit right to the end of a ghost story. Last night, Mary Grimes was telling us about the Black Dog with red eyes roaming about the big houses in Palmerston Road. She swore it was as true as God, because her mammy worked in one of the houses and didn't it cross her path – a sign of terrible trouble – and disappear through the iron railings into the bushes in the park, howling at the moon. How could I get up in the middle of the story and break the spell? I had to know what happened, or I wouldn't be able to sleep at all. Mam kept calling me in and I had to let on that I didn't hear her.

Mam is fed up with illness and worry. She always seems to be taking Joan to St Vincent's hospital. Even if I have the flu, I'll have to have a terrible dose for Mam to be convinced.

I wake with something worse than flu. Every breath makes my chest hurt. Coughing is painful. I just want to lie still and sleep. Grandilla comes in and feels my wrist, then my forehead. He says when he gets to work in the dispensary he will pay Dr Lemass three shillings to visit me. I hope Mam won't be too cross with me, and say a little prayer to St Jude to make me just a little bit better.

'Dearest Jude, I know I asked for a temperature, but I did not expect more than I asked for. I don't really want the pain in my back and chest and all. I don't mind if you make them go away now. Thank you.'

He isn't listening. Maybe he can only do miracles, not undo them. I'll have to find a more reliable saint next time I want something.

Auntie May comes up with a drink and opens the window to let in fresh air.

'There. That's better. A bit of a breeze won't hurt you. The doctor will be here after dinner. I called in to the dispensary to see me da when I was getting the messages. The dispensary was packed, so it was. In all me life I never saw so many wretched people. I'll be glad to get away from all the misery. If it wasn't for Paddy and Garry, I'd have been gone years ago. Now I'm left with no choice.'

She sounds angry. It can't be with me, because she keeps smiling at me and patting my hand.

'What do you think is the matter with me, Auntie May?'

She can't look me in the eye. 'The same that's the matter with half the population. Overcrowding. Under-nourishment. Hopelessness and helplessness. That's what makes us sick.'

'That St Jude seems to be going mad infecting all the lost causes of Dublin. I wish I'd never done the novena to him now. Maybe it's the novenas that are making everyone sick.' I mean every word.

She smiles, even laughs a little. 'It's not St Jude we have to thank for our poverty, love. It's Judas. All the feckin' Judases running the country and the Church.'

The doctor wakes me. He doesn't speak, but lifts me up to a sitting position and sounds my chest with a stethoscope, then leaves. Mam is home from work now and I hear him murmuring to her on the landing. I wait for her to come into the room, but she goes downstairs instead.

Joan is in Granny's bed in the parlour. She has been there for weeks, and Granny sleeps on her chair in the kitchen. When Mam finally comes in to see me, she is crying. I suddenly think of Sammy Dempster.

'You've to come downstairs with me if you can manage it and get into bed with Joan in the parlour. You'll be better down there when I'm at work. Your granny won't be able to get up the stairs to look after you, with her bad feet. Auntie

May won't be here any more after Saturday, when the school holidays begin, so that's the best arrangement.'

I can't understand so many things at once. Why is it OK now for me to sleep with Joan in the parlour, when I wasn't even allowed in there to see her in case I caught TB? Why won't Auntie May be here in the school holidays? Why does Granny need to look after me? I try to ask Mam, but I feel too tired to bother.

Auntie May and Mam help me down the stairs slowly. I am feeling exhausted by the effort. Joan has her comics spread all across the bed, but moves them without fuss to make room for me. I have never felt so important. I wish I was well enough to enjoy it.

Joan tells me what is wrong with me when we are on our own. 'They think you have TB too. I heard them saying you'll have to see Dr Dorothy Price at her TB clinic. You can't go yet, though. She has so many children to see to, you'll have to wait.'

Joan knows all about the clinic and needles and blood tests and inoculations. She isn't even frightened. I am. I put my hands over my ears so I can't hear any more and fall asleep watching the painting of Auntie Rosie on the wall talking to me. I wake up. She is still moving her lips. She looks like a witch, and I think she's going to get me. When I start crying, Joan calls Mam. She's not angry that I am sick, like she usually is. She gets a damp flannel and puts it on my forehead, then sits on the bed blocking out the sight of Rosie in the picture. I sleep deeply at last, glad at least that I won't be going to school for a while.

Auntie May is amazed at what she is reading in the *Irish Times*. 'God bless this bloody country. Listen to this, Mother. "In large-scale tests using the Tuberculin Standard, it has been found that a far higher percentage of persons give a positive reaction in urban communities than obtained among people living more widely apart . . . comparatively few city dwellers reach adult life without becoming tuberculin positive . . . 55 per cent of children tested were positive before fourteen years of age"!'

'It's lack of nourishment as well as overcrowding that causes it,' Granny says. 'Does it mention that?' She doesn't wait for an answer. 'No, I don't suppose it does. It might mean that they'd have to do something about it. It's not just TB and famine that kills people, you know. It's the long, slow hunger at the end of every day. It's the hunger at the end of every meal, the half-filled plate and the watery stew made with half a pound of beef for eight people and a few pot herbs thrown into it.'

Granny rarely comments on anything in the paper. She has taken it personally, Joan and me being sick. She makes us soup with fingers of brown bread to dip in it and colcannon with dollops of melting margarine on top. She is also upset that Auntie May is going to England.

'Whatever I do over there, I'm not going to be a skivvy. I do enough skivvying here,' May says.

'How will you get on working in a factory, May?' Mam asked her when the two of them were reading the advertisements in the *Evening Herald*.

'I have two eyes, two hands and two hungry children here to support. I'll have to get on all right.'

Mam continues to read out notices. 'It says here that they want laundry workers. I might join you.'

'I know it will be hard for you here, Sally, when I'm gone. You'll have to undertake everything on your own. Especially now that Ma is suffering so much. If I don't try to make a home for me and the boys now, I never will. Paddy O'Toole might knuckle down too, if I give him a bit of encouragement. In all our married life, we have only lived together for four and a half years.'

Mam looks upset. 'Nearly the same amount of time I lived with Paddy O'Brien,' she said.

'Do you know what I'm thinking, Sally?'

I hold my breath, praying that she says she is thinking of changing her mind. She is staying after all.

'I'm thinking that our family, Ma and Da's family, were never meant to have any luck.'

'Well, you're luckier than me, May. That's all I can say. At least Paddy O'Toole remembers he has children. At least if you go over there, he'll give you a bit of support.'

I close my eyes, too tired to listen any more. Resigned to the fact that Auntie May is going. She will never come back. Never. Except perhaps for a holiday. Or maybe she'll be like Dad and disappear. The pain in my chest is crushing, even though I take several deep breaths.

Dr Dorothy Price asks not just about our health, but about conditions at home.

'No, doctor, they don't have a bed of their own. They have to sleep in bed with me.'

'I see.'

'No, doctor, they don't have eggs and milk every day. Nor butter. Nor fresh fish. Nor a lot of things I could mention.'

'Well, if they don't, they won't be well enough to fight the infection. I want you to see the Lady Almoner. She will give you dockets to help you feed them properly.'

The dockets are for the Monument Creamery in Ranelagh. You feel clean just going in its door. The counters and shelves are of cool marble and eggs nestle in straw-packed baskets. The milk is in glass bottles instead of churns and it is pasteurised, according to the labels. The shop assistants are dressed like doctors in crisp white coats and they smile at the poor as they exchange their dockets for food. I think there must be something in the dockets, because the shops where just money is handed over are not so pleasant. Priestley's or Paddy Kane's on Oxford Road put the groceries on the book all week, hoping to be paid when their customers get their wages or money sent over from England. I can't imagine Bill Priestley or Paddy Kane in white coats, bothering to nestle hen eggs in straw. Poor Simmie in his shop opposite the One Rooms is in need of a few dockets for his own family.

'Why,' I wonder aloud to Grandilla, 'if we have to have nourishing food, don't they give us the money in the first place? Then we wouldn't get sick and if we had the money, we could spend it in Simmie's and Paddy Kane's and they wouldn't have to wait in hope for money from their customers.'

'Because that would be too simple. The dockets serve two purposes. Sure, how can the poor be trusted to spend their money on good food? And would they know good food if it hit them in the mouth?'

We laugh, but I still need the complete answer.

'What's the other purpose, Grandilla?'

'Well now, the dockets system is a type of rationing up. That way, the select few can remain just that by having subsidies by indirect means. They couldn't be expected to get in a queue with a neon sign advertising help for those who have plenty. Oh no, indeed not. But if they give it to them by way of the pockets of the poor, sure won't they all benefit. And by benefiting, they can be seen as benefactors.'

I understand, but not completely. 'But the shops that take the dockets are still only shops?'

'Yes, they are, but just imagine how many cows grazing on green grass your one who owns the Monument Creamery has to have, to keep all her creameries supplied with milk. And how many chickens for the eggs? Now, with the best will in the world, I can't see Paddy Kane branching out in Oxford Road. There's not so much as a blade of grass to graze a worm.'

Grandilla knows so much about everything. Sometimes I think he wishes he didn't, because knowing things is not like being able to do anything about them. I don't know very much about anything at all, but as soon as I am given another thing to think about, I'm driven mad with new questions until I wish I never asked the first one in the first place. Like now, Grandilla stops talking to fill his pipe. I wait for him to put it in his mouth to smoke it, setting me free from what is becoming a lecture instead of a simple answer. He even stands up and moves to spit in the fire.

'And,' he continues, as my spirits sag back into the chair, 'never mind the upkeep of Mrs Ryan's farm and all her Monument Creameries. What about the upkeep of Burton Hall, her country estate?'

I'm bewildered. One woman owning all that and so many owning nothing at all.

Grandilla is far from finished. He rubs a lump of tobacco in his fingers, then presses it into the bowl of his pipe. He often does this, so he can gather his thoughts between his ravings.

'And what of Mrs Ryan's talented son, John? Wouldn't he be lost altogether without the docket system? How could he pursue his hobbies of music and fine arts without the dockets? Isn't it in that splendid apartment of his mother's in Grafton Street that he entertains the budding literary geniuses of this fine city? Where would they go to discuss ideas? They can't be in the watering holes of Dublin night and day, now can they? Their pockets would prevent them. Thoughts need watering if they are to take shape at all. Then the shape needs an airing with like minds. I suppose you could say the dockets are doing a grand job all round. If we didn't have TB, we'd have to invent it. It's the hub of the economic wheel of all our lives.'

I am glowing with pride. For once in my life, I have something to be proud of. I lie back on the chairbed in the warm kitchen, near the table and the smaller pine press stacked high with newspapers, and admire my world. I look at the range, snug in the chimney, its edges gleaming silver against the black. I consider the torn oilcloth, its pattern worn to brown in the middle by the constant trudge of feet before I was even born and the small holes in it, in which we search for silver sixpences and find farthings. I count the hard-backed chairs around the scrubbed table and try to count every single person who ever sat on them, including visitors and priests, and in this briefly religious moment, I study the print of *The Angelus* and make a quick sign of the cross from habit. I luxuriate in the soft-faded shades of comfort of the walls surrounding my haven and try to imagine something more lovely than this, like John Ryan's splendid apartment in Grafton Street, and I cannot. All that comes to mind is Mr Grogan's left-hand parlour in the Purcell Rooms, which can be the only other room of splendour in the city. I bet it is better by far than John Ryan's. Still and all, I reflect, isn't it wonderful altogether the way the TB is keeping us going? Without it, we'd all be living in England. And the country would be like one of them ghost towns in American westerns. God really does move in mysterious ways.

Four

I have another year off school to reflect on a range of subjects, from sickness and religion to families and emigration. I am as cosseted as my sister's cat, Fluff. All I have to do all day is lie on the chairbed and daydream. I hear all sorts of secrets when they think I'm asleep. 'Spy on the Coombe', Mam calls me. She's the only one who knows that I'm ear-wigging. It's not that I'm nosy, it's just that I love the stories.

Auntie Moll, Mam's half-sister, comes over from Clanbrassil Street twice a week to see Granny. She comes in the daytime when Grandilla's at work. She married Alec Hemingway against their wishes and it was years before she was let back into the house. 'After all,' Mam said, 'he was a Protestant and twenty-five years her senior. It had a terrible effect on the family.' And didn't they have to get married beyond the gates of the side altar after the Saturday Mass, with only Mam and Auntie May as their witnesses. Mam said that as God's her judge, she never got over the shame of it.

She forgets I'm there while she is telling this to Paddy, who at fifteen and a half is just of an age to be introduced slowly to the skeletons crammed into the family cupboard.

Shake hands with your Uncle Mike, me boy
And here's your sister Kate
And this is the girl you used to swing
Down on the garden gate . . .
Shake hands with all the neighbours
And kiss the Colleen Bawn . . .
But check that she's a Catholic first
Or we'll shoot you against the wall.

'Go 'way,' Paddy says, 'and how old was she?'

Mam's arms are crossed at the chest, protecting herself from what she is about to tell him. 'Old bloody enough at nearly forty and him nearly sixty-five.'

'Go 'way,' Paddy says again. 'Why did she want to marry an oul' fella like that?'

'Not because she had to. "Will you promise to bring up any children of this union as good God-fearing Catholics?" the priest asked them, before he consented to the marriage. "Father," she said, "if such an event occurs, there'll be a star over Dublin lit up like the *Princess Maud* and there'll be statues of me in every church in the land. I can't make such a promise, because it, like Alec's banjo, would be idle."'

Mam and Paddy laugh as if something funny has been said. I remember Uncle Alec before he died and I never saw him with a banjo.

As Joan and I get better, Granny is getting sicker. She sleeps in the daytime and cries with the pain in her feet. Only Mam can wash them for her. They are all swollen and, where the skin breaks, yellow pus seeps out. This morning,

58

she is not in the kitchen and the fire is just embers in white ash. The big black kettle, usually boiling its head off, is stone cold. In all my life in the house, Granny has been in the kitchen every single morning. Mam is making porridge. In all my life in the house, Mam has never made porridge. If Auntie May were still here, she'd have lit the fire. The changes have started. The house seems smaller and colder. Without music, it occurs to me, and I turn on the wireless. The song reminds me of Auntie May and I turn it off.

Joan is in a convalescent home called Linden. I'm not delicate enough to be there with her, but too delicate to go to school yet. When the house is silent, after Grandilla, Mam and Paddy have left for work and Garry bangs the hall door on his way out to school, I sit at the table, unsure what to do with the day ahead of me. At one o'clock, I've to heat the pot of soup to have with the bread, already sliced so I don't have to use the saw knife. Granny is to have just the soup, she can't manage the bread. I'm to take her in drinks of water until Garry comes home. Then he will make her a cup of tea. They don't trust me to strike a match. The clock ticks loudly. I can't remember hearing it before. I can't remember being on my own in the kitchen before either. Not for a whole day anyway. Fluff watches me slyly, so I suppose I'm not really alone. I wonder if cats count like people. She must miss Joan like I miss Auntie May.

I decide to write her a letter full of news. I don't tell her that Granny is dying. I tell her that Joan and me are getting better, thank God, and that I even went out of the house last Friday for a little while. Mam took me next door but one, to

Mrs Patterson's house. She was in bed with a headache and Mam took her up a cup of tea, allowing me to follow and see her bedroom. She had a dressing table stocked like a chemist's shop. Full of creams and lotions and perfumes of all description. Blue Grass by Elizabeth Arden is her favourite and I sprayed myself with it generously.

'Isn't that a delightful perfume, Sally?' Mrs Patterson asked Mam proudly. Showing off.

'Oh it is. It's very fresh, isn't it?' Mam agreed, until we were outside the house. 'Blue Grass, me arse!' she said then, careful that her voice did not carry up to the open window.

We laughed at the absurdity of a grown woman idling in bed, her main worry what she sprays on her wrists. Auntie May will love that, I think, and end my letter with a line of xxxx's. 'PS,' I write, because I have just discovered that letters from England always have one. It is usually the main point of writing, but so as not to cause anxiety, is added as if it's just an afterthought. 'PS, the house is changed without you.'

We walk down to Westland Row, Paddy, Garry, Joan and me. The sun is splitting the trees and the city itself is humming with summer. Boys ride bikes with their shirt sleeves rolled up and girls' skirts billow as they walk, like colourful umbrellas. Old women still wear their head-scarves, trusting nothing. Not even the weather. And they clutch their shopping bags tight to their chests, plotting their plunder of the bargains in Camden Street. Old men wear mufflers at their throats and are going nowhere, and the younger ones hang out on the street corners, wishing they were. As we near the station, we have to slow our pace. Half of Dublin must have someone coming home and the other half must have someone leaving, judging by the suitcases and bags being carried and dragged along the street. The only other time I've seen such crowds is on Sunday mornings going to and coming from Mass, when the streets are thick with people too.

We join the queue to buy our platform tickets, then line up along the railings to wait. Paddy takes charge, checking the expected time of the mail train from Dún Laoghaire with a guard. Waiting to go, people are standing five and six deep, either emigrating or seasoned travellers, returning to the sculleries and building sites of Britain. When their train comes in, the smoke and the carriages obscure everything for minutes. Then, I see people clinging to each other, saying their endless goodbyes. Even coming home is shadowed with goodbyes.

We will be over there on the goodbye platform next week when Auntie May goes back. My dad left from there alone. I wonder how he felt, sitting with his back to his life and his family as the train chugged him out of Dublin forever. Forever. Ever and ever. I hum to myself:

> For ever and ever
> My heart will be true
> Sweetheart, forever
> I'll wait for you . . .

Waiting forever is something I never considered. Waiting means something, or somebody, will arrive at the end of forever. There is no point in waiting for a train if it is not coming. The thought comes into my head that he might be on the train we're waiting for. That possibility hadn't occurred to me until now. Maybe forever, like my sickness, has passed. I whisper it to Joan. Her eyes widen and she nods. We make a silent pact to watch out for him. I wish I had not had the thought, though, because now a need to cry comes over me, dimming my joy at the prospect of seeing Auntie May again.

'Are you all right?' Paddy asks me and I lie that I am.

Paddy is tall, nearly a man. He has begun to keep a watch out for us since his mother went to England. What with Mam working all hours and Granny lying in bed all the time, there is nobody else to mind us. He lets Garry and Joan climb up on the low wall and run up and down the slope to the road below to pass the time, but he makes me stand beside him. I'll be nine next week, just before Auntie May goes back, and then I'll run wherever I like.

Great billows of steam precede the boat train into the station. It slows and shunts its way to the platform and, as it does, all the people waiting surge forward, craning their necks for their own people. I watch the faces of the returning men and women as they alight and pass us, lost in their own worlds of reunions and hopes for times that can never be again. They have left these streets and these open spaces, the hills and mountains, strands and rivers and, while they were gone, the rivers took a little more of their banks, more mosses grew on the peaks, and in the streets and houses they left behind, people died, grew up, moved on. They are coming back. Coming home, but home as they remember it is gone forever. Home only exists for us, the ones they left behind. My heart surges with grief for them as I watch them and I vow that I will always remain here. Always. Always is more solid than forever.

I am preoccupied with these thoughts as I seek out familiar faces in the crowd. I cannot see my dad, no matter how hard I look. Why can't he come back? Margaret Hall's dad works in England and he comes back every summer and every Christmas. So many dads do the same. Look at all these men striding down the platform. How many of them are dads? All coming home to see their children. Why are we so different? I can't find the answers within myself. I've tried before whenever I am reminded of dads, which is nearly all the time. I am silly to think he will ever come home. I watch a boy run through the people to his dad. He is about my age. His father picks him up and carries him on his shoulder, his case in his free hand. My cheeks are aflame with embarrassment and rage.

I haven't noticed Auntie May standing quietly beside us. She loves tricks and she hid herself between her friends Lou White and her husband Harry to sneak past us and come up behind us. I screech with joy and cling to her while she kisses her sons and Joan. Lou White is large and bag-laden and Harry looks like a priest out of uniform.

'Say hello,' Auntie May tells me.

Lou smiles and tweaks my cheek. Harry shakes my hand.

We walk down the slope to the street and Auntie May hails a hansom cab. Together with her and Lou and all the cases and bags, Joan and me sit in the carriage like princesses for the journey home. The boys walk back with Harry and arrive at the house when we do. Even though we only have cups of tea and sandwiches, it's like a wedding celebration, except for poor Granny, who is still lying in the parlour.

Auntie May goes in to see her, creaking open the door and calling her name. 'Oh, Mother, I wish there was something I could do. Is there anything I can get you?'

'Only release, May. I can't bear the pain.'

Granny is propped up on pillows and a fire is lit in the parlour grate. She keeps clutching at the quilt and letting it go, as if she is counting. 'Where's Paddy O'Toole?' she asks. 'Did he not come home with you?'

'No, Mother, he couldn't manage it this time. Next year, please God, we'll all come home together, Paddy, Noel, John and me. Won't that be great?'

'It would so. Better than strangers in the house.' She keeps clutching the quilt. Holding on. She means Lou and Harry.

'Shh, Mother, they'll hear you. They've been very good to me, so they have. I have a lovely room in their house and they treat me like one of their own.'

'Is Paddy in the house with you?'

'No. He has to live in Leytonstone near his work. I live in Kensington near mine. We're doing the best we can, Mother.' Auntie May sounds weary.

I recall the Up and Up Park and the promises Uncle Paddy made, still to be kept.

'I'll come in and see you again before you go asleep,' she promises Granny.

It's my ninth birthday. I line up my four cards on the press and count my money. The Whites gave me a ten-shilling note. Auntie May gave me half a crown and Auntie Moll sent me a postal order for another half-crown. One present, a cardboard dress doll in a box, is from Mam. Somehow, Joan has been able to buy me some paper scraps to stick in my scrapbook. Mam has the day off from work, which surprises me, because it's the middle of the week.

'Where would you like to go today?' Mam asks me as we eat breakfast. 'You can choose, Birthday Girl.'

I have no hesitation. 'Killiney. And the Up and Up Park.'

'Ah no, Mam,' Joan says, 'not Killiney again. Why can't we go to Blackrock?'

'Or the Scalp?' Garry suggests, not really wanting to go anywhere at all. He'd much rather be out in the Buildings kicking the toes out of his boots with the boys.

Paddy is off work for the day too, because his mother wants to see a bit of him before she goes back to England. 'I know, we'll vote on it,' Paddy says. 'Eight votes and no abstentions.'

'We have to agree the options first,' Auntie May rules. 'I'm not slogging me way up to the top of the Scalp in this heat and Lou and Harry aren't cut out for it either.'

'Right, then. Here's the choices. Killiney. Blackrock. Howth Head as the outsider,' Paddy shouts over us.

'No,' Mam chips in. 'I'm not having Howth Head as an

option. It's right over the north side, and you know very well I can't even put a foot beyond the Pillar without getting a raging headache, can I, May?'

'That's a fact, Sally,' Auntie May concedes. 'The air over there is nothing compared to our air over here. I don't know how they manage with breathing it in all the time.'

The vote, when it is eventually taken, is six to two in Killiney's favour. I narrow my eyes to give Garry and Joan a withering look.

'Torca, it's called.' Paddy has learnt something.

His mother is making the tomato sandwiches. 'What?'

'Torca. That's what it's called. Torca Head. The park at Killiney. The one that young one calls the Up and Up Park. Torca.' He dances round the kitchen shaking his bum. 'Oh Torca, Torca, Torca . . . Torcha, Torcha, Torcha . . .'

I make up my own song: 'I'm agoin' Up and Up. Uhu ho. Up and Up. Aha, ha', and I shake my bum too.

Joan and Garry make an effort and we keep it up all across the Buildings and down the Hill.

Lou and Harry keep raving about the scenery and I begin to like them for the first time since they arrived. We sit on the steps of the memorial high on the hill, a little nearer to heaven, and pose for photographs. We are so high that I have a sense of falling through space and time into the unknown. I reach out for Auntie May's hand and hold on. Uncle Paddy has been replaced by strangers. In two, maybe three years, Auntie May herself will not be here. Her life will be lived out amongst strangers from now on. Don't ask me how I know it, but I do.

Lou White loves cucumber. She brought three huge ones over in her luggage and she's been slicing it onto her sandwiches ever since. Cheese. She has cucumber. Ham. Cucumber. Egg. Cucumber. She's sabotaged our picnic with the stuff. I pick it out of my tomato sandwich, cursing her under my breath. Only she gave me the ten shillings for my birthday, I'd pick a wing off a dead fly and put it under her cucumber. I'd never set eyes on one in my life and now I can't open me mouth for a bite of bread, but it's full of cucumber. And it smells awful.

And Auntie May smells of just-unwrapped soap.

Five

Summer is ended and Auntie May has gone back to London, to her room in Lou and Harry's house. From there, she can walk to her job in the Beecham's vitamin factory. Where does she walk to on Sundays when she walks alone? On Sundays here, after dinner, she walked with us, usually out to the Dodder to let us fish with jam jars on pieces of string. There was no point buying fishing nets on bamboo canes, even if they could be afforded, because you no sooner put them down on the river bank, than they vanished into thin air. A look along the river provided several probable culprits, all of them lined up with tell-tale green nets dangling from their canes into the shallow water. Anyone could have jam jars, that's why nobody wanted them, so nine times out of ten, if we went out with a jam jar, we came home with one too. The pinkeens in them were usually emptied into an old basin and observed for common habits until they died, fishes out of their own waters.

On a map of southeast England and Greater London, I try to work out the distance from Kensington to Leytonstone to see if a Sunday walk would take her out to meet Uncle Paddy. I see that it is impossible. If we knew where my dad lives, she could meet him for a cup of tea. Or Uncle Paddy and him could go to the pub together and talk about old times. John, Auntie May's second son, lives in Earl's Court, quite near Kensington on the map. I am relieved. Noel, her eldest, lives in Yorkshire, wherever that is. Wouldn't you think they'd all get a house and live together? They have all gone over there to work and earn money, because there is no work and money here – except for my dad, who does not want to be hemmed in – yet they have no money left over to do anything with, once they have paid for their digs and sent money home.

I will never go over there, except for a holiday. I can hear the hidden trickling of the oul' Swan River and feel the promise of my velvet curtains in my empty hands. When I get my house, they can all come home and live with me and we will talk all day and every day.

Before that, I have to go back to school. I'm declared fit as a fiddle. Sister Madeleine, the head nun, talks to five of us in her office. We have all been off school sick for a year or more. We are still not fit, by her standards, to join the classes we left until she has given us essential warnings about the expectations placed on us.

'There'll be no allowance made for slackness of any description. If you are not well enough, there is no place here for you. We are not a convalescent home, though that's the way we are treated, with the amount of sickness there is. The classes you left are the classes you will return to, without exception. You will all be behind and you will be expected to catch up. Hard work and application of purpose should do it. Good day.'

We all stand up to leave, relieved that none of us had been singled out. I whisper, 'Howaya', to a girl from the Buildings as we go.

'Patricia O'Brien, come back here now and close the door.' Sister Madeleine is red in the face with rage.

I turn, keeping my eyes cast down in case I provoke her further.

'Do you remember the rules of this school?'

'Most of them, Sister.'

She leans over her desk, her face twisting into a mask, behind which she can become anything she wants to. 'What ones have you forgotten?' she shouts.

I feel uncomfortable, because she is leaving me no option.

'How can I know, Sister, if I have forgotten?'

She hammers the desk with her cane. 'Don't get smart with me, you . . . you . . . wretched urchin.'

I stand in silence, waiting. I know she wants to use her cane. She wants to lash it down until she can no longer lift her arm. Small lines of sweat ooze on my back. I want to run, but my legs won't move.

'What was the matter with you, to warrant a year of absence?'

'I had TB, Sister. A spot on my left lung.'

'So, you are as diseased as most of this city. And you want this school to nurse you, don't you? Would you like a bed in the corner of the classroom. Eh?'

'No, Sister, I have no disease any more. I'm well now.'

'Until the next time. And your sister. Is she well now too?'

'She's nearly well. When she's better, she'll be back. She

loves school, so she does. Honest.' I lie, may God forgive me.

'Well, I'd like to give you something to remind her that I expect her manners, as well as her health, to be beyond doubt when she does return. Hold out your hand.'

She rolls up her right sleeve to get a better swing on the cane and lashes it down across my fingers. I shout out and withdraw my hand, placing it under my arm. She orders me to hold out my other hand. When I do, she lashes me again. A small fire is burning in my soul. When she orders me to hold out my hand again, I stand still, keeping my hands under my arms. She will have to pull them out, if she wants to keep beating me. We face each other. Both intent on victory.

'Hold out your hand. Do you hear me? Hold your hand out!'

I recoil from her. She smells chalky and spicy and I feel sick. My stomach turns over and over, but my hands stay put. If she touches me at all, I decide, I will kick her in the shins and run. I hope she hasn't locked the door. We both jump at the polite knock.

A voice enquires, 'Am I early, Sister Madeleine?'

Her terror mask changes before my eyes. I'm witness to another transubstantiation. Here she is in the blink of an eye, a flirty girl, soft and coy. Father Fahy spits hello. He smiles. She smiles. And I wait for the music. He transmutes into Pat O'Brien playing the priest in *Angels with Dirty Faces*. And I transmute too. I am no longer Pat O'Brien, schoolgirl. I'm James Cagney, an angel with a dirty face. School carries on, business as normal beyond the door. Beyond the miracles.

'Oh no, not at all, Father, do come in, won't you. This poor child is just back to school from TB and we're having a little chat.'

'And are you fully recovered?' he asks, as Sister Madeleine nods at me to leave.

'I am now, thank you, Father,' I say and walk down the corridor to my class. Very relieved.

When I examine my hands, they are swollen and blistered. So is my soul, or spirit, or whatever it is inside me that sets me apart.

Granny died last night. She will be buried on the day before Christmas Eve. Auntie May will be home for the funeral and for Christmas. Noel is coming home with her, his first time back from England in years. I wonder what he looks like now. People change. Grandilla has changed in the last few days. Instead of being the smartest man in Dublin, all polished and sparkly, he sits in his old man's singlet without a shave. People keep knocking on the door but he refuses to see them. Mam has all the arrangements to make on her own. Joan and I go with her, walking backwards and forwards across the city to see men in pinstriped suits and positions.

We walk along the canal to Sally's Bridge and turn towards Mount Jerome cemetery, where Mam has to see about reopening the family plot. I've been worrying all morning.

'What will we do about Christmas, Mam?'

'What do you mean, what will we do about Christmas?'

'I mean, will we have a turkey?"

She stops, stunned. 'Will we have a turkey? A bloody turkey! Will we have a turkey, and me mother not even in her grave. Is that all you can think of? Feckin' turkey?'

Mam starts crying. Not just tears, but sobs, and we are on the street. People are looking at us and she doesn't care. Joan begins to cry too. I won't. These things have to be discussed.

'What sort of a child are you at all?' Mam manages as she sobs. 'You're your father's daughter, that's a certainty. He'll never be dead while you're alive, with your runaway gob. Selfish to the core. That's what you are, the pair of you. Well, we'll see about turkeys soon enough, after the funeral. There won't be enough money for the potatoes to go round it in the dish, no less the penny to light the oven.'

Mam is gathering control of herself as we walk through the cemetery gates. I peep at Joan behind Mam's back and she smiles at me. Death and money are all they seem to be talking about in the house. Too much death and not enough money. It costs money to reopen the grave.

At the wake, the night before the burial, Noel begins singing 'Keep right on to the end of the Road', making all the women cry. It is strange having the wake without the body in the parlour. We weren't allowed to have her home, because the gangrene had rotted away so much of her body. I hear Mam tell Auntie May that the smell was terrible altogether at the end. Death was a merciful friend.

In the bleakness of this dark day before Christmas, we stand around the only thing we own in Dublin, a small patch of earth, the grave in which we bury our dead. When they lower Granny's coffin in, there is space for two more. One of them will be Grandilla, then who else? Who will be left to place on top of them?

I walk back between the rows of angels and Celtic crosses with women in black. The only face I recognise is Auntie Moll's. Even in black, in a graveyard, she manages to look slightly glamorous, different altogether from the other women. Without exception, they are wearing black head-scarves. Moll is wearing a small hat with a black feather in it. The feather is set with small pieces of jet and when the wind ruffles it, they shine. All the other women have hand-bags with handles clasped in gloveless hands, but Moll carries a long grey crocodile clutch bag with matching grey leather gloves. In her other hand, between raised fingers, she holds a lit cigarette. Instead of talking to the other women and entering the competition they have going about the number of times they have buried someone in this cemetery, she walks among them, but not with them. She ignores them and, try as they might to ignore her, they are drawn to look at her, as I am, mesmerised. I know her husband Alec is in the cemetery too, but she does not feel the need to mention him. In my house, as well as my green velvet curtains, I will have a hall table on which will lie a black feathered hat and grey leather gloves.

When all the mourners have left, Auntie May, Mam, Noel and Paddy sit long past one in the morning, going over old times. Granny, that old, bent, decaying woman, had been born to comfort, the only treasured daughter amongst three sons. A daughter of publicans and property owners in Pimlico, in the Liberties. Mary Reynolds had been a raving beauty, with coal-black hair and green eyes, and Grandilla, Jem Colgan, had fallen in love with her the first time he clapped eyes on her and she only fifteen. She served him a pitcher of porter in her mother's pub. The women in her family held all the wealth. The men gave it all back to Arthur Guinness. She was a spirited girl, though I cannot imagine it, and she ran away to marry her first husband, Paddy Fleming, when she was sixteen and a half. They went to Arklow, near the Meeting of the Waters, and lived in a cottage on the estate they worked on, he as a coachman and she as a parlour maid. It would have been lovely had they lived happily ever after, except that none of us would exist. Paddy Fleming died in her arms in their tenement in Thomas Street, leaving her a widow at twenty-seven, pregnant and with four young daughters to keep. She had already buried three children.

Grandilla loved her still, though she didn't believe him. Her burden was his. He married her and gave her children a home, including the son born after his father's death. Grandilla makes a habit of giving children a home. What will he do without her now? What will he do when all the children have gone? I cannot bear to hear any more and I go up to bed. For once, the talking is beyond me.

Joan nudges me awake. 'Can you hear it?' she whispers in the dark.

I can. In the scullery below us, the brass cold water tap is filling the big black kettle. Hairs rise on the back of my neck.

'It's Mam. Or Auntie May,' I say to Joan, to reassure myself.

'No. They're both asleep in Granny's bed in the parlour. They went in when I came up to bed.'

Joan is sitting up, pulling the blankets over her face. We hardly breathe.

'It can't be Granny,' I say, though it cannot be anybody else.

The shuffling from the scullery into the kitchen sounds like her shuffle. Nobody else in the house shuffles. If the house caught fire, I could not get out of bed. Now, unmistakably, the dying embers are being raked in the range, to clear the ashes, just as she always did in the early hours as she pottered about to ease the pain in her feet. In the morning, as usual, the kettle will be singing and the kitchen will be cosy. It will also be Christmas Eve.

Grandilla lies on in bed. The dispensary is closed, giving him an excuse. The kitchen is cold and white ash covers the grate and hearth. Mam is going to clear it when she has a cup of tea. It won't be the same with water boiled on the gas stove in the aluminium kettle. It will never be the same, because no one will light the fire in the early hours again.

'Did you hear me granny shuffling round in the night?' Joan asks Mam and Auntie May.

They looked at each other.

'No, of course not. How could she? You must have been dreaming,' Auntie May says.

'Of course you were dreaming,' Mam agrees. 'It was a terrible day yesterday.'

'We must have had the same dream then,' I say loudly, 'because I heard her too.'

'Oh, dear God in heaven, protect this house and all in it,' Auntie May says, then speaks more firmly to us. 'You may think you heard her, because you wanted to. Maybe it was real and you did hear her. They say it sometimes take a while for a poor soul to depart from this world. We just don't know about these things.' Mam puts a cup of tea in front of her and sits down, silently urging her to pick the right words. 'If you hear her again, because you might,' she continues, 'just say a little prayer for her and offer up thanks to God and his Blessed Mother that she was with us for so long. If you do, she'll be gone in a day or two.' She smiles at us, letting us know things are OK.

Mam adds, 'Whatever you do, don't say anything about it to your Grandilla. It'd kill him altogether.'

We make our promises and keep them. Granny stays on over Christmas, though there is no celebration, apart from the red candle burning all night in the parlour window. If others in the house hear her, they say nothing. Nor Joan and me. Not even to each other. She shuffles along the hall and rakes the fire a few more times, then she leaves, leaving a silence more unbearable than the noises in the early hours.

Noel has gone back to Yorkshire, laden with bacon and black and white pudding, and Auntie May will be returning to London tomorrow.

'I wish I could stay, Sally, I really do. But I've been

promised a house out in Crawley when the factory relocates. It's the only chance for the boys. They'll have more than they will ever have here.'

'When do you think you'll get the house, May?' Mam asks, her voice trembling.

'I'm on a waiting list. First, they have to want to move my job. Then, I have to want to move. Then, on top of that, I have to qualify. With children. I've ticked all the boxes. Now I just have to wait. I'm good at that!'

Mam's black jumper makes her face even whiter, especially with her black hair. She has large black circles under her eyes too. She looks a bit like Dracula's daughter, I think, and turn my face away in case I see new growth on her eyeteeth. I feel frightened. All the talk is of movement and change and people leaving. If not right now, then soon. I can't imagine the house without Paddy and Garry. Maybe Auntie May won't get her house in Crawley. Maybe she'll come home. We'll all manage somehow. We always have.

Grandilla sits in the corner listening. He has not been out of the house since we came back from Mount Jerome. Maybe he thinks he'll be left on his own. I don't see how, because Mam, Joan and I have nowhere to go. I want to hug him, but he never hugs anyone. Mam never hugs anyone either. They are alike. The distance from my side of the table to Grandilla's side is more than I can travel. Mam has taken to sleeping in the parlour, giving us more room in the bed.

Since Christmas, through the worst of the winter, Grandilla gets up in the early hours to make up the fire. He fills the kettle, sweeps the hearth and sets the table too. Life is the same and different. This morning, Grandilla even has Fluff sitting on his lap. He is stroking her fur and she is purring as if he is her long-time friend. His usual comment when he sees her is that he is tempted to give her a toe in the hole.

'I don't think she's well,' he says, when he sees the amazement on my face.

After school, I find Joan sitting on the step with the invalid in her old tin doll's pram. I peep in and pull back the blankets, shuddering with disgust. The cat is lying there like a hairy withered child with a yellow bonnet on its head. Usually it is hanging from her arm as if it's been boned and rolled, so relaxed is it. Joan is sobbing.

'What's up with it?' I ask, hoping it has the mange.

'I think it has the measles.'

'Cats don't get the measles.'

'Ah, they do,' Sylvester Merrins says.

Sylvester hangs around with Joan, mainly for her cat. He is an expert on them. His own cat is the best cat in Dublin. It gets the post from the door and frightens the postman. On a day that Mrs Merrins had no money at all for food, didn't Marmalade, the quick-witted cat, slink out to Findlater's and drag a string of sausages home for her to cook. Then it went back out to Ranelagh and carried chips back from the chipper, neatly wrapped in newspaper, to go with the sausages. 'Did it remember to put the salt and vinegar on?' Paddy asked when I repeated the story.

Sylvester is asked to manage the crisis.

'Right then, Joan, you'll have to take it to the free vet. It could infect everybody with them lumps if you don't find a cure.'

Together, Joan and Sylvester push the pram across the Buildings, almost running in their desperation to get the cat seen to. I wonder if we should be wearing masks or maybe hankies around our faces. I run to keep up, risking everything. Before we get to the bottom of the Hill, a small band of kids are running along behind us. They have picked up the scent of disaster.

We make them wait on the path outside the vet's. The waiting room is full of lame dogs and old ladies glad of somewhere to sit. We can't wait. The cat is curled dying in Joan's arms.

'Mister, Mister,' Sylvester shouts through the sliding window, 'there's a cat here covered in lumps all over. I'm startin' to get them too. Can you see to it, Mister? We don't know what's wrong with it.'

This appeal brings the vet out.

'Right, whose cat is it?'

'Mine, Mister,' Joan says.

'You come through to the surgery. The rest of you wait outside. He eyes all the kids peeping through the door.

'Can me sister come in with me?'

He looks me up and down. I pass. I hope he doesn't do an operation in front of me.

He takes the cat, now struggling, out of Joan's arms and sits it on a table. 'Tell me what the matter is.'

Joan pulls up the matinée coat.

'It's these spots. They've come up while I was at school. Is it going to die?'

Her sobs would wake the dead, so she's no worries there. I don't know where to look for the best. I wish she'd control herself. The vet looks. Then he laughs. He throws his head back and laughs so loudly, I think he has taken a turn. Each time he starts to talk to Joan, he laughs again. He's an eejit. We wait for him to compose himself. And him with a white coat on and all.

'This little lady is perfectly healthy. There is nothing at all wrong with her, except that she is going to have kittens.'

We stare at him, is he mad or what? He waits for the penny to drop. When it doesn't, he adds, 'These spots will feed them. They are not spots, they are nipples.'

On the steps, Joan gives an audience to the concerned fans. 'The spots are for feeding her kittens,' she says with pride.

'Ah yes, that's right, so they are,' Sylvester says.

'How will it have kittens?' I ask the expert.

'Oh, now, I can't tell you that. It would be a mortal sin,' says the fount of all wisdom. Joan allows Sylvester to carry Fluff home in the crook of his arm like a proud parent, while she pushes the tin pram along, clanking all the way back up the Hill.

'We better get a few tins of condensed milk in,' I resolve, ever the practical one. 'They must be mad altogether if they think a few oul' spots will feed them.'

Six

On Shrove Tuesday, Grandilla decides to make pancakes.

Joan looks at the mixture in the bowl. 'It's too watery,' she says, as if she's been cooking for a family of ten for forty years.

'Do you think so?' he asks the room in general.

'Add an egg,' I tell him, because it sounds better than too watery.

'Righto,' he agrees, cracking an egg into a cup and beating it.

'And a pinch of salt,' Paddy says.

By the time he's finished adding a bit of this and a pinch of that the mixture looks so thick, he decides to throw a handful of raisins in and bake a cake.

'Did you ever cook, Grandilla?' I ask him, because he never has in my lifetime.

'Now and then. Once in a while. I made curry in Burma and I made bread once for me mother in Francis Street. Never pancakes. Never pancakes. There's an art to them, I'm told. They're more difficult to cook than your French cousine.' He is beating the second pancake mixture, whipping it like a spinning top round the bowl.

'Can I toss one when it's cooking?'

'Indeed you can. But the mixture must stand for at least an hour. Maybe two. We'll have them when you mother comes home.'

'Or we'll have tuppence worth of gur cake from MacGurk's Dairy,' Paddy states, not fancying either Grandilla's pancakes or his improvised cake.

A domesticated Grandilla is a novelty. If he doesn't die before I get my house, I'll let him live with me and do the cooking. I have no intention of ever cooking. 'Oh that's lovely,' they say, when you've done it once, and before you know where you are, you end up like me granny.

He misses her. His way of showing it is to try to do all the things she did. All the years he sat at the table, never lifting a finger, except to his lips, while she sat and chopped vegetables, diced meat, made bread, strained dripping, lifted pots, lit fires. Now, when she is gone, he has become her. It is like he died and she moved into a better body called Grandilla, so that she can continue to look after us.

The pancakes, stacked high on a plate, smell delicious. Each one he lifts with a fork, squeezes it with lemon and a sprinkle of sugar, then folds it, sprinkles it again and serves it personally to us in turn, like he is a waiter. His face is puffed with pride and he watches us take every mouthful.

'Are they nice?' he asks us.

'Massive, Grandilla,' we all say and mean it.

Joan is sick again. The doctor is so worried about her that he arranges for her to go into St Anthony's in Merrion. At the last minute he sends me too, which is puzzling, because I am not sick at all. Mam takes us out on the bus after work on a summer's evening. Auntie Moll comes with us.

'Why have I got to go too? I'm not sick.'

I am feeling resentful at leaving my small gang of girls, Catherine, Ann and Eithne. We sit for hours in Dunne's hallway making up stories, discussing the ins and outs of this and that. We mainly talk about the latest musical showing in the Stella or the folley-uppers at the Princess. Musicals are best. We watch all the steps, learn all the songs, then put on concerts for the kids in the hallways of the Buildings or round the back of fairs in the Villas under the long wall. I am Doris Day and Catherine is Betty Grable. I am constantly defending my star role and if I am away for too long, one of my understudies, Ann or Eithne, will take over.

'I never heard of a healthy child going into hospital,' I complain on the bus.

'It's not a hospital, it's a home.' Auntie Moll nudges me, trying to keep me quiet.

'What sort of home?'

Kids get sent to all sorts of places in Dublin. There's Approved Schools, like Glencree and Artane, where boys are sent for stealing bicycles and robbing shops. They get beaten with leather straps and dipped in cold water and when they come home, they are white and quiet, like they have secrets from the world. I rob shops. Only biscuits and sweets and lemonade bottles. When people return their empty bottles for their sixpence deposit, Jimmy in Coffey's shop puts them in a crate outside. Before him, Mrs Brophy put them under lock and key in her parlour. But Jimmy is a culchie, so what can you expect? He doesn't understand the Dublin kids. We take them out of the crate and back into the shop for another sixpence. Sometimes Jimmy pays more out on the bottles in returnables than he's made when he sells them with the lemonade in.

Then there's convents for bad girls and orphans, like Goldenbridge. Mam's always saying she'd have been better off if she'd left us there when Dad walked out, instead of working her fingers to the bone to keep us.

I ask again, 'What sort of home?'

'A sort of convalescent home,' Auntie Moll says.

Mam says nothing. Joan, who has been in so many places for sick children, says nothing either.

The nuns wear white, as if they are in Africa. Nuns at St Louis's wear black, so there is a small novelty in watching them. It's creepy at night when they float around the dormitory with their candles and hover over the beds of crying children. The nurses are nicer than the nuns. Maybe because they can go home every night. There is one consolation about being in St Anthony's, I think, when Mam and Auntie Moll have waved goodbye from under the trees in the grounds, and that is, no more school.

It seems not even that small advantage will be mine. After breakfast, a nun calls the names of the new children and marches us to the schoolhouse. It consists of one room, one teacher and a rickety tin roof, through which the rain falls. It is like Mr Grogan's back of beyond and we only a few miles out of the city. The teacher is small and old, with a bun on top of her head. She is kind and careless, letting us talk whenever we want to and throw chalk at each other and her. Boys at the back keep locking each other in the store cupboard and she pretends not to see them. I like this school. I'd come here every day if it wasn't in a home.

At two o'clock school finishes and we have sandwiches and milk brought out to the field. The teacher sits with her back against a haystack and falls instantly asleep. We go mad, throwing straw all over each other and climbing on the roof of the barn. If we are sick, then it's a strange sickness we all have that has given us a massive injection of energy. In the sunshine, my arms go golden and so do my freckles. I live for the two o'clock bell and the fields.

Some afternoons, a few of us are allowed to help in the kitchen garden. It is a mysterious place full of strings and poles and greenhouses and colours and smells. The old nun wears a hat low on her forehead, over her veil, and a navy overall, full of pockets. Like a magician, she pulls out scissors and knives for pruning and string for tying. Her face is like the uppers of my old shoes, crinkled and brown. We learn more from her than we do from the teacher.

She works while we gaze in wonder around us, then walks off between rows of strawberries, leaving us to recover our senses, which have been stolen from us. I have never before been in a garden. I've been in several parks and walked around many fine Dublin squares, including Mountpleasant, Stephen's Green and Palmerston Park. It would be wrong to count them, though. I can only measure this garden against ones with walls and paths and toolsheds full of spades and shovels and baskets.

Most days, I hurry to the garden after school. I have a lot to learn, if I'm to have a garden when I get my house. It is becoming complicated, moving on from velvet curtains. I learn to recognise weeds and can name flowers other than daisies and buttercups. I eat more of the soft fruits than I pick. The only raspberries I ever tasted before were in jam.

Joan is quiet most of the time. Too quiet, I think. We hardly get to see each other. She sleeps in one dormitory with older girls. I sleep in another with boys and babies, as well as ordinary girls. I wave to her if I catch a glimpse of her and she usually waves back, but today, my birthday, I will be able to see her properly. I am having a tea party after school. Mam has sent me a tipsy cake and a nurse has put ten candles on it. I have six cards to open and two presents. Auntie May sent a card from London with a five-shilling postal order. There's a card from Mam and a card from Auntie Moll. One from Lou and Harry White and one from Catherine, Ann and Eithne. They haven't forgotten me. I'm still Doris Day. I sigh with happiness. I hold out my last card, still in its envelope, trying to think who else could have sent it. Not Joan, she is here. She would not have needed to post it.

'It could be from Dad,' I whisper to Joan.

'Open it and see,' she tells me.

It is a lovely card of a pop-up dog and a number ten badge.

'Who sent it?' Joan asks.

'It's from Grandilla. I can't believe it. He's never sent me a card before.'

87

She takes it from me and reads: 'Wishing you a very happy birthday. Hurry home soon. Love, Grandilla.'

We both start crying. It's all right for Joan, she's used to it, but it's agony for me, because I never cry. Not as a rule.

'Why can't we go home, Joan?' I ask, as wave after wave of homesickness washes over me. 'What have we done wrong to be sent here?'

'We've done nothing wrong. It's not us. It's Mam. I don't think she can cope with us.'

'Why? She copes with Paddy and Garry. They haven't been sent away. It must be our fault.'

'If I tell you something, will you keep it a secret?' Joan asks.

The nurse urges me to blow out the candles on the tipsy cake and make a wish. I have never had a birthday party. We are always invited to the Henley girls' birthdays. Mr Henley is great gas. He dresses up every Hallowe'en. I try to behave like Maura, sitting still and smiling. I'm not sure I like it, with everyone waiting for me. I blow, despite myself, and all the candles go out together. The kids all cheer, shouting at me to make a wish. I close my eyes.

Let us go home, I wish.

After the party, I try to find Joan. I must know the secret. She is nowhere to be seen. My presents were two jigsaws. I hate jigsaws.

The apple trees are weighted heavy with ripe fruit. We are allowed to eat the ones we find on the ground. They are bruised and maggoty, so the only solution is to shake the tree and catch the new falls for ourselves. The garden's end-of-summer lushness hides us from the nuns, nurses and ourselves. Our real selves belong on paved streets with buses and bustle, with people talking in our own rhythms. Our ears are used to voices, not birdsong. I miss them, the voices. Even the ones I have listened to and never really heard what they were saying.

I want to go home.

Across the grounds, St Anthony's Asylum for Blind Children hides in the trees. Sometimes, drifting on breezes, we hear the children singing. We never see them. Except when we go over to their chapel for Mass. We stand at the back, creatures apart, because the nuns think we are rough city urchins, fit only for each other. Our place is always at the back, just like we are always at the back of the class. These children have come from all over the country, from all sorts of backgrounds, for one reason only, lack of vision. We have come from one background only, lack of money. We are needy of the nuns' charity. While the nuns grow virtuous and nearer to God with their good works, we become victims of deeds they call 'good', like discipline of work and prayer.

Polishing all the shoes in the boot room is the job I usually get. I'm supposed to pray while I work in solitude, rubbing a rag across summer sandals or whitening all the runners, mixing the paste with water and applying it evenly with an old toothbrush. In theory. More goes on myself than the runners. The first time I did it, I mixed all the runners up and I spent the whole evening acting like Prince Charming, trying to find the foot to fit, instead of roaming about the fields or the kitchen garden.

We are not allowed to look the nuns in the eye. If we are meek enough, they will inherit the earth. I know the secrets the Artane boys know.

'After breakfast,' the head nun announces, 'we have a special treat for you. We are taking you for a walk along the strand at Merrion. And we are also taking the blind children. You must behave yourselves. No pushing. No swearing. Just best behaviour, please.'

What more can she expect from city children?

'The blind children will set you their good example.'

Joan walks across the field with me towards the Blind Asylum. The sun dances fairies in the trees.

'Special treat?' I say to Joan. 'We can go out to Merrion any time we want when we're at home. We've been here for weeks and this is the first time we've been allowed out. It's like we're in prison. How can it be a treat? Suppose I say I want to stay and help the gardener, would they let me?'

'Of course not.'

'So how can it be a treat if we have to go whether we want to or not? Just like we had to come here, whether we wanted to or not. All I want to do is go home.'

'I know. Mam is coming to see us tomorrow night. With Auntie Moll. She might take us home soon.'

'How do you know?'

'She sent a note in with a woman who works in the kitchen.'

'How can she see us? It's not visiting day. She can only leave a parcel at the gate.'

'That's when she's coming. She's going to leave us a parcel

at the gate, then she'll sneak into the grounds and wave to us at your dormitory window. I've to try to be in there about eight o'clock.'

I don't understand. 'How can she take us home, if we have to wave at her through a window?'

Joan is tired of explanation. 'No. Not tomorrow night. Soon. She's going to see about it.' Joan squeezes my hand.

I am still confused. 'I don't know why we're here in the first place. I'm not sick. Even you're not sick any more.'

'It's not about being sick,' Joan says. 'It's about Mam. She can't cope with us.'

'Is that the secret?'

Joan nods.

'Why is she trying to get us out if she can't cope, then?'

Cope? What does that word mean? Wasn't there a fella in Dublin called Paddy the Cope? He was running around the streets about the same time as Biddy the Burster-Bucket, long before Johnny Forty-Coats or Bang-Bang.

We are queuing in the drive of the asylum, waiting for the blind children to come out. Some have white sticks; some, dark glasses, like Joan used to have. Some are just holding hands with others better equipped. We walk in crocodile through the gates, back into the world. I am elated. People stand aside to let us pass. They see only white sticks and assume we are all blind.

'Ah, God help them,' a couple of old women murmur at a bus stop.

'Isn't it a terrible pity all the same. Blighted for life they are.'

Along the strand, people stand up from their deck chairs and move them out of the way. I pick my way over the sand in unsuitable laced-up shoes and stumble.

A man races over, picks me up and holds my elbow, gripping tightly. 'Hold your horses, love, until I find your white stick.' He kicks his foot round in the sand, searching.

I burst out laughing. 'It's all right, Mister, it's all right now.'

Mam and Auntie Moll are waving from under the trees. Joan stands beside me. We look down on them, as if they are a pair of garden ornaments. They have smiles on their faces. We don't smile back. I want them to go so that I can get into bed. They will go back on the bus, feeling as if they have done their good deed for the day. I'm sick of good deeds. They will go into the kitchen for a cup of tea and an examination of their visit. When Auntie Moll leaves to walk back to Daniel Street, she will stand on the doorstep and tell Mam not to worry, everything will be all right. But it won't. Don't they realise that? Looking at them through glass, with them on the outside, places us inside. Captive. They are still there waving as I turn my back on them.

For a few weeks longer, we serve out our sentence, getting up to one bell and going to bed to another. I think that there is no escape, but just as swiftly as we arrived here, we are told to leave. No preparation, apart from stripping our beds and changing out of the dresses we have had to wear.

We wait in the porch with two brown paper parcels of our clothes. The children remaining behind have been taken on another 'treat'. We didn't have time to say goodbye to them. It is just as well we made no special friends. I wonder if Catherine, Ann and Eithne will remember me. I can't believe we're going home. I feel nervous in case the nuns change their minds and grab us back again without warning. I count, as if I am a clock ticking off the minutes. I must keep counting. If I speak to Joan, it will break the spell. Time will stand still. We will be here forever.

'Here's Mam now,' Joan shouts. 'Here she is.'

Mam is coming right up to the front door to collect us. I realise she is quite a small person. She walks along the gravel in slingback shoes, taking an eternity, smiling and waving. We wave back, encouraging her to hurry up. We are still prisoners. Even if we go home today, we might be brought back tomorrow. We will have to be more watchful from now on.

Grandilla has shrunk. The kitchen is smaller than I remember it.

'It's only relative,' Grandilla says. 'You've been living in a bigger space for so long, you've constructed different boundaries. We all do it.'

'I kept thinking about the kitchen, even though I wasn't here.'

'Well, you're here now and that's what matters,' Mam says, as if the home can be removed with our coats.

I want to examine things for change. I want to count the cups and saucers and the knives in the drawer. I want an explanation.

'Why were we in that home, Mam?'

'Because Joan wasn't very well. That's why. I told you before. You're never satisfied.' Mam is going to cry. She always does when she doesn't want to say things.

'I was all right, though, Mam. You never took me to the doctor.'

'The doctor thought it was for the best. He thought it would do you good.'

Joan sits silently.

When Paddy and Garry come home for their tea, things seem nearly normal again. Now we are six. After tea, I am allowed out to play. I run across the Buildings, delighting in their greyness. The kids are gathering near the ball alley, getting set for another night of running and screaming. There's a fight being planned, the Buildings versus Chester Road. We'll murder them. We pick our leader, one of the tough Conways.

'Ee-aye-adio,' we chant, making war noises by banging the flat of our hands against our open mouths. We run in file like warriors through evening light and the dusk of autumn, past men in shirtsleeves playing a game of pitch-and-toss against the long dividing wall. Women sit outside the hallways, surrounded by children, enjoying the last of the evenings before winter sets in.

The Chester Road kids are waiting with recruits from Rugby Road. We charge them and they run, some in fright back into their houses, others, good runners, along Oxford Road, down Charleston Road, out through the shops in Ranelagh.

'Bloody street Arabs,' an old woman shouts and picks up her lapdog.

We run ourselves to a standstill and disperse without prisoners at the bottom of the Hill.

I knock on Ann's door. Mrs Elliott invites me in to wait. Eithne is already there, squeezed onto a seat at the end of the table, eating bread and dripping with the family.

'Would you like a slice, love?' Mrs Elliott asks.

'Ah, no thank you, Mrs Elliott. I've just had my tea.'

'Have you? I bet it tasted great, after being in the home.'

'It was lovely altogether, Mrs Elliott. And we had bread and dripping too.'

Eithne, Ann and I go up to Gulistan to Catherine's cottage. Mr Downes is setting off on his bike to visit his wife in St James's. She's had a lung removed and she can't come home yet, but she's getting better. Mr Downes does everything for his children while his wife is away and he still makes jokes when he sees us. I wish I had a dad like him. He wouldn't let his children go into a home.

'Catherine,' he calls through the door, 'better get on your dancin' shoes. Doris Day is back.'

Seven

It helps that the rhythm in us is as natural as our breath. In and out. In and out. Kick and stamp. Kick and stamp and lift and lift. I do a great Johnnie Ray number called 'Walkin' My Baby Back Home' for the kids sitting on the path. It's easy to bluff with tap-dancing as long as you keep time. I bluff and await the applause, wallowing in it. Catherine is next. She does an Irish jig, which is all right for her. She goes to Annie Berry's Saturday School of Dance in the Buildings. 'One, two, three and on your heel. One, two, three and on your heel,' Annie instructs, while her brother plays the accordion and kids without the sixpence a lesson look through the window, trying to absorb a few tips.

God alone knows how, but we have managed to slip into the Radio Éireann studio in Rathmines as they prepare to broadcast their *Céilidhe Music Show*. Catherine is forever trying to outdo her brother, who won a competition at the Four Provinces Ballroom with a perfect take-off of Nat King Cole. She is just waiting to be discovered, like Connie Smith, who lived in the Buildings, so she tries to be in the right places in case her opportunity knocks.

She's dead lucky, because the compère asks, 'Are there any Irish dancers in the audience?'

Catherine's hand shoots up, 'Me, Mister. Me.' At the same time, she's pulling the rest of us to our feet. 'Come on. Oh, please get up. I can't dance on me own.'

Before we know it, we are up dancing on the boards to 'The Walls of Limerick', without any rehearsal at all. The small audience applauds us loudly and the music swings into another set.

The four of us fall giggling out onto the Rathmines Road. Our feet have danced on the wireless. We're stars.

'If we are interviewed for the papers,' Catherine says, 'and they ask will success change us, I'll say, too bloody true it will. Didn't success do wonders for Maureen O'Hara!'

Mam is not impressed when we tell her we danced on the wireless, even though she was listening to the programme.

'Sure how the hell could I tell it was me own daughter dancing on the wireless? One pair of clattering hobnails is just the same as another, as long as the timing is right. They saw you coming, letting you in for free so that you could dance for nothing.' She draws breath, before heaping the final insult on us. 'Ginger Rogers wouldn't dance for nothing!'

Our bubble is burst, we sit dejected.

Mam settles her feet on the other hard chair. 'Exploited. That's what you were, the lot of you.'

Catherine is outraged. 'Now that you've pointed it out, Mrs O'Brien, I will never dance for Radio Éireann again. Not if they pay me.'

When we are not dancing, we walk by the canal alongside couples, arms entwined, and old men with no money for pubs, sitting on the daisies. We splash stones in the water, frightening the ducks and watch snooty swans gliding through reed lanes with their young, still tinged baby-brown. They head towards the setting sun, turning to shadows in the twilight glow. Perfect pairs. Perfect families. Perfect examples. We sit on the grass silently, not wanting to end the evening.

'What do you want to be when you grow up?' Eithne asks of no girl in particular.

'A dancer,' Catherine says without having to think, clearly over her exploitation.

'I want to be a nurse,' Ann says, surprising us, because she can't stand blood.

It's a hard question. I think it's a wrong one.

'Nothing at all,' I say.

'You can't do nothing,' Catherine says, wishing she had thought of it first.

'I can so. I can sit all day and all night doing nothing in my own house.'

'Well then, smart arse, where is your own house going to be?' Catherine is annoyed now and stands up to hurl big stones into the water. She never thought about her own house or sitting still in it.

We all stand. It is getting really late. I'm confusing myself, because just as Catherine can't dance all the time, I know I can't sit in my house all the time either. I'm trying to think up a solution to this dilemma. The only one I can arrive at is a husband. Not one like my dad. Definitely not. One like Mr Grogan might be suitable, but he would have to be my age. I think of Auntie Moll and realise why she married Uncle Alec. She needed her own house where she could cook and listen to operas. I can't see what else I can 'do' in order to let myself 'be'.

'Well?' they demand, chasing my dreams.

'My own house is going to be here, on the banks of the Swan River, and I am going to be a writer.'

I never before thought of being a writer. I thought I would work in the laundry like Mam or clean other people's houses like the aunts. The word 'writer' just came out of my mouth from nowhere. It sounds a lot better than 'husband'. They are as surprised as I am.

Whenever Mam catches me writing, she asks me if I have nothing better to do. If she's really annoyed, she insists on reading it before throwing it on the fire like rubbish. 'That won't get you anywhere,' she says. 'Your bloody father fancied himself as a writer. Always down with that bloody Father Sylvester in Adam and Eve's on the quays. Intellectuals they thought they were. I ask you. One a priest and one a military policeman in the Irish Free State Army.'

We are walking up Mountpleasant Avenue, past the giant's house and the Leinster Cricket Ground, where the magician made Catherine disappear at the funfair. Anything is possible. If Catherine can get in a basket and disappear and if a river runs under our feet and we don't see it, even someone like me can be a writer.

'Where's the Swan River?' Ann asks, and I tell her.

'Right here.'

'You're mad, Patty O'Brien, so you are. There's no river here. And you can't be a writer, you'd have to be posh and go to Trinity College,' Catherine says, as if she is right.

Perhaps she is.

'Do you remember last year at the funfair when the magician put you in the basket and made you disappear before the audience?' I ask her.

Catherine remembers. She rests against the cricket ground wall, giggling and coughing. 'Janey Mac, when he asked for a volunteer, we all put our hands up, remember? He had already given me three shillings outside his tent and told me I had to climb in the basket and curl up until someone opened the trap door underneath in the stage. He promised he wouldn't stick in the sword until I was kneeling on the ground.'

'Yeah, and we were screamin' as if he was killing you and he kept runnin' the sword through the basket an' all,' Eithne says.

'Then, after all the screamin' an' shoutin', he puts his sword in his belt, opens the basket and you step out. Remember? And you told us you went to a magical land full of palaces and white tigers lying around like pussycats?' I continue.

'Yeah, and you were under the stage all the time,' Eithne shouts, let down.

Catherine needs to explain herself. 'I made it up because he told me I mustn't tell anyone about the trap door or he'd take me money back. That's all. And anyway, I told you all after I bought the fish and chips out in the chipper, didn't I, Ann?'

'That's right. She told us all the same, so she did.'

The point I want to make is becoming clearer to me. 'Well, all I'll be doing if I sit in my house on the Swan River and write all day is make up stories. Just like the one you made up to keep in with the magician.'

We are all surprised by my answer. Catherine, not only a magician's assistant and a dancer, realises she has the makings of a writer. All any of us can say now is good night.

It's always the same. After Hallowe'en, we think about Christmas. From the time the clocks go back and the nights start to draw in, we spend more time in the house. Joan wants to make paper chains for Christmas. She would also like a Christmas tree, lit with small white candles on every branch, like Dolores Holden's, her best friend from Rugby Road. Every year, Mrs Holden lets us in to see it. We didn't go to look at it last year out of respect for Granny.

Granny hated paper chains and the 'paraphernalia of Christmas'. 'Dust collectors, that's all they are and a waste of good money,' she'd say as soon as she heard the first carol. 'All they're good for is kindling for the fire.' Though she is up in Mount Jerome, her voice is still in our heads. We begin to cut and paste paper chains from old scraps of paper, making bells and lanterns and misshapen reindeer, working against our consciences, awash with guilt.

'Jaysus,' Grandilla says when he sees them spread across

the table, 'it's like a cottage industry. Are you doing them for everybody in the Buildings as well as the Villas?' he asks, irritated by the mess.

He is not too well. He hardly ever goes out now, not even over to McGrath's on the Hill for his couple of glasses of stout. Mam has taken to going across for them, bringing them back in brown paper bags, ashamed to be seen carrying them.

'No, Grandilla,' Garry says, 'we're doing them for us. They're all for us. We can decorate the whole house this year . . .' He stops, mindful of what he is about to say, knowing that pleading will get us nowhere.

'If you put them up, you'll only have to take them down. There's no purpose to them that I can see, except to stop the dust settling on the presses. We can light a red candle in the parlour window as we've always done and put a few sprigs of holly over the pictures. We can have a good dinner. What more could you want?'

Grandilla has given us our answer. We clear the table, throwing the fruits of our labour on to the fire.

'Why do we always light a red candle?' I ask him.

They used to say that it was to help Santy Claus to find the house, but we no longer believe in Santy Claus.

'It's for them who might come home,' he says, and from nowhere, I think of Dad.

'Who do you mean, Grandilla? Auntie May and Uncle Paddy know we'll be in. They don't need a candle.'

'I mean, all them that's left. Emigrated. As well as them that's dead and gone.'

'Janey,' I say, 'I hope they don't all turn up together!'

Holding his chest for a minute to catch his breath, Grandilla walks to the door. 'If they do, make sure you invite them in. In no time at all, there'll be strangers in the house.'

It is only eight o'clock and he's gone to bed.

'Take no notice of him,' Mam says. 'He's rambling. That's all.'

In bed myself now, I count all the family on my mother's side who are dead or gone. Just the family. Not cousins or anything. There's the three children from Granny's first marriage to Paddy Fleming. They died as babies. Then Paddy Fleming. He died at twenty-eight. That's four. Then there's the five from that first family who lived. Only Auntie Moll is still here. Three of Moll's sisters, Maggie, Essie and Rosie emigrated. Rosie ran away to Rhodesia with a fella from Terenure. He was bitten by a snake and died. Do I count him? No. Stick to family.

Maggie took her illegitimate daughter Gussie with her to Hertfordshire when she finally married Gussie's father. And Gussie married the man who managed the London Palladium. That's ten. Two years before I was born, Auntie Moll's only surviving brother caught TB and died. He was thirty-six. But I've already counted him. Granny never got over it. Then Granny died. That's eleven. Auntie May's baby girl Rose died from meningitis when she was nine months old. That's twelve. Then Uncle Paddy went to England. I have to count him, because he's Garry and Paddy's da, and I really like him. After that, there's Noel and John who went to England. Noel to Yorkshire and John to Earl's Court. They make fifteen. My little brother, sixteen. If I include

Grandilla and the rest of us in the house, Paddy, Garry, Mam, Joan and me, that makes twenty-two. I nearly forgot the six children who died from Granny's second marriage to Grandilla. Mam told us about her little brother, Buddleigh, who died when he was four, and her cute little sister, Angela, who liked to dance. That's twenty-eight.

In body or in spirit, it's going to be a crowded house. I can just see them all standing round the red candle in the parlour window, waiting to be let in. Wouldn't it be a great hooley all the same if they all turned up?

'And how have you been these past fifty years while I've been bringing up all these children?' Grandilla would ask Paddy Fleming over a bottle of stout.

'Ah, grand. Grand altogether. Not a care in the world. It's a great life if you don't weaken.'

There's all these extra beds to be found. I've decided to count Uncle Alec in after all, out of fairness to Auntie Moll. Twenty-nine. What about Dad? Where will he go? Limerick maybe. Grandilla would never let him in, not even if I only whisper his name around the candle. Of all the people past, present, living or dead, he is the only one who can't come in. Banished for eternity. I fall asleep sorting out beds and blankets for all of them. Some people count sheep.

Next morning, despite the chill and the smell of mists brought in on damp coats, as if to make amends for his mood last night, Grandilla makes a pot of steaming porridge for breakfast. He lollops large helpings into bowls and passes the milk and sugar round the table. 'There, now. That'll set you up for the day.'

I watch him, inspecting him for a halo or a sign of significance.

'We'll take a run out to the zoo. It's years since I had a ride on an elephant's back,' he'd said, just after we came home from St Anthony's. We couldn't believe it, but hurried up in case he changed his mind. He never usually took us anywhere. In the monkey house, he put his arm on my shoulder when I got too close to the bars. I pulled away, more nervous of him than the baboon, but by the time we got round to the elephants, I was holding his hand.

'Elephants never forget,' he told us, 'and they grow old and die and mourn their dead.'

'And what do they put on their headstones, Grandilla?' I asked.

'Tusk, tusk,' said Garry.

I wonder if the elephant who gave us a ride on his back will remember us if we go back next year. I wonder if Grandilla will still be here.

Even Mam was relaxed that day, pleased for once that her father was spending time with her. She took a photograph of us with her Box Brownie camera. 'I hope it comes out,' she said, as if the day is a dream and she needs the photograph to prove it happened. It is stuck behind the clock, curling at the edges and fading fast.

The banging on the hall door wakes us all up. It's still a few days to Christmas, and Grandilla has been lying in the Meath hospital for the past week. Mam jumps out of bed and puts on her coat, which was lying across our feet. A frosty moonbeam lights her way down the dim stairs. I am shivering at the loss of the coat's bulk, then my knees start to tremble. The Angel of Death has sent his herald yet again. Urgent voices, then Maggie Heffernan's, catching as she tries to speak, making it difficult to grasp. 'It's the hospital, Sally. You're wanted on the phone.'

Phone calls and telegrams have replaced the screech of the Banshee and the Dead Man's Rap, but are just as feared, just as chilling. People in the Villas associate the Heffernans with the dark side of life. If Maggie or Alfie are seen knocking on the door, people bless themselves.

The phone call this time is about Grandilla. I know he is already dead. I have known since spring that he wanted to die. A strange thing happened to him then, when he turned nice. The previous Christmas, after Granny was buried, he had been as mean and miserable as he'd ever been. We first noticed the change on Shrove Tuesday when he made the pancakes. Though he'd mumbled excuses and shouted at us several times before tea to reassure us and himself that he was still the same miserable oul' so-and-so he'd always been, he could not hide the sadness in his eyes. All fight had gone.

Winter began to hang in fog around the Villas and seep in through seldom opened doors. He took to coughing fits that turned his face blue and stole his breath. He seemed always to be asleep. Once, he dozed off in a rambling sentence about the Boer War. His old man's face relaxed, taking on the blush of a child. The old soldier vanished, leaving just the boy in the used body. He should have made pancakes a long time ago.

We all go to see him in the morgue. His hair is silky and his moustache is newly clipped. In death, my shiny Grandilla has returned. He could be stretched out on the kitchen table, he looks so comfortable and at home. The only clash of concern is the rosary beads twisted through his lifeless fingers. He never prayed. Not that I know of.

Before the funeral, which can't be held until Auntie May manages to get home, people call to the house and sit in the kitchen drinking his whiskey.

'I think he pined for Mary,' is the general opinion.

'Ah, he did so. I think he did,' people say, who haven't seen him since she died.

I think he was sad for himself. He had become a man too soon, fighting wars. Later burdened with the children of other men. He had nearly left it too late to let us know him.

Again, it is the eve of Christmas Eve. Black plumed horses pull all the carriages and the hearse. All the women are in black once more and Auntie Moll is wearing her hat. I have a black armband on my sleeve and a black ribbon in my hair. So does Joan. On our hall door, a large wreath hangs with a black-edged card commemorating him. Even the carriage window has a small black blind. I pull it up to see where we are. Mam slaps my hand. For the rest of Grandilla's last journey, I sit with my head lowered, listening to the sure and regular clip-clop of the horses' hooves on rain-drenched streets.

We walk in file behind the coffin, from the gate, through the vaults topped with angels, some standing with folded wings, some kneeling in demented grief, hands joined in prayer, weighed down with the sins of the world. Even the Dublin Mountains, looming watchful beyond, are wearing black clouds of mourning and they weep inconsolably. I know that Grandilla is not special, even in death, because all across the cemetery, at the end of every path, lie row after row of graves, most with up to six people in them. They can't all be special, I think, not even Grandilla, though he was once the smartest Grandilla in Dublin, but I hope they all are missed, like he is already. It would be really nice, I think, and can't help myself, though I know it is wrong, if, in one of these graves holding the remains of people who were not special in any way at all, my dad is lying. Then I would know where he is at least. Death has a certain security.

Again, we sit and listen to the talk around the table before we go to bed. If Grandilla roams around the house in the small hours, we don't hear him. We listen, willing small noises, unable to make them manifest, falling asleep at dawn. Next morning on the Eve of Christmas, we cut and paste new paper chains and hang them from the kitchen ceiling in the gathering dust. At midnight, we light a new red candle and place it in the parlour window, a small light in Dublin, just for him.

After the funeral and Christmas, Auntie May is going back to England. She takes me with her down to Cooke's at the end of Grafton Street, to get her sailing ticket and change her money up. We run into Auntie Moll as she is about to go into Cavendish's.

'I'm just going in to get a bit of oilcloth for the scullery,' she tells us. 'If you're not in a hurry, I'll meet you in Bewley's for a cup of tea. I've had the insurance policy pay-out. The one I took out on Jem Colgan. It'll help Sally with the burial costs, but there's enough for a treat or two.'

We sit waiting for her under the speckling windows. Auntie May is wearing a navy suit and her dark hair is tied back with a slim velvet ribbon. She never wore suits before she went to England and I think how nice she looks. I wish she didn't have to go back. She won't order until Auntie Moll arrives, in case she's faced with the bill. This is our first time in the coffee house, although the aroma of the freshly roasting coffee gives us pleasure every time we pass.

When other customers keep glancing towards the door, we know Auntie Moll is making her entrance.

'Will you look at the cut of her?' Auntie May says, embarrassed.

Her grey swagger coat is casual on her shoulders and her neat little hat is tilted forward for the kill. In one hand, she holds a lit cigarette, and in the other, a shopping bag so laden it is almost sweeping the floor. She reaches our table, flinging the shopping carelessly underneath.

'Have you ordered yet?'

'No. The waitress hasn't come over yet,' Auntie May lies, without a blush.

Auntie Moll slides her coat onto the back of the chair and

keeps her hat on. From her throat, she unpins her scarf and sticks the safety pin into the collar of her jumper.

'There, that's better. Right, May, what will you have?'

'A cup of tea will do me fine.'

'And you, Patty, will you have a glass of milk and a cream bun?'

I am in heaven. 'Yes, please.'

The waitress, standoffish in her little black dress, turns to Auntie Moll. 'And yourself, madam?'

'Oh, I'll just have a cup of black coffee and an ashtray,' she indicates her cigarette, taking her down a peg or two.

The waitress ignores Moll, gliding away to whisper our order like a confession, through a hatch.

Auntie May winks at me. 'Black coffee? For Jaysus' sake!'

There are only five of us in the house now. Five out of ten. At one time I thought everyone was forever. Forever and ever, Amen. Mam is cross more often and finds it hard cooking and cleaning after work, though we try to help her. We peel the potatoes and set the table and make the beds. I even scrubbed the floor, but it just made her angry, because I left pools of water on it and she had to get down on her hands and knees to mop it up, wringing it into a bucket.

'Leave it till I ask you to help in future. You're more of a hindrance than a help. If you think or imagine that I've nothing better to do after a day's work than mop up after you, you're mistaken. Get out of this house and don't talk to me again.'

I stand out on the doorstep until I think she's feeling

better. When I go in, she doesn't say anything. Nothing. Not even in anger.

'Are you not talking to me then, Mam?' I ask.

She doesn't answer. She doesn't answer me all week. I think a letter might work.

Dear Mam

I am sorry I made the floor so wet and that I made you extra work. I hope you are better now and will talk to me soon. I promise I'll be good from now on.

Best love, Patty

I fold the letter and take it up to the Kelso Laundry.

'Will you take this into me mam?' I ask the woman at the counter.

I stand waiting for an answer and a queue of people form behind me. I can feel their eyes on me, searching me for sins. What sort of young rapscallion would torment her mother?

Instead of Mam, who I hope will come out, the woman comes back. 'You'd better go home, love. Your mam is busy.'

I walk back down Richmond Hill, wondering how I can get her to talk to me again. If I do anything to help her, she'll go mad. I'm more of a hindrance. Maybe she hasn't read my letter yet. That's it. When she does, she'll know I'm sorry and forget all about it.

I watch the clock all afternoon. It takes forever for the hands to get to six. When I hear the Angelus bells, I hurry out to wait in Coffey's Lane. It's too dark to go any further. As I wait in a doorway, I rehearse what I will say to her, going over and over it until I hear her footsteps. I'd recognise them anywhere.

'Hello, Mam,' I call out softly in case I frighten her. 'It's only me. I've come to meet you.'

She doesn't alter her pace at all. Nor does she speak. I walk with her in silence into the house.

Eight

The shamrock is lying in a saucepan of water, waiting to be pinned with our badges to our coats. Joan and I have green ribbons in our hair. Our shoes are polished, ready for the St Patrick's Day Parade.

'There,' Mam says, after pinning in my shamrock and inspecting me, including my fingernails, 'you'll do.'

There's an excitement everywhere. Everyone has a touch of green on them, even if it's only a sprig of shamrock. The nuns at school have made much of the parade this year. 'It's only the fourth year of Ireland's nationhood. A Republic. A true army of a true republican country will be leading the parade this year,' they told us. 'We are no longer a Free State of Britain. We are ourselves alone.'

Whatever we are doesn't seem to be doing much for our poor city, but I love the parade, with drums and pipers and decorated lorries, soldiers in greatcoats and leather boots. We stand squashed on the curve of the Bank of Ireland, screaming ourselves hoarse. People usher children to the front. We stand, enchanted, until the last lorry has passed, leaving us lonely and lost after all the excitement. Everyone seems to be heading back through the Green, like us.

Walking by the tailored lawns, an image of my dad walking through the arch comes to mind. Where is he today? He could have been marching in the parade. It's no good asking Mam what she thinks. His name is still forbidden.

I'm sitting on the steps of Dunne's hallway, enjoying Saturday without school, waiting for Catherine. It's still early; only daily Mass-goers on the streets. A telegram boy rides his bike from Alma Terrace, a toy soldier in his uniform. He takes out an envelope from his belt bag, examining it, inspecting the numbers on the doors in the Villas. I'm not worried. Sometimes, if people have to come home quick, they send telegrams. We only get bad news from the Heffernans. He decides which house his telegram is for and props his bike on the kerb. I am still watching. He walks to our house, slim shoulders back, preparing himself. Mam puts her hand to her mouth. He hands her the envelope and she signs a piece of paper against the doorframe.

'Are you all right, Missus?' he says.

She watches him cycling away before closing the door. I sit where I am as if I am posh, no curiosity. Mrs MacInerney passes me on the steps, her plaid coat buttoned to her neck and her hat pinned securely to her hair, though there's not a breath of wind to blow it off. She'll take no chances.

'Is that all you have to do on a lovely day like this?'

'Ah no, Mrs MacInerney, I'm only waiting for my friend.'

I wonder what she'd say if she knew we had a telegram. If she knew Mam had gripped her throat, speechless on an ordinary day. Ordinary days are full of surprises. I wonder if Mrs MacInerney has discovered this yet.

When Catherine comes, I tell her I have to go into the house. 'What's wrong?' she asks, knowing already about bad news slipping slyly into days for dancing and days for doing nothing in particular.

Mam is crying. So is Garry. Joan makes tea. I have never seen a telegram out of its brown envelope. Each word is printed in capital letters and stuck on paper. I read it. I read it again. It's from Auntie May.

PADDY DEAD STOP LETTER FOLLOWING STOP
FUNERAL NEXT FRIDAY STOP

Stop. Stop. Stop. Stop all the people leaving. Stop all the people dying. I pray and I don't know who I am praying to or if I am being heard.

When Auntie May's letter arrives, she says she wants Paddy and Garry to go over for their da's funeral. They can travel across with Christy O'Toole. Garry may as well stay on with her in Lou and Harry's house for the time being. Paddy may as well stay until the flat comes up in Crawley around September time. She'll wait to settle Garry in a new school then. Poor Uncle Paddy, who traipsed all over London looking for a home for his family, will not be sharing it with them after all. He will be lying eternally in an unmarked plot in Whitechapel.

'Cancer of the liver,' Mam tells Auntie Moll. 'He thought he had ulcers. There was nothing they could do. Poor May. Just when she gets a home for them all. And it only five months since we buried me father.'

115

I try to imagine Uncle Paddy. I can't get his face in my mind. I am finding it hard to get Auntie May's face too. Soon, I'll find it hard to get Garry's and Paddy's. I won't be able to remember them at all. I sing, but I can't sing it out loud, only in my head.

Ten green bottles, hanging on the wall
Ten green bottles, hanging on the wall
And if one green bottle
Should accidentally fall, there'll be
Nine green bottles, hanging on the wall . . .

Who will be next to fall? In Listers', next door, they live lives where not much happens. It's the same the other side in the Maguires'. Nothing happens and they have nice coats and say good morning, smiling, meaning it because every day is good for them. They walk out to Ranelagh for their papers and stroll back the long way round, not a hurry on them, knowing that things will still be the same when they come home. What do they do? Is there something to living easy that we have never learned? People die. People emigrate. It's always been the case. But not one after the other. And now it's speeded up. They die and emigrate in the same week. I try to picture Uncle Paddy in the Up and Up Park, strolling like he owned it, carrying all our bags. Bending finally to blow out the flame.

Most days in the summer holidays, we go up to Palmerston Park. We go in packs, boys and girls spreading wide across the paths on the way up; into the roads, hitting each other, running in case we are caught and hit back, screaming as if our lives are in danger. Loving it. It's fair to say we don't go into the park, entering like strollers and nursemaids. We invade it, coats buttoned at our neck like capes. We storm the gates, whooping and hollering our arrival.

The park-keeper encourages us on to the rough side, where swings and seesaws are ridden off their hinges. He protects the posh side for ladies in straw hats, ensuring the flowers stay in their neat beds long enough to spread and perfume the air. He watches us, just letting us know he is there and we have no right to be.

On the way home, we've taken to going into the Methodist church on Charleston Road. The devil is there. If you go in far enough, he bangs the doors shut behind you, keeping you in all night. You'll never be the same again. We take it in turns to run in as fast and as far as we can while everyone counts. Most counts wins. If we walk round the outside three times holding our collar, we will be safe. It's like waving garlic in front of Dracula. I try to avoid going in by pretending I'm too grown-up for such games. Besides, didn't I hear me own granny's ghost and survive a night in the room over the scullery? It's a mortal sin you'd have to tell in confession. Mam had to confess when she went into the Tin Church on the Ranelagh Road when Mrs Patterson's daughter got married. I used to make my sins up after I made my First Communion. I have real ones now.

Mam forbids us to go up to Palmerston Park. 'It's full of ruffians, so it is.'

Joan only goes now and then. She is growing out of running around. She spends time with Dolores Holden or Pat Henley at the shops in Ranelagh. My friends are changing too. New kids chase us through the bushes. Marty Corcoran and Douggie Davis know how fast we can run. They're not much fun any more. New boys from places beyond the Buildings have yet to get our pace. The boys from beyond go to Synge Street school. They wear watches and ride bikes. The boys from the Buildings try to fight them, though they talk to girls from beyond as if they are perfect gentlemen. Summer in Palmerston buzzes and sizzles. I wish I never had to go home. Home is an empty table in the midst of empty chairs.

Christmas again. Nobody can get over from England. It's just the three of us. And our lodgers of course, Mr and Mrs Killan. She comes from Camden Street. Newly married, she is pregnant. We are not supposed to notice. Every other woman in Dublin is pregnant. I used to notice women walking around with bulges under their coats. They always wear coats in the street, winter and summer. I thought it was a strange way of carrying bags, like African women with loads balanced on their heads.

'They're babies, stupid,' Catherine told me. She knew because she had little brothers and sisters.

'Why don't they get prams then? It's terrible keeping the poor things hidden under their coats. They could suffocate.'

Mam gave the Killans Grandilla's room.

'He'll turn in his grave,' Auntie Moll said.

Then they went and papered it pink. There's no stopping them. She brings the evening meal down to the kitchen, cooking it, an offering covered with a white cloth. She takes forever, slicing onions and carrots and peeling potatoes under running water. He sits up in Grandilla's room, in the pink, reading the *Evening Herald* while the sacrificial dinner is prepared. I plan revenge for Grandilla. He spent a lot of time in that room, before it was pink, like he was on small retreats. Every trace of Grandilla has been removed. They have laid his ghost. He could never haunt a room with pink wallpaper. He needs bottle-green gloom, darkened more with blue blinds on the windows. He needs lamps on every top and turn to illuminate his books. When he died, we put our ears to the door, listening for his cough or the squeaks of the bedsprings. Just because we didn't hear them, didn't mean all trace of him had gone. Not until the pink wallpaper.

Mam charges them ten shillings a week for the use of the room and facilities. We are not supposed to show our irritation at any time, no matter how irritated we might feel. We can't eat until she has prepared the meal, cooked it and washed up. We sit, smiling like eejits, while she flutters round the kitchen, all airs and graces. 'Molly from Clare with a Rose in her Hole,' Auntie Moll calls her.

On Christmas morning, they go to Camden Street to be waited on. She couldn't cope with our arrangements, what with the sink being in the scullery and the gas stove in the kitchen, too much for her altogether. Mam listens, sympathy and concern on her face, her fingers crossed behind her back.

'Did you ever hear the like?' she asks us when they have left. 'Mind you, it's just as well we're so primitive with our arrangements, or she'd be fiddling and farting all day. We'd be eating our Christmas dinner at midnight.'

'But we're not having our Christmas dinner here, Mam, we're going up to Kimmage,' Joan says.

'I know we are. How could we be expected to stay here on our own on Christmas Day and it on top of the anniversaries of me mother and father? If Molly and Peter hadn't invited us, where would we be? Me father didn't realise how near to the truth he was when he warned us about strangers being in the house.'

'Maybe he did, Mam. Maybe he knew how poor we'd be with him gone,' Joan replies.

'Poor? Poor? We're not poor, we're destitute. If it wasn't for the Killans, we'd be on the street.' She sits with her hands in her lap, helpless, then stirs. 'Anyway, we'd better get ourselves ready. It's a long walk to Kimmage. There's no point lighting the fire now. We won't be back until gone midnight.'

Mam was Molly Leonard's bridesmaid on the day she married Peter Dingle. Dad was at the wedding too. The Dingles didn't go to Mam and Dad's wedding the following year. Nobody did except Julia Bolger and her boyfriend. Afterwards, the four of them went to see a film in the Green picture house, then sat on a bench in the Green eating fish and chips. Grandilla had forbidden Mam to marry Dad, but she loved him so much, she went against him. They never spoke again until Dad left.

Molly and Peter and their three daughters, Annie, Marie and Julianne, live in a Corporation house on Lismore Road. It's like going out to the country when we visit them. Uncle Peter keeps pigs on a piece of scrubland up off the Kildare Road. I'm let push the handcart round the streets with the girls, collecting slops for the running rashers and buying sherbet dabs from the women in the houses at the same time. Every other house is a sweet factory. It's the same in the Buildings, where candyfloss and ice lollies seem more the rage.

Julianne, the youngest, is a constant reminder of Mam's dead son. John is allowed to grow up, a shadow boy, whenever we visit.

'He'd be almost twelve now. Imagine that,' Molly says, looking at Julianne. 'It breaks my heart to think about it.'

'Paddy O'Brien always wanted a son. Me mother always said John's death was the death of our marriage. But it wasn't my fault he died. Half the babies in Dublin were dying with gastroenteritis. Bluebottles lighting on every surface and unswept crumb.' Mam can't bear to think about it.

Marie is tinkling the keys on the piano. In minutes, we're having a concert, singing and dancing, the accordion going like the clappers with Annie's touch. We all have to do a turn. Mam sings 'I'll take you home again Kathleen', embarrassing Joan and me, making Molly cry. At every wake and hooley she sings that. I'm Frankie Laine, up in the sky with the Ghost Riders, and Joan is Ella Shields, a.k.a. Burlington Bertie, pacing up and down the Strand, correct and easy.

We walk home through midnight streets. Smartly we walk to keep warm, past the Sundrive picture house, through Rathgar, Terenure and Rathmines, conscious that the shadow boy is pacing behind, tormenting Mam. 'Poor John, my poor baby. My poor lamb. God rest his soul.'

The Killans have had enough. She couldn't possibly bring a child into a house with such arrangements.

'Good riddance,' Mam says as the handcart of furniture is trundled out of the Villas and across the Buildings. 'We'll manage. We'll have to.'

Mam's wages are just a bit more than the rent. Then there's the gas and electricity. We practically live in the back bedroom now. There's only one room to warm and we get into bed after tea, before the fire goes out. From Monday or Tuesday, until Mam gets paid on Friday, we have little or nothing to eat. Mrs Maguire has begun to call over the back wall on a Thursday with a plate of mince and potatoes or stew. 'Sally, I've made far too much dinner. It's a sin to waste it. Do you think Fluff will eat it?'

Fluff does, but only the scrapings we leave on the plate. Auntie Moll brings a bag of groceries once a week. Bill Priestley on Oxford Road will no longer let Mam have anything on the book because she's run up such a large bill.

'I don't know which way to turn,' she tells Auntie Moll when we visit her in Daniel Street.

She's invited us to Sunday dinner and the spread before us is more than we've eaten in weeks. Tender corned beef, floury potatoes, cabbage and baked onions, homemade brown bread slivered with best butter, not margarine, then apple tart and custard.

'Look, Sally, get a trace put on Paddy O'Brien. It's a disgrace, him living the high life in England and not a penny piece for his children. Does he think they can exist on fresh air and charity? If I had me way, I'd have him put in Mountjoy. Hanging's too good for him.'

'You don't know what you're talking about, Moll. How can I put a trace on him? Even if I knew, it'd cost money. I have no way of making him support his children. He knows perfectly well the state of things here.'

Moll lights a cigarette and begins to pace. 'What about Limerick, his mother? Don't you think she'd like to help her grandchildren? Why don't you write to her?'

Mam stands, facing Moll. 'If I was breathing my last, I wouldn't ask her for as much as a farthing. I've never met her. And I never want to. He ran away from Limerick and never went back. They know we had the children. They've never sent them a birthday card or a postal order in thirteen years. I don't want my daughters having anything to do with him, or Limerick. Do you hear me?'

They stand looking at each other. I think Moll might hit Mam, she seems so angry. Instead, she sits down and twists her cigarette into the plate.

'What about what they want, Sally? Have you ever asked them?'

'They'll do what I want. I'm their mother. I'm all they've got. They'll have to get used to that fact. And so will you.'

Auntie Moll has put the idea into my head that I am entitled to have an opinion about my dad. The realisation shocks me. Wishes are not opinions. Wishing we could see him, or worse, his mother, our grandmother, are thoughts that can never be voiced. An opinion is another matter. I think dogs are better than cats. Dogs chase balls and lie at your feet, guarding you. Cats are sly watchful creatures shitting everywhere, leaving smells in old houses. In Joan's opinion, cats are better than dogs. Cats curl purring in your lap. Dogs chase you and bite you. Our opinions are different, but that's OK, it's only cats and dogs. Mam let Joan have Fluff, because, in her opinion, cats are better than dogs. She wouldn't hear of me having a dog.

How can I have an opinion about our grandmother? I've never met her. I wish I could see my dad, but do I want to? I'll have to want what Mam wants. It's less confusing. Safer. When I'm older, I'll get myself a dog. I have a dad. That's a true fact. Mam is wrong. That, too, is a true fact, but it's also a fact that I'm not able to tell her so.

Auntie Moll lights another cigarette. She sits by her fireplace, her feet on the fender, head against her lady's chair, one of a pair Uncle Alec bought her when they married. His was the gentleman's chair, plush and carved, fit for a king almost. Mam is sitting in that, looking uncomfortable. Auntie Moll's present for Alec was a pair of silhouettes, one of her, one of him. They were placed low on either side of the fireplace in jet frames – not on the mantelpiece or hung high – his by her chair and hers by his, so that seated, they are at eye level. As Auntie Moll smokes, she glances at

Uncle Alec's silhouette and I see that she has her own sadness in her.

I sit on our window ledge, bored, waiting for something to happen. A sense of something about to happen has been with me for weeks. It's been quiet for too long. Mrs Shallon and her sister pass, too wrapped up in their conversation to notice me. 'Hot in their leather,' Mam would say if she could see them, fake tan legs and fluffed out hair. Big women they are, from the country. Dublin women are small and dark like Mam and Auntie May.

'So, I told him, if you only knew how difficult I have it bringing up three children near that hell hole of Mountpleasant Buildings, you'd know all about it, so you would . . .'

I'm straining to hear what her sister says, when a fella on a bike with a girl on the crossbar nearly runs them over.

He steadies the bike, laughing. 'I'm sorry, ladies. I'm new here, I don't know the layout at all.'

He is stocky and handsome, with his shirtsleeves rolled up over muscular arms.

The sister puts on a high voice. 'Oh, not at all. I was going to ask where you were going with no bell on your bike!' she shrieks.

'We were going to number nine. We're looking for Sally O'Brien.'

I jump off the window ledge, straightening my skirt. Thank you, God. Thank you very much.

The happy couple are Jane and John, our new lodgers. Life is looking up. Mam has given them the return room we used to sleep in, and the back bedroom. We move into Grandilla's pink one. Mam buys new beds on a Cavendish weekly payment card. Joan has a single bed all to herself, with her own sheets and bedspread. I'm not allowed to sit on it, not for a second. I'm the hot-water bottle in Mam's semi-double, put in a few hours before she comes up. When she tells me to move, she lies in the warmth and I have to start all over again, my face squashed to the wall. She is saving the bed in the parlour in case anyone comes home from England. Sometimes, when I walk past the parlour door, the hairs on the back of my neck stand up and I have to hurry in or out of the house. Granny is sitting in there, her poor feet bandaged. Her poor heart broken. I can't open the door in case she rises and takes me by the hand to sit beside her. I am ashamed. Nobody is frightened of their granny. Only me.

Jane and John have brought changes, starting in the scullery when they line up their gleaming saucepans. All with lids. It's not that they don't like our arrangements, it's just that they have so much stuff they think we might as well all use them and save running up and down stairs causing disturbances. John doesn't sit up in their rooms like Mr Killan. He sits at the kitchen table. He's a butcher and he brings home big cuts of meat for all of us. He's fixed the catch on the kitchen window so that Jane can raise it up when she's cooking. Breezes blow in, she raises it so high. It was only ever raised an inch or two and propped up with a cut of wood.

126

*

Joan is fourteen today. No school ever again. She can't stop smiling. She started work in Harcourt Street Laundry this morning. Mam is relieved, what with Joan working and Jane and John's money, she'll be able to pay off the debts she has built up with Mr Davidson, the rent man. When Mam was unable to manage, he offered her a loan with a few shillings interest. She could pay him a few bob every Saturday morning when he collected the rent. He used to arrive on a bike, now he has a car and it's better than Alfie Heffernan's. He's taken to wearing a Crombie overcoat, looking more like George Raft in a gangster picture than a rent man.

When Mam cleared her first loan, he offered her another. He listened to her problems every Saturday, telling her she was marvellous altogether with the way she was managing.

'If I make it seven pounds, Sally, you can get a bit of coal as well as the shoes for the girls and the oilcloth for the kitchen.'

Mam didn't know. 'Seven pounds is more than I've had at one time in all my life.' She hesitated, tempted with visions of a perm in a shop instead of getting her friend Sheila White to do it with a Toni. She might be able to run to a pot of distemper to brighten up the kitchen walls.

He took his wallet, crammed with notes, out of his inside pocket. He counted slowly, stopping at five, prepared to go further. He was about to put his wallet away when Mam decided.

'Ah, go on then, I may as well be hung for a sheep as a lamb.'

Although it was a struggle, she cleared the second loan and the interest. It was the third loan that crippled her altogether.

Life is good. Mam is so happy talking with Jane and John, she lets me go up to Palmerston Park most evenings. To meet Bernie Logan, a girl from a tenement on Charlemont Mall. We walk home together singing Guy Mitchell songs and telling our secrets. I've never told secrets to anyone before. Not Catherine or Ann or Eithne. Not even Joan. If I haven't got a new secret, I make one up. I tell her it's a secret that Grandmother O'Brien from Limerick is making arrangements to bring me down on holiday soon. Bernie knows how Mam feels about the O'Briens and she swears on her life she won't tell anyone. She tells me it's a secret that she likes Tony Corcoran, but she'd die if I told him. I swear to God I won't, but I can't wait until I see him.

Tony is over by the swings talking to Jimmy Redmond. I could never go near him if he's with Jimmy. I think Jimmy's great. Like Robert Mitchum. He even has a dimple in his chin and a tie with a Windsor knot pulled away from the neck of his shirt. He is pure sophistication, meant for profit while I am meant for loss, a Redmond from Mountpleasant Square. They flick stones at us and we shout at them to stop, hoping they won't. Bernie is jumping in the rope skipping high. We sing at the top of our voices:

> The wind, the wind, the wind blew high
> And Bernie Logan said she'd die
> If she didn't get a fella with a marble eye.

> She is handsome
> She is pretty
> She is a girl from Dublin city,
> Let them all say what they like
> For Tony Corcoran wants a wife.

She stops skipping and runs away, cheeks flaming, delighted that her secret is in the open. Tony is red-faced and smiling. My turn next. The rope swings faster.

> Round apple, round apple,
> In a carriage go round,
> To see Patty O'Brien
> In a carriage go round.
> In a carriage,
> In a carriage,
> By night and by day.
> She's dying to see
> Jimmy Redmond today.

Now the secret I didn't know I had is out. Jimmy is smiling. It's fine with him.

Joan is coming up Mountpleasant Avenue with her boyfriend Bob.

'Don't you dare tell Mam, or I'll brain you, so I will,' she whispers as we pass.

It gets me thinking about Paddy Larkin, the soldier from Cork. Once or twice he met us coming out of Mass on a Sunday morning, and came back for a cup of tea. He reminded me of Dad. A few times we walked along the canal. Mam said she used to be engaged to his brother, Dennis, until she met Paddy O'Brien with his gift of the gab. It made Mam seem more exciting, knowing she had a past. If Dad is dead, Mam could marry Paddy Larkin and we could move to Cork and live happily ever after.

The next Sunday, Paddy had one of his sons with him and I knew how impossible it all was. He could never leave his wife and Mam is still married to Dad, wherever he is. After that, we never saw Paddy Larkin again.

At school, the nuns still rule with their crucifixes. Their main aim is subordination of spirit, not veneration of the Holy Spirit. I am on my knees in front of the statue of the Blessed Virgin, an example. I will not be able to stand up until every girl has left the school. Two other bad girls keep me company. Our sins are Chinese rings, made by rubbing the skin on the backs of our fingers raw, allowing small scabs to develop. There are so many Chinese rings in the class, an example had to be made. Fatherless children make the best examples; poor fatherless children even better, because it wouldn't do to go upsetting the likes of Harriet Massey's father in the funeral business. Mind you, in fairness, Harriet would never be caught dead with a Chinese ring on her finger. Three is just right for an example, enough to create a small detour at the statue. Enough to make the point.

Sister Madeleine watches to make sure we do not speak or move a muscle. The parquet flooring makes ridges in my knees, the injustice makes me seethe. I become a small revolutionary, revolting against religion and its enforcers.

My thoughts frighten me. I know the penalties for doubting God's existence.

The freedom of summer evenings are a total contrast to the misery of school. It is our habit to walk along the banks of the Grand Canal as evening melts to night. We try to impress each other, while appearing not to try at all. Bernie walks ahead with Tony. I stroll behind with Jimmy along the tufted, daisy path. Swans, Lir's children, glide by, a fleet of toy gondolas sailing into legend.

'Do you think you will sail away from here one day, like them, Jimmy? Like everyone?'

'Not at all. Why would I? I've too much here, haven't I?'

His red-gold hair is a Brylcreem gleam and his silver watch shines on its leather strap. He is clearly meant for banks and business, certain where his ship will take him. It will not be docking in a strange country, only somewhere along the Swan River.

'Do you know that Mountpleasant Square is on a hidden river?'

'Who told you that rubbish?' Jimmy takes everything for granted.

'Mr Grogan. He told me years ago. All the houses running down to the right of your house were built on its banks. That's why people came out of the city. To be away from the running sewers.' I want to tell him that my house will be on the Swan River too, but I don't. 'And do you also know that passenger barges used to sail from Portobello Bridge right down to the Shannon. Right down to Limerick in fact. Isn't it strange that an old river is driven underground and a new stretch of water is made by man to transport things from new developments? People used to stroll by the banks of the Swan River, just like we're strolling now along the canal.'

We stand still, imagining, our faces reflecting and shape-shifting in the darkening water, distorting into memory before our eyes.

Mr Davidson is not too happy when Mam tells him she can't pay him anything before Christmas.

'What am I supposed to live on, if them that owe me don't pay me?' he demands.

'I know I'm already in arrears, Mr Davidson. If you only knew what a struggle . . . If you give me a chance to get over Christmas, I'll pay a bit extra off the arrears.'

Bear-man, wrapped in his Crombie, he looms in the parlour, blocking the window. Mam can't ask him into the kitchen any more in case he sees Jane or John. We'd be evicted if he knew about them.

'You manage to pay the rent all right,' he complains, 'but you seem to think it's OK to give me nothing but excuses week in and week out. You were all right when you were asking to borrow. Oh yes! You're all the same.'

Mam is shocked by his outburst. I hope she doesn't start crying. She excuses herself for a minute and he turns to me.

'My, my, aren't you growing up. You'll soon be out to work like your sister. How old are you now?'

'Thirteen,' I answer, raging.

'And what would you like to be when you go to work?' he

asks, as if I'd have a choice.

'A moneylender, Mr Davidson.'

He gives little coughs while I watch him. I will not leave the room. He might open Granny's mahogany sideboard and put something precious in the folds of his fine coat.

Mam comes back with her purse and counts out five shillings.

He checks it before putting it in his pocket. As he enters the amount in the book, he reminds her, 'You do know I'll have to put a higher interest on the outstanding balance to cover the arrears, don't you?'

'If that's the case,' Mam says, 'I'll always be in your debt.'

He tips his hat to her as he leaves.

After Christmas, Mam is back to pawning things to meet her Saturday payments. She hasn't had to pawn things since Joan started work. Joan gives her a pound a week and keeps half a crown for bus fares and going to the pictures. Jane and John's money goes to paying the rent and most of Mam's wages of three pounds ten shillings a week goes to Mr Davidson. Her outstanding balance never seems to shift.

She finally tells Auntie Moll how she is placed, unable to keep it to herself any longer.

'Bloody bastard,' Auntie Moll says, 'I'd like to report him to the Rental Agency. Except they're probably all a band of moneylenders on the side, with the tenants their golden harvest. The style of him, living off the backs of the poor, with his painted-up house in Clanbrassil Street. I'll give him interest.'

Her anger is a moment of revelation for Mam, making her face up to her situation.

'Every day brings us nearer to hell. If I miss a payment, he adds it to the original loan, plus interest on top. The total debt is more than I'll earn in months. I'm at me wit's end with worry. I feel like putting me coat on and walking out the door like their bloody father. He doesn't lie awake night after night worrying about food for his children or keeping a roof over their heads. Bad cess to him, wherever he is.'

They sit on either side of the table, looking for solutions until they hit on the inevitable. Auntie Moll opens her packet of Sweet Afton and searches in her handbag for her lighter. She inhales and we wait, knowing what is to come. She blows the smoke slowly from pursed lips, and touches Mam's arm.

'You'll have to see what's advertised in the *Herald* tomorrow. I'm sure there'll be no end of opportunities for laundresses in England. And Joan might be able to get placed with you.'

She does not mention me. Will two more green bottles tumble from my wall? All gone. They are not even aware I am in the room.

'Yes. I will. I'll start looking tomorrow, Moll.'

Joan is out, another blissful hour of ignorance with Bob. Then she'll come home to a changing world. What of me? What becomes of a girl without a mother or father who cannot even call herself an orphan? Will I be sent to a home? I keep waiting for others to make up their minds about me. On the turn of their minds, like the turn of a halfpenny on a feck board when the caller shouts, 'Feck off', I wait to see which way I will fall. I walk from the kitchen, my separateness complete. She will do whatever she wants to do. I no longer care.

134

Nine

A light fall of snow, fairy dust, covers the paths outside. Lights from lamps make it sparkle. I watch for Auntie Moll from the window, rubbing my breath from the pane. I don't recognise her at first, because she is linking her arm with a man for support against slipping. He is Terry Cooney, her gentleman caller, an old friend of Uncle Alec's, always been a fixture in her background, emerging at times of need. We need him now, for practical purposes. He volunteered to help us carry our cases out to Dún Laoghaire. We are going by bus because it is cheaper than the goodbye train. Two buses really. The number twelve into town and then the bus from the quays out to the boat. I run down the stairs and open the door.

They come in, shaking snowflakes around like confetti.

'It's a terrible night altogether,' Terry says, meaning the weather.

'Yes,' Mam says, 'terrible.'

Our three cases are in the hall. The mahogany table is clear of coats. The parlour door is ajar. I wonder if Granny is listening behind it. 'They're all gone now, Jem,' I can hear her saying. 'That's the last. The end of an era.'

Mam walks like someone recovering from an operation; small halting steps. Joan is weeping. She doesn't want to go. She wants to stay with Bob and Dolores and May White.

Nobody asked me what I want. Jane and John stand at the door, waving us to the end of the Villas. We walk steadily across the Buildings, glad the weather is keeping people off the streets.

'Are you all right, Patty?' Auntie Moll asks me for the third time.

'I'm all right,' I say, wondering if numb is all right.

'Are you all right, Patty?' Mam asks.

'I'm all right,' I say, feeling number.

'Are you all right, Patty?' Joan asks.

'Yes. 'Course I'm all right,' I tell her. 'Are you?'

'I feel numb,' she says.

The *Princess Maud* rocks against the quay under the bleak February sky. Snow falls on hundreds of shoulders. At some point, the crowds going are separated from the crowds just saying goodbye and everything becomes confusion. People cling to each other, refusing to part, knowing they must. Cases are picked up and put down again and again as they grab an extra second with each other. Mam is sobbing loudly and Terry keeps encouraging her. 'Ah, come on now, Sally. You'll be all right. You'll be grand, so you will.' The doubt rises with his voice.

I stand back from them all, an in-between. A purgatorial spirit, not living, not dead. Mam reaches for me and I pull away.

'Hurry along now, please,' the stewards urge the desolate

people, shepherding them up the gangways onto the boat.

Mam is moved along against her wishes. Joan is too, and Terry passes their cases along to them over the heads of the crowd.

We stand and watch them until they can no longer be identified in the swarm.

'Come on, love,' Auntie Moll says.

Terry picks up my case. We walk back to the harbour entrance and the buses, stopping every so often to wave until the boat evaporates at the milky horizon.

Auntie Moll is kind to me. Her feather bed is softer and warmer than the one I shared with Mam. The twill sheets smell of fresh air. The quilt is of goose-down. I drift into sleep to the rise and fall of Auntie Moll's voice talking, as much to herself as to me. I do not know how to be in Moll's house. It has different smells that become part of my dreams. Its rhythm is different to mine, its heartbeat rising as mine falls, falling as mine rises.

I wake early. I want to go home.

Auntie Moll gives me her advice.

'Jane and John won't want you turning up whenever you want to. You live here now. The sooner you get used to it the better. You'll make friends here too, if you give yourself the chance.'

'What chance can I give myself, when I can do nothing except what other people decide for me? Jane and John don't belong there.' My voice is shaking. 'They only rent two rooms. It's not their house. It's Grandilla's.'

She shakes her head, despairing of me. 'Sure isn't your

Grandilla dead and buried? What does he want with a house? The house belongs to whoever pays the rent. It won't be long before Jane and John realise that, even if your mother has a private agreement with them.'

She doesn't understand my bewilderment at the changes. This is her house. Nobody can make decisions but her.

'They have the run of the place now that your mother is gone,' she continues. 'They'll soon let you know all about it if you intrude on them.'

She is setting the fire in the neat grate. The wood crackles, inviting me to stay in the warm.

'I'm going home. I need to get me comics.'

'What comics? Why didn't you put them in your case?'

I feel tired trying to explain things.

'Because they wouldn't fit. That's why. All I could get into that stupid case was me school skirt and things and me blue cardigan. Anyway, I forgot all about the comics.'

They hadn't seemed very important until now.

The snow in the Villas lies almost undisturbed, except for a few snow harvesters, making snowballs and snowmen. When they see me, they fall silent. Suspicious. Not understanding me coming back when I have already said goodbye. I wave casually as I knock on my old front door. I am an alien. An intruder. When the door shut behind us last night it was our home; the only one we have known since Dad left. Now I have to wait like a stranger before the breath-of-fresh-air couple let me in.

John opens the door, peeping out in case the cold creeps in. He stares at me, as if trying to remember who I am.

'It's only me,' I mumble. 'I forgot me comics.'

'Patty. We never expected you. Not so soon. Come on in. Jane will be pleased to see you.'

Jane stops cooking the breakfast. 'Well, look who it is. I was only saying to John when you left last night that it's a pity you're not a couple of years older. Then you could have stayed here with us. Wasn't I, John?'

He is pouring me a cup of tea from Granny's brown teapot. 'You were, Jane.'

John passes me the cup. I don't take it from him, forcing him to place it on the table; a supplication.

'If I'd been a few years older, Mam would have taken me to England with her and Joan.'

I will not allow them to lie to me to cover their embarrassment. They sit smiling, wishing I would go. I may be too young to work, but I am old enough to know that eyes tell truths that words deny. I am older than they are in certain ways. It's not as if I can take the house off them or anything. I can only come in if they let me.

I search through a pile of old newspapers looking for my comics.

'What are they called?' Jane is looking through another pile.

'*Girl* and *Schoolfriend*. I always leave them here.' As I say it, I remember that I have no right to be here myself, never mind my comics. I feel confused. 'They must be up in the bedroom.'

I run upstairs. Something is different. The books from Grandilla's wardrobe are in neat piles on the landing. I wonder why. John couldn't possibly be planning to read them. Nobody is allowed to read them. I open the bedroom door. Mam said she was leaving the beds and the wardrobes to show that she was still the tenant. I stand in the doorway, not understanding the changed scene. The clothes from the wardrobe are in neat piles around the floor. The curtains have been taken down from the window and the beds stripped. There are no pictures of elks on the pink walls. No comics.

John is standing behind me. 'There's no point having the biggest room in the house all locked up,' he says. 'We thought we'd move in here and put your mother's things in the back bedroom. They'll be there when she wants them. We have to pay the rent.'

'It's OK,' I say. 'I don't think she'll be coming back. Can I just see if there's anything I want to take over to Auntie Moll's?'

His head is hanging on his chest, ashamed of the haste of the clearance. 'Yes. Of course you can. Take as long as you like.'

There is nothing I want in the room except the past. The one thing I cannot have. I sit on the end of the bed and listen. I hear only silence. No more friendly voices. All gone now, except for me. And I should be going too.

'You can come over whenever you want to, Patty. You know that, don't you?' John says, not able to wait until he can close the door.

'I will have to come over to collect the rent every Saturday morning. That's all. If you're out, leave it in the parlour. I can get in through the window if the door is locked.'

That shocked him. I feel better.

'And Auntie Moll has a key as well. For emergencies.'

The snow has turned to slush. Instead of going straight back to Auntie Moll's, I walk into the city, turning up along the quays. The Liffey walls marginalise the river, cutting it off from pavements and people, so that it becomes a sly lick, set on its own seaward journey. No turning back. I watch the snow swirling onto its surface, then melting and vanishing. Now you see it, now you don't. People. Now you see them. Now you don't. All sly licking as the Liffey. All on their own journeys, marginalised between the walls of birth and circumstance.

I go on by Christchurch and Winetavern Street, across into Patrick Street and the cathedral on to Clanbrassil Street, then, as dark clouds gather in the afternoon, I turn into Daniel Street.

Auntie Moll is pacing the floor. Her friend Jessie Goldberg is sitting in the lady's chair. Auntie Moll holds her chest, sitting at the table, allowing ash from her cigarette to hang grey-wormed and drunken.

'What kept you? I've been going out of my mind thinking you've been run over or run away. I'd to send a boy on his bike up to Jessie with a note asking her to come down to be with me in case I got bad news.'

She is shaking with relief. I feel sorry I caused her such worry.

'I just went for a walk, that's all. I didn't even think it mattered.'

I am still standing in the green raincoat Mrs Patterson

gave me. It drowns me. She must have been the height of fashion in it before I was born. I am also wearing her brown suede boots. I have them well lined with newspaper against the cold, but they are still too big. Sleety snow had been falling since the temperature dropped, swirling around me like a belly dancer's seven veils, which are now dropping in murky puddles on the oilcloth. Jessie gets up and leads me to the fire. 'Will you relieve yourself of that oul' raincoat this minute and get warmed up. You're perishing with the cold. You'll be in bed with double pneumonia in the morning if you're not careful.'

She fusses, busying herself, finding a coat hanger and wiping the floor. Auntie Moll sighs, relieved I'm back, but burdened with me at the same time.

'She can have a bit of a lie-in tomorrow, Jessie. School is the last thing she needs right now.'

As we lie in bed in the dark, Auntie Moll wonders how Mam and Joan are getting on. 'Kent is right on the heel of England you know, and Christ knows where Bexley Hospital is. It won't be very pleasant for them living-in, but they were lucky to get jobs with accommodation at all, God love them.' She nudges me. 'Did you hear me?'

'Yes.'

'Well, answer me when I speak to you. A bit of civility costs nothing.' She has a sharp tongue, but she always relents. 'Are you all right? You've had a bit of an ordeal yourself. A good cry would do you the world of good.'

'Good night, Auntie Moll,' I say, wondering how I can ever cry again.

It's a couple of days before Mam's letter arrives. The hospital in Bexley is a mental hospital. Every part of the hospital is locked, including the staff quarters. They have to carry a master key at all times to get about from one part to another. Joan is terrified. Some of the patients are in a terrible way and some of them work in the laundry for pocket money. The manageress, Mrs Pryor, is very nice and she is turning a blind eye to Joan only being fifteen. Although it is OK to work in England at fifteen, you have to be sixteen to work in a dangerous environment. They get danger money. Only a few shillings, but it covers the hospital in case anything happens.

'God bless us and save us,' Auntie Moll says as she reads the letter aloud. 'They never made mention of it being a mental hospital when they advertised. I suppose it's the only way they can get people to take up the jobs. Deceit.'

She tells me to get a pen and notepaper and dictates a letter. She can read anything, including *The Irish Times* every day, because it was the paper Alec used to read. We always had the *Evening Herald*. She can't write anything except her name. 'If I went to school,' she boasts, 'it was only to meet the scholars coming out.'

'Dear Sally,' she says, as she paces up and down, cigarette smoke curling upwards. 'In all my life, I've never heard of such deception. I know it will be hard, but if you can stick it now you're there, it won't be long before you can clear you debts. Then you can make your mind up to come home or maybe get another job over there, better suited to you. Tell Joan to keep her chin up. Never let anyone see she is frightened of them. That's the trick. As for Patty, she's swanning around Dublin like a Yank, crossing every bridge before she even comes to them and going back on herself before she sets off. She'll be able to get a job as a tour guide before she's finished. But here's what I'm going to tell you, Sally, in the heel of the hunt, the girls will be up and married and then where will you be? That's all I can say for now. Moll Hemingway.'

She loves that name and often gets me to writes letters, so she can use it. 'Read that again,' she'll say. It's always the end bit she wants repeated.

'God bless us, Patty, you have a lovely hand,' she says, studying the finished letter, focusing only on the letters spelling her impressive name. Moll Hemingway.

I haven't been to school since Mam and Joan left last week. If I don't mention it, I hope Auntie Moll won't either. When I walk down Daniel Street, the kids look at me and smile. I know them a bit from visiting Auntie Moll, but living here is different. I want to go up to Portobello to see Bernie, but when I walk up that way, I find myself turning corners, on different days, walking down different streets. Bernie must wonder why I am not at school. I can't bear to think about the Buildings or the Villas, but I manage to find my way to Mountpleasant Square, walking into it from the Ranelagh Road end instead of the avenue in case I run into Jimmy. I never said goodbye to him and now I don't know how to say hello.

Mr Grogan lets me in. Taking my raincoat, he shakes it out onto the steps. In his left-hand parlour a turf fire hisses.

'That oul' turf. If only they'd give it a chance to dry out, before sending it to the depot, instead of it spitting everywhere like a wildcat.' He rakes the smoulder and puts another sod on, then hangs my raincoat from the picture rail as if it is the most precious thing.

'Take off them oul' boots and get your feet warmed.' He places a footstool in front of me, moving newspapers. 'How is your Auntie Moll adapting to having a young girl to take care of, then?'

Should I tell him how confusing it all is, living with Auntie Moll? Should I mention that the meals I'm expected to eat are more than I can manage? There's breakfast, when she has a liking for kippers with a sup of black tea poured over them, soaked up with a cut of brown bread. There's dinner, with rashers and egg or black pudding. There's tea, when Terry comes over, with stew or steamed haddock. Sometimes a piece of stuffed steak, all served with a dish of floury potatoes. Then, when I've let the button out on my skirt, there's supper. Usually, this is brown bread and marmalade.

'Don't go turning your nose up at wholesome food. If you were in Africa, you'd eat it. A week's starvation would do you a power of good,' Auntie Moll says.

'Ah, now, leave her be, Moll. Sure she's not used to it. Let her ease herself in, why don't you?' says Terry when there's tension building.

I want to tell her that I know what it is to be hungry. Hunger doesn't make a glutton of a person. It makes a person delicate in their eating, slow in digestion of each morsel so that it is savoured and tasted fully.

145

'It's OK, Mr Grogan, but all she does is get meals ready. Every time I go back in the house, there's something simmering or roasting. The worst thing is kippers for breakfast.'

His eyes twinkle. He makes steaming cups of cocoa on the back window table, almost vanishing in swirls of turf-dust. 'What wouldn't I give for a woman who cooks kippers for breakfast? Tell me, has she a spare room over there, or is she spoken for?'

'Terry wouldn't be inclined to visit her if there was another man in the house.'

He hands me the cup and rakes over the old ashes again. 'And have you heard from your mother yet?'

I tell him about the state of the hospital.

He gets annoyed. 'We are like lambs to the slaughter. They need roads, send for the Irish. They need nurses, the Irish. Factory fodder, the Irish. Jobs they won't do themselves, the Irish. Yet they perpetuate the myth they have created of us a lazy, ignorant, drunken nation, dishonest and unreliable. Holding mirrors. Why should they advertise the truth in Irish papers when an Irish government aids and abets them? Sure isn't it a great solution for them to export the unemployed to England instead of having them crowded into the tenements, upsetting the good-living people whose only need is to look after their own?'

I feel guilty. I feel as if I should have been able to point out all he has said to Mam before she went.

'I didn't want Mam to go, Mr Grogan. I didn't want Joan to go either. I wanted them to stay here with me. Mam isn't lazy or deceitful. She's always worked hard in the laundry, even when she was sick.'

I don't like the way Mam is lumped in with the ideas people have about us Irish. I don't understand why he seems annoyed with me, except that I could not make Mam stay. She would not have left Joan behind, even if she was not old enough to go to work. She would never have considered going to England without her. Mam went because it was the right time to go for herself and Joan. She could not wait for me. I know this absolutely to be true, but I cannot put what I know into words that will match Mr Grogan's. I think the best thing I can do is leave and go for a walk along the canal.

'I have to go now, Mr Grogan. Thanks for the cocoa.'

He is disturbed by our conversation. 'Are you not going down to the underworld to see Mrs P and Bella? They won't be too pleased at all if they know you've been and gone without as much as an hello.'

It seems I can't please anyone.

'I have to go now,' I insist.

It is not so much school I'm missing, as my friends. I never thought in all my life I would yearn to go to school. It is three weeks now since Mam left and still Auntie Moll has not mentioned it. When she comes in from her early morning cleaning job at Guinness's at James's Gate, I'll suggest going back on Monday.

Auntie Moll leaves the house at five every morning before the streets are aired and she is home before nine with the kippers for breakfast, *The Irish Times,* and a packet of Sweet Afton to while away the day. She is a great fan of Arthur

Guinness, saying he's done more for Dublin than God in heaven above. Haven't I to thank him for this cottage as well as me widow's pension and me little cleaning job. He looks after his workers and when they're dead and gone, he looks after their widows and children. A great man is Arthur.'

'True enough,' Terry says whenever she sings her hymn to Arthur, 'but where would he be without his legion of workers or the terrible thirst brought on by their sweat?'

'Auntie Moll, I was thinking about school. Will we get into trouble if I don't go, do you think?'

She is grilling the kippers in her tiny scullery with the back door open into the whitewashed yard.

'There'll be trouble if we carry on as we are,' she says, 'trying to manage on my money. I think you can consider your schooldays over and done with. It's a job you're needing to put shoes on your feet and clothes on your back. Them oul' boots are falling apart and you've nothing to replace them. You could do with a new coat and a couple of dresses. I don't know how your mother thinks or imagines that I'm able to clothe you as well as feed you and give you a bed. You'll be starting work on Monday if I have anything to do with it.'

The hill up to Carrickmines Golf Course is steep, winding up past tucked-down houses and wide-open fields. At the hilltop a large gate bars the way, admitting only golfers or the family who lives in the house and runs the golf club. We stand to catch our breath and admire the rolling hills.

'Will you look at them lunatics, dragging them bloody bags of clubs on their backs.' Auntie Moll laughs. She laughs so loud and so long she brings on a coughing fit and has to throw her cigarette into a hedge. 'Businessmen they are. Out from Dublin for relaxation. If that's how they relax, I'd hate to see how they get their kicks.'

She is in kinks, creased over with delight. I laugh with her.

'Now remember,' she says, recovering, 'if they ask how old you are, you're fourteen. Don't say you're only thirteen. Tell them you'll be fifteen in July. You've been working for Jessie and her brother Hymie for over six months. Jessie said she'd give you a reference.'

'What have I been doing for them?'

Auntie Moll's voice is urgent, we have already rung the bell. 'How many more times must I tell you? You've been helping them in the house, especially on Saturday, when they can't even light the gas.'

'Why can't they light the gas on Saturday?' I've never heard of the like.

'Holy Mother of God, what sort of thick are you? It's against their religion. Saturday is the Jewish Sabbath. Spent in prayer. No work or menial task to distract them. These people are very respectable. They'll never employ you if they think you are mitching from school. Straighten yourself up and try to look intelligent.'

The child I am to mind is brought into the kitchen to meet me. She is a two-year-old called Marie. Margaret, her mother, is pregnant and needs to rest. Her husband is in America, so she is living with her parents, Mr and Mrs

Golfcourse, an elderly couple who cook lunches and book golfing parties as well as maintain the course. It seems I will do, although I don't know how they arrived at that conclusion. I've never looked after anything breathing in my life, not even a cat. I'm to arrive at ten and work until six, six days a week. I may have half an hour break for a light lunch, which they will give me, between twelve and two when there is a lull. I may be required to help out in a general way if they are busy or if Marie is having a nap. I will be paid a pound a week and supplied with a weekly return train ticket from Harcourt Street Station to Carrickmines. I can drink as much tea as I want and the light meal will not be deducted. Although any indulgences will be charged for.

'She'll take it and she'll start on Monday,' Auntie Moll says, standing to make a dignified exit.

I have never been to Carrickmines on a train by myself before. I have never been on any train anywhere by myself before, so I check every nameplate at every station, jumping up and down like a jack-in-the-box, annoying the other passengers. At Carrickmines, the guard touches his cap and bids me good morning, making me feel important. I walk out into the dusty lane. An heiress returning home to my country estate.

Marie is waiting for me at the gate, holding her granddad's hand. I am to take her for a walk around the edges of the golf course, avoiding the sheep and the flying balls. If someone shouts 'Fore!' I am to stand stock still. I am to return her to the golf house for her milk and biscuits at eleven.

I don't know what to do with her while we walk. Her fat little legs take her towards the sheep and I have to keep diverting her attention with songs and rhymes. The hour with Marie is one of the longest in my life. I just can't fathom what I should do with her. If I pick her up, she wriggles free. If I sit on the grass, she runs away. If I want to walk, she wants to sit. And she cries all the time, wanting her mother. Why can't she look after her?

My only distraction is the sea beyond the timid hills. I am drawn to it, fascinated by the way the clouds and wind keep changing it. I want to stand and count the swelling waves so that on the seventh, I can make a wish, but Marie is screaming for attention.

'Bloody brat,' I tell her, taking her hand. 'Time for your milk and biscuits.'

It is clear to Mr and Mrs Golfcourse and Margaret that I am not cut out for minding a child, so I am put to work in the kitchen, freeing grandad to entertain Marie, allowing Margaret to sit and knit tiny jackets for another child who will exhaust her even more. Granny is lovely, the only one familiar with work, baking bread and scones, cooking breakfasts and lunches for the golfers, washing and ironing in minutes she should call her own. I help her wash up and peel potatoes. When meals are finished, I clear tables in the dining room, wiping them down, laying out knives and forks again for the next diners. After a week, she thanks me for my hard work and gives me a pound note and next week's train ticket; satisfied, despite my failure as a nursemaid.

I run down the steps of Harcourt Street Station and dash across the road. In a dark, seductive confectioner's and tobacconist's, I flirt with the varieties on offer. I buy three bars of Fry's Chocolate Cream, one each for myself, Terry and Auntie Moll, and ten cigarettes for her too.

Terry is walking along Clanbrassil Street ahead of me. I follow his dapper Dublin dandy shape, falling into step behind him. He is unaware of me, strangely, because he must have been acutely aware of everything around him when he umpired the cricket in Leinster Cricket Ground. He often talks about the players and how he dealt with them when they thought he'd misjudged a Leg Before Wicket or a dropped catch. 'Gawkeye, last of the Balbriggans,' Uncle Alec used to call him.

'Gawkeye,' I shout and duck in a doorway.

He turns, scratching his bald head, walking on, looking behind him all the time. He'll see me soon if I don't make a dash. I run up and grab his arm, linking him, given new courage by my wealth.

'Was that you calling me?' He is smiling, glad to hear Alec's old nickname.

Auntie Moll has the table laid. Kathleen Ferrier is singing on the wireless, the fire red in the grate. I am so excited. Before I take my raincoat off, I empty the pocket onto the cloth.

'What's this?' Auntie Moll voice rises.

'Presents. I bought them from me wages. Here.'

I distribute the gifts between them, waiting for appreciation.

She bangs a dish onto the table. 'How dare you spend that money before I see it! How dare you!'

I reel backwards, shaken. I hold out my hand, offering her the clenched money. 'There's more than sixteen shillings here for you. I can buy me shoes next week.'

I can't understand what I've done to upset her. She picks up the money and places it on the mantelpiece. Terry gives me back his bar of chocolate. Auntie Moll throws hers on the fire, making it roar.

'It is not my responsibility to feed you. That privilege rests with your mother. If and when there's enough money left from your wages for the like of chocolates and cigarettes, I'll let you know. Until then, you place your pound under the clock when you come home every Saturday. Do I make myself clear?'

Speechless, I pull a chair out and sit to the table.

'And don't you dare sit to my clean table with that filthy bloody raincoat on you. Get up at once and hang it behind the door.'

I do as I am told. Kathleen Ferrier ends her lament: 'Oh, my be-lov-ed father, I miss you – so – today.'

I leave the cottage and walk to Portobello to wait for Bernie. Whatever the weather she will have escaped from her canal-side tenement. She will have to come home. I stand on the lock gate watching the swans. I have not seen her for such a long time. She knows where I live. Though we promised each other we would not lose touch, she never came to see me. I felt too confused to visit her. How do you leave all you know and begin another life no more than a long walk away in a cottage with polished furniture and a goose-down quilt? Every day, a new rule is introduced which can only be broken until I am made aware of it. Familiarity is found only in my face in the mirror. Like Mrs Patterson's old raincoat, Auntie Moll's cottage wraps me in an ill-fitting cloth. I am a disruption to Auntie Moll's long-established way of living and a threat to the way of living Jane and John are seeking. If I were to fall into the canal and float away, all the way down to Limerick, it would be a conclusion of sorts. 'Young girl, aged about thirteen found floating in the Shannon,' the Limerick papers would say. Granny O'Brien would bless herself, whispering a small prayer. Never knowing she is praying for the soul of her own granddaughter.

I construct images in my water-watching, too engrossed to notice the tramp leaning against the arm of the lock gate. He smiles, not worried about his bad teeth. He is young, with long, greasy hair falling liberally on his old army coat. We smile.

He extends his hand, offering me a piece of bread and dripping. 'You can feed it to the swans if you don't want to eat it.' He demonstrates. 'An oul' one in them houses over there left it on the step for me.'

Stupidly, I say, 'I've never seen you here before.'

He has never seen me here either. 'No, I've made my way up from Avoca over the last week or so. I spent last night out beyond in Rathfarnham.'

'Where do you sleep?' I ask, expecting him to tell me he sleeps under the stars.

'Oh, in barns and outhouses. Or railway stations. Anywhere I can tuck meself into. I try to avoid the grass at all costs. The damp is bad for the bones.'

He moves to the bridge. I follow. It worries me that he doesn't have a bed.

'Would you like to sleep in a bed?'

'Not at all. To have a bed, you have to have a house to put it in. Then you have to pay the rent.' He looks me square in the eyes. The look tells me to mind my own business. Bread and dripping will not change him. When he knows I understand, he continues. 'No. I wouldn't like to sleep in a bed.'

We lean on the shoulder of Portobello, two alone people on a bridge of maybes.

'Where are you going now?'

Until he speaks, I don't think he knew his direction at all.

'I'm going as far as that stretch of water will take me. When I get there, I'll turn back and contemplate it all from the other direction.'

I ask if I can walk a bit of the way with him.

'It's your road as well as mine,' he says, surprising me with his generosity.

I walk with him as far as Sally's Bridge, wondering if I should turn down Clanbrassil Street, or carry on walking beside him to the where the sun sets on the Shannon, or to nowhere in particular, maybe just as far as Inchicore. I hesitate at such freedom, not knowing what I can do with it. He stands patiently while I make up my mind.

'Maybe I'd better not go. I might get told off if I do.'

He smiles at me. 'Being young is hard. Not a piece of yourself can you call your own. Maybe it would be as well if you didn't come.'

Ten

I notice the arrival of summer, seeing the changes from the fields of Carrickmines. Buttercups turn the grass to gold, and twig-like hedges become green walls at path edges. When lunches are done and the tables are cleared, I stroll along the tops around the golf course contemplating the sea stretching between Ireland and the Welsh coast.

I cannot make sense of it. I am here. Mam, Joan and Auntie May are over there. Beyond the sea, beyond in a country that makes strangers of families, doing ordinary things. They could just as well be doing them here. If Mam had sent me to work here and not to Auntie Moll's, Mr Davidson could have his interest and we could still be living in the Villas. If only she had waited. If Auntie Moll knew she would have to send me to work, why didn't she mention it to Mam before she made the decision to find work in England? I could be leaving my wages on the mantelpiece in the Villas instead of the one in Daniel Street. I can't make sense of it, no matter how hard I try. Three weeks. Three weeks is all that separated her new job and my first one. I want to scream my rage across the mocking divide.

Auntie Moll gives me two shillings for myself every week when I leave my pound behind the clock. She has bought me two pairs of shoes and a blue waffle dress. Jessie has made me two summer skirts. I meet Bernie some Sunday afternoons. Jimmy and Tony too. It is nearly like old times, except that they tell jokes I have not heard and fall silent when I tell mine.

Other Sundays, I sit on the grassy banks around St Patrick's cathedral, watching the life I am trying to cling to drift by. People are different here. Only in small ways, like the way they have of hurrying past doorways and lingering on corners. In Ranelagh, apart from in the Buildings, people stroll. Some saunter. They never linger. The Liberties are not for sauntering. The old houses have lost their curiosity for the locals. They know them like the backs of their hands, living here, seed, breed and generation. They walk from A to B with their eyes shut. Whereas in Ranelagh, populated as recently as two hundred years ago, they still need to stand and take stock of where they are, admiring the long gardens, eyeing up new families moving in from the country.

It's only now I realise that Mr Grogan was wrong. I can't be Paddy O'Brien's girl from Swan River. His river was the Shannon. He was just passing through Mountpleasant, as I am just passing through the Liberties. At liberty to go anywhere but home.

Auntie May and Garry are there when I come home from work, sitting at the table, with the air drifting in from doors open for the August heat. They are amazed at how grown up I am.

'You're taller than me now. I'll be looking up to you from now on,' Auntie May jokes, giving me a hug.

Garry is the one grown tall. He doesn't want to sit and listen to women talking, he is excited to be home. 'Come on, Patty, let's go into town. I'll buy you something to eat.'

Separation has changed us both. He has an air about him, crew-cut hair, sharply dressed. His shoes are leather. I can tell from the softness and the shine. He has his hands in his pockets as we stroll across O'Connell Bridge. A photographer snaps us, catching me with my mouth open. I take the ticket and put it my cardigan pocket. I have learnt that small recorded moments prove our lives.

He buys me egg and chips in a café near the Metropole.

'Listen to this, Patty, you've never heard anything like this bloke.'

He puts a coin in the machine, presses a button and this mesmerising sound spreads around the café and down my spine like honey on hot toast. People strolling past stand still. The juke box becomes a pulpit, a vibrant platform for a special preacher man. His voice, his message, his energy is a massive transfusion, if I could only understand. His words are slurring heartbreak in a lonely street hotel.

I stop being Catholic. Garry is moving to the music, singing the words.

'Feckin' fish on Friday, Garry, who the hell is that?'

Garry keeps singing until the music dies. Then says, 'His name is Elvis Presley. Don't say you've never heard of him? He's everywhere.'

'Garry, I haven't even heard Doris Day for months. Radio Luxembourg is banned.'

The world had changed since I went to live in Daniel Street.

He understands. 'She's just not used to kids, that's all.'

'Would you like to come down to see Christy and Kathleen with me this afternoon?' Auntie May asks as I'm eating my kipper.

'I can't. I won't be back from work in time.'

She winks. 'You will, because you're not going to work.'

I look to Auntie Moll for permission. She does not turn her head. She is upset with me about something. What is it? She let me have the unsuitable shoes instead of the ones with thick soles and laces. She even let me have my hair cut in a sort of teddy girl effort and said it was all right. 'A week soon rectifies a bad hairdo.' Now she won't look at me.

'Do you know what I'd love to do, Moll, before we go to see Christy and Kathleen at the college? I'd love to have a stroll over to Joe Courtney's in Thomas Street. It's years since I saw him. Do you remember when we were kids up in the brickfields? The last time I saw him was at me da's funeral. He promised he'd make the headstone, but we never had the money.'

Auntie May doesn't want to waste a minute of her time at home.

Auntie Moll moves her head. She does not look at me. 'I may as well come with you in that case. I have a cup of tea with Joe whenever I'm in Thomas Street. He's a great oul' skin.'

Sometimes I go with her and watch him chiselling angels, or read the inscriptions on the headstones lined up for the dear departed.

Joe clears a bench for the aunts. I lean against the wall, watching the people caught in the opening of the gates, passing by, staying for another day. Some staying until Joe chisels out their name on stone, chipping them into memory until their stones and stories are overgrown with time. Near me on a stand, Joe makes three cups of steaming tea. He is caked in dust, his hands so ingrained they appear almost black. I listen to them talking, recovering their shared past from cobwebs and clinging ivy.

Joe sings:

> Oh, I live in Faddle Alley
> Off Blackpitts near the Coombe
> With my poor wife Sally
> In a dirty nasty room.

Joe sings, and the aunts crease up.

'Great times, indeed,' Auntie Moll said. 'Great times.'

Joe is Grandilla's first cousin on his mother's side.

'He was a man before I was even thought of, so he was. I remember when I first clapped eyes on him and he strolling along Meath Street. Out of uniform he was. "Isn't that a great lookin' fella," I sez to me oul' man. "Sure that's your mother's sister's second son. They don't make them like that any more," sez he, eyeing him up. "There's me first cousin," I'd say whenever he passed, though he didn't know me from Adam there was so many of us. I'm tellin' you, you'd have to stand and watch him till he turned the corner.'

'Indeed so,' Auntie May says, his favourite child.

'So, if he was my first cousin,' Joe tells me, 'that makes you my third cousin, once removed.'

'She'll be removed all right so,' Auntie Moll tells him, 'because she's off to England at the end of the week.'

I swallow hard, nearly choking.

Auntie May leans over and touches my hand. 'I was going to tell you when we were our own. I'm taking you into Cook's to get your sailing ticket this afternoon. Afterwards, I am taking you to say goodbye to Christy and Kathleen. Your mother has agreed that you can come and live with me in Crawley.'

What is she saying? How can I just go over there as if I'm off on a day trip. What about school? I just can't go to a school in another country. It was hard enough here.

'Will I be old enough to work in Crawley?'

I am just old enough to be working officially here, since I turned fourteen last month.

'Don't worry, love, you won't have to work at all. You'll be going back to school. The one Garry went to. It's beautiful altogether, so it is. Like a private school, set in its own grounds. I have the space in the flat now that Paddy is called up for his national service.' Auntie May brushes the dust from her navy suit, concentrating on the one speck like it's a devil of a job.

Nobody asked me what I want to do. They just fitted me into their own plans. Sly licks.

I'd been thinking of getting a living-in job in one of the big houses in Rathgar. I see them advertised nightly in Terry's *Evening Herald*. I skim over the ones for nursemaids and concentrate on kitchen helps.

I look at Auntie Moll in her summer blue suit, her small hat with the veil. She has tears in her eyes. Who are they for? For me? For herself, the last one of our family able to remain at home? For all that was and all that now will never be? I go over and sit beside her, wanting to tell her I will miss her, unable to say it.

She puts her arm around me, forgiving me everything.

'Can you chisel me an angel while you're at it, Joe, one who does as it's told and might get to heaven? One without wings.' She smiles at me behind Joe's back. 'The one I have is just about to fly.'

No more green bottles.

Before we go to Thomas Cook's and on to Christy and Kathleen, we go into the GPO. Auntie May has a bundle of postcards to send to her mates in Beecham's factory.

'Why are you sending them? You're not on holiday, you're at home. I thought you only sent postcards if you went somewhere strange.'

She is working her way through the cards, stopping to think of twenty different ways to write, Having a great time, weather could be better, see you next week.

I have the job of licking the stamps.

'It's expected, sending cards. They stick them on the walls.

I wouldn't like to let them think I forgot them.'

'Why don't you tell them something interesting? Like what we're actually doing. Things like that.'

She laughs. 'There'd be no room on the card. Who'd be interested in what we've been doing this week anyway? Can you just see it? "Dear Anne & Co., spent today in a stonemason's yard in the back streets of Dublin. Sat in Moll's night after night talking about old times, promising we'd do something constructive tomorrow, perhaps go to the Olympia or the Gaiety. Never did. Off to say goodbye to my brother-in law and his wife who live in the best building on Stephen's Green. Sailing tomorrow. Love May."' As she is saying it she is writing it, surprising herself at how great it looks.

There is one card left over.

'Here, you write something interesting, since you're so gifted.'

I have few words and lots to say. I don't want to waste them. I write.

Dear Tramp,

Hope you got as far as there and back. I am going further, though neither of us knew it when we met. Think of me at Portobello.

The Girl by the Lock

'Do you want to waste a stamp on that?' Auntie May hates waste. She is turning into Granny.

'People got messages before stamps. Now I've written it, he'll know it.'

I tear it up and put it in my pocket.

I read my sailing ticket. Single. Dún Laoghaire to Euston via Holyhead. No return. This is only a dream. Grafton Street won't exist if I'm not here. Will it? It was here before I was. It's here when I'm over in Ranelagh or asleep. It won't even know I've gone, because it never knew when I'd arrived. I'm nothing at all but a sneeze in its existence. The people are going home, to tenements and fine houses and families. They don't realise how easy it could be for them to walk along Grafton Street with a one-way sailing ticket in their pockets. They probably wouldn't believe me if I told them. I examine their faces as I pass, a futile search for a dark-haired man with steely eyes.

A soldier walks towards the three of us in the lane by the College of Surgeons. Long easy strides that tell us he is staying put. Auntie May grips my arm. We stand aside to let him pass. Should I look at his face? My heart will explode if I don't. My breath will never return. Though I know it isn't him, I glance slyly at his face. The soldier moves past us, a ghost who has stolen my father's way of walking.

Just before I follow the aunts through the gate, I give a backward glance but the soldier is gone. Across the cobbled yard, the small rear lodge of the college is lit yellowish beside the mortuary, a pale beacon to the unknown.

Kathleen pins a St Christopher medal to my cardigan.

'Patron saint of travellers. Even if the ship goes down, you'll be safe.'

Christy is taking Garry on a tour of the college. As head porter for several years, he feels entitled to give private tours.

'You'd think he laid the foundation stone himself,' his brother, Uncle Paddy, said after one of his misguided tours.

Girls are not allowed. Nor women, because Christy's interest in his workplace is centred round the laboratory. 'There's things in them jars that's not jam or pickles. Eyes as big as babies' heads and humps that never saw the back of a camel!' Though it's my last day but one in Dublin, he refuses to take me with them.

He lets me down lightly, forgetting he's promised that one day I'll have the grand tour. 'Anyway, Skin, two's company, three's a crowd and four's a feckin' excursion. Sure I've only one pair of hands. What would I do if you both fainted together?'

His daughter Elizabeth takes me up to her bedroom above the mortuary. Her St Louis's uniform is on a hanger behind the door, pressed, though she left last year.

'Did you like school?' I ask her, wondering if she understands my question.

She smiles. 'I liked the girls. I missed them when I left.'

'So did I.'

Downstairs, after tea, like so many other times, we sit beside each other in the corner, listening. Auntie May, Auntie Moll and now Kathleen repeat again some of the stories, mythological and true, told earlier in the stone-mason's yard. Like a rosary, they run the decades through their hands with light touches and small movements. I say them too without moving my lips, in perfect time with the stops and starts of their recollections. I think I was born with their memories in my head. I shiver. Someone is walking over my grave and their litany becomes the extreme unction of the emigrant. The emigrant now is me. I pay rapt attention, knowing I will never hear the likes again.

Eleven

Crawley is a sprawl of square little houses set in square little gardens. It has no canal or river, no smells and sounds of street traders and street children. It is the land of permed hair and contemporary homes. Looking through lighted windows, walls are painted red and grey, except for Auntie May's walls, which are creamy soft. Mam is waiting for us on the steps. So is Joan. Mam cries when she sees me. I am unimpressed. She has dispatched me to England like a parcel, but not to live with her. She didn't ask me if I wanted to come here or stay in Dublin. People change when they come to England, losing their real selves. I am already changing.

'Now,' Auntie May says, 'will you have a bath before your dinner? It's been a long oul' journey to the Promised Land.'

'A bath? I didn't know you have a bathroom. And have you running hot water too?' I ask, thinking of the tin bath on Friday nights in front of the fire.

'Yes. And what's more, you won't have to wait till anyone else is finished with the water.'

Auntie May's flat overlooks a playing field. I sit at the

window and watch the children. Their English accents chant their childish songs and my eyes are stung with tears. How will I learn all the things they know about here? Things they don't know they know, like 'ta-ra' for goodbye and 'wotcha' for hello. I said 'Howaya' this morning to the lady underneath and she said, 'Pardon?' A milkman in a striped apron delivers the milk from the back of a strange little cart. The bottles are different and some bottles have orange juice in them. When I asked for a sliced pan, the woman in the shop said, 'Pardon?'

'Now, listen, love, you've been here four weeks and it's time you went to school. You'll be getting me into trouble if you don't,' Auntie May says out of the blue.

I thought if I kept quiet about it, she'd forget. I wish she needed the money for my keep like Moll did. Then she'd be forced into finding me a job, regardless of the rules. Mam is sending her ten shillings a week for looking after me and she has promised to buy my clothes. I'm well provided for, just when I could do with a little desperation. I've watched the kids from St Wilfrid's going about the town. Apart from the kids from Notre Dame, they are the poshest. I know I won't fit in. They all have mummies who work just for pin money and daddies with Ford Prefects dropping them out in Goff's Park.

Auntie May is cooking Sunday dinner, bustling about with pans, moving from one side of the kitchen to the other as she speaks, as if starting school in another country is a cinch.

'There might not be a place for me until after Christmas,

now that the term is under way.' I am ever hopeful. I move from sink to worktop too, transferring places with her in the narrow space.

'Here,' she says, handing me a bowl, 'make yourself useful and whip the cream, before you lose the use of your arms. I'm having tomorrow morning off work to take you up to see the head teacher, so you may as well prepare yourself.'

The road out through Ifield and along Goff's Park would make a nice stroll on this autumn day if we were going to turn around again and go home. Instead, I feel like I felt that time in Baggot Street Hospital when I was four and a half and the porter pushed me along white corridors, strapped on a trolley, to the operating theatre. My neck was hurting and they were going to cut a lump out of it. Lying flat on the trolley, watching the bright white lights flying past my head was the most frightening moment of my life. Until now. When the trolley stopped, I was in a room with shining lights and silver knives for slicing people. A woman in white with a mask on her face stuffed a cloth over my mouth to stop me screaming and the smell turned into a sound which turned into a white tunnel sucking me down into blackness.

Now the smell is here again swirling about us on the path to this terrifying school. St Wilfrid's nestles in shrubbery and trees with elegant windows gazing in perpetual boredom on late September lawns. Fearful as I am, I spy myself sprawling beneath a shady tree swotting at prep. I know that is what pupils do in English schools, not that I know what prep is, though I've read about it in books from Rathmines library, where girls had names like Bunty and adventures.

'I suppose they'll have a tuck shop and play tennis too,' I say to Auntie May.

She is trying not to laugh at my mortification, though she nods her head to confirm the worst. 'And detention if you misbehave,' she warns.

Mr O'Reilly, head teacher, shakes my hand warmly and welcomes me to St Wilfrid's. 'It is always a pleasure to have pupils from home,' he says with a fine Cork accent.

The shock of his warmth renders me silent. Whenever one of the nuns extended their hand to me it was to slap me down. I resolve to wait and see how he behaves when Auntie May is gone. I bet his voice changes the minute she walks out the door, but with his permission, we leave together.

'You can start on Monday next, Sarah. Take a few days to get used to your new home and surroundings before having to cope with a new a school as well. I just wanted to meet you today and find out a little bit about you.'

He is the first person ever to use my right name. The nuns called me by my second name of Patricia and everyone else calls me Patty, which rhymes too easily with scatty and fatty for my liking. He is smiling all the time he is talking, walking about his study – that's another word I'll have to get used to, 'study'. Only offices in St Louis's. A restless man, he can't stop pacing. 'I'll get one of the prefects to show you around, so it won't be too strange on your first day.'

Prefects – another new word. We called them creeps or pets.

'Your aunt has already spoken to me about you, Sarah. I understand you've actually been working back home. That must have been difficult for you.'

'Not really. I liked it. It was out in the country and the woman was nice.'

He is still beaming at me. I wish he'd stop. Schools are places where smiles are sins. As for laughter, it's a sure sign the devil is playing his tricks. Yet I want to laugh. I don't know how I can stifle the laughs collecting in my belly. I feel like I'm auditioning for a part in a picture. Any minute now someone will shout, 'Cut!' and I'll be sitting on the steps of Dunne's hallway telling the kids about this weird school. I can't come here. I really can't.

The prefect is a spotty shy boy of about sixteen. He stutters at every question of Auntie May's and blushes into the collar of his maroon blazer. I am blushing every time he knocks into me as we walk through doors. How I'll manage in a classroom full of boys, I don't know. As for how I'll manage in such a place at all, brimming over with confident girls and boys at every turn, girls in shorts on tennis courts and playing netball, boys in whites on the cricket field, more lounging against the back wall, all shouting and laughing so much that the noises of each group are collected together under a humming dome which echoes in our ears out beyond the gates.

'What do you think, then, love? Will you like it?' Auntie May asks, wanting me to say I will.

So I do.

I can't believe the noise. I could walk from the front hall right to the end classroom in St Louis's and hear a pin drop during lessons. When lessons were finished and we'd said our final prayer of the day, we walked in silence two by two, back down the corridor and through the gates. No wonder we ran like lunatics in Palmerston Park. Maybe I'll be all right on Monday. Maybe in all the noise and bustle, nobody will notice me at all.

On Monday, I meet Nellie George on the back stairs.

'I'm Nellie,' she says, as if being Nellie is great.

'I'm Sarah Patricia O'Brien,' I say, thinking it might make a better impression than being Patty. I like Mr O'Reilly calling me Sarah.

She is having none of it. 'We'll call you Pat, then. For short.'

So that settles that. After I hang my blazer in the cloakroom, I follow her down the front stairs, all wide and polished, across the hallway to the classroom. I want to run away, just like I did on my first day in St Louis's. I have no business being at school. I've already been to work. I hope Mr O'Reilly hasn't told anyone about that. They will know I had to go because I was poor. I can't expect them to understand something they have never experienced.

The teacher is in front of the class, tall and slim with the face of the Pope, dressed like an undertaker. He peers at me down the length of his nose, over the frames of his glasses, making out he doesn't know what or who the hell I am, interrupting his class and he in full swing. I follow Nellie to the desk, while I am inspected by the hushed girls and boys. I know I look awkward in Garry's old blazer, even though Auntie May reversed the buttonholes to the girls' side. The grey skirt is a bit long, because I have to grow into it, and my

172

white shirt is buttoned too high. All the girls, including Nellie, have their collars turned flightily up and two or three buttons casually undone. They are wearing their ties like necklaces. I'm a gobshite.

'This is the new girl, sir. Her name is Pat.'

He looks at his notes. 'Pat? I have Sarah down here. Sarah O'Brien.'

'That's my real name.' I look at Nellie, not wanting to get her into trouble. 'But they call me Pat. For short. Patricia is my second name.'

He screws his face up, puzzled-like. Mr Pope, I think to console myself, I'll call you Mr Pope, sir. Sir Pope, whatever your name is.

He puts on an Irish accent, giving the boys and girls permission to laugh at me. 'Ah sure and begorrah, Pat will do or else we might have to call you Mick.'

The class is in an uproar. I manage to smile, as if he is great gas, hoping he'll choke.

The playground is empty this evening as I look out from the kitchen window to glimpse Auntie May coming home from work. It's only six o'clock. In Dublin, the kids will be just going into Palmerston Park. After tea here, the streets are deserted, children spirited away by 1950s Pied Pipers, piping seductively from flickering boxes in the right-hand corner of every front room. Switch them on and all the children disappear. I feel like the only girl in the world. I've lit the fire in the sitting room, set the table, peeled the potatoes and read two more chapters of Mickey Spillane. Two chapters a day is about the limit because I have to sneak it back to the top of Garry's cupboard before he gets home from work. I've my eye on *Tropic of Cancer* because my birthday is in July, then I'll start on Edgar Allan Poe's *Tales of Mystery and Imagination*. I'm saving them for the dark days before Christmas to read in the glow of firelight. I miss the ghost stories in Dunne's hallway where you can't bear to listen to another word, yet you can't bear to miss the ending. Kids in Crawley don't tell stories, ghostly or otherwise, and they don't dance in the street. Instead, I have to dance by myself in the marley-tiled hall remembering the steps, singing the words. Trying to still be Doris Day.

There she is, Auntie May, huddled in her raincoat against the driving rain, coming up the Close with her shopping bags. Bringing home the bacon. I race down the stairs to open the front door.

'How did school go today?' she asks, puffing up to the flat.

'OK.'

I don't know how to describe the panic I feel in school. It is like a gas jet between my ribs, burning low and steady, bursting into high magenta flame around my heart when I am singled out by Sir Pope to answer a question or burning red on my cheeks when I am trapped in a corner by a bunch of mocking kids.

She takes off her coat, lights a cigarette and takes a few long drags before setting about transforming the kitchen from a lonely room in which I pace into a genie's shush of sounds and smells. Chops sizzle in minutes and tomatoes

174

ooze and spread through frying onions. Cream slurps onto peaches and spoons chinkle in dishes.

'I told you everything would be OK, love,' she says.

'What does your dad do?' Angela asks.

'He was a soldier,' I say to satisfy her curiosity.

'Was? Is he dead then?'

'No. I don't think so.'

She lives with her own mam and dad in the old part of town, not in one of the new housing districts littered around it.

'You must know what he does. Unless you haven't got a dad.'

I sit beside her near the netball court. Notre Dame Convent is playing our school. I'm supposed to be interested, but I can't get excited about an oul' ball falling through a net. We played netball for one term in St Louis's. I only played twice because each match cost thruppence.

'I have got a dad. He lives here too, but he's working away.'

That should cover it. For now anyway.

'Is it strange coming to a different country?'

My stomach knots. Nobody has asked me a question like this before. I have to be careful. If I admit that it is indeed strange in another country, I will have to explain all the differences, like I have to always explain about my dad. I think of things that are the same.

'You do lots of things like we do. You know, going to

Mass and things and going to the pictures. Our seaside is nearer and our houses are older, but there's not much difference.'

'You sound different, though. I always thought the Irish were different; not like us. Strange. Some people don't like mixing with the Irish because they're always getting into fights. We are more self-controlled. Cool. Disciplined.'

I like Angela. She sits beside me in class and we've begun walking home from school together. Still, I can't let her get away with such stupidity. I don't want to lose my temper with her. It wouldn't be fair when I can't lose it with Sir Pope because he's a teacher and he enjoys passing remarks.

A Notre Dame girl elbows a St Wilfrid's girl in the back just as she's about to shoot for the net. In seconds, girls are screaming at each other, pushing, poking, spitting.

I nudge Angela. 'Oh look! They must all be Irish.' I stand and brush the dirt from my skirt.

In the changing rooms, a group of girls surrounds me.

'Say somefing Irish,' a big girl, 'Miserabletta', shouts, insisting, forcing her face into mine.

Miserabletta wants to be a Comptometer operator, whatever that is, a Cockney with ambition, as confused by the green lawns of Crawley as I am. Every weekend, she traipses back to the Smoke with her mum. She, like me, is a fish out of water, but unlike me, she is the biggest fish in the pond. I don't know about being a Comptometer operator, but she has the makings of a nun: the self-importance, the need to control. Early on, we got the scent of each other. Fear smells. Dogs can smell it and some humans.

176

'Go on then, Paddy-girl, let's hear you. Say somefing Irish.'

I refuse to perform, keeping my head down to change my shoes.

She hits me on the back of the neck. I don't look up. She hits me again. All the other girls stop talking, expecting a fight. I might not be a practising Catholic any more, but cowardice reminds me of my prayers. Tying my shoelaces, I beseech God's Holy Mother, before rising to walk to the back staircase. Miserabletta follows me, pulling my cardigan, dragging it off my shoulder. I keep walking down at my own pace, into the playground.

'Lucretia', her dainty little friend with the moo-cow eyes, is leaning so far out the window that with any luck, she might fall out altogether. She screams, 'You filthy Irish bogtrotter. Go back home. Go back and sleep in your pigsty. That's what you have in your houses. Pigs.'

I think of Uncle Peter's pigs out on the scrubland off the Kildare Road and their mud-scurrying.

I stand and look up. 'I would love to go back to my pigs. I wish I could, instead of having to put up with feckin' smelly gobshites like you two!'

Miss Brown, the deputy head, another nun in disguise who watches from windows and doorways, is standing just behind a hedge.

'Sarah O'Brien, you will report to my study first thing in the morning. I have never heard such language from a young lady. Never.'

Resentment must be written all over my face. I've only

been in the school four weeks and I'm collecting enemies like badges. Maybe Miss Brown didn't hear Lucretia's abuse. Maybe she did. I don't think she likes me though. It was just an impression I had when Mr O' Reilly introduced me to her. Whenever she sees me, she seems to be inspecting me for flaws. I walk on my own in the middle of a large group of fourth-years, heading for the gate, remembering Auntie Moll's advice to Joan about the hospital in her letter to Mam. 'Chin up, never let anyone see she is frightened.'

So I set my chin for Auntie May's and I follow it. They might well be able to smell my fear, but I vow never to let them see it.

Twelve

I keep going over the directions in Mam's letter. Get the 710 from Crawley to Croydon. Ask the driver to point you in the direction of the 725 bus stop. It goes every hour, so if you miss it, you'll have to wait. Get off in Old Bexley. There's a bus goes right up to the hospital main gate. Go into the gatehouse. The porter will be expecting you. You can wait there with him if I'm not at the bus stop.

I have to press my face to the window to see where we are. Lights stringing misty towns run steaming down the glass. Maybe the driver's forgotten to put me down in Croydon. What will I do if I get lost? The longest distance I ever went on a bus in Ireland was out to Enniskerry. Or was it Howth? You couldn't get lost in Dublin no matter what bus you got on. All you had to do was get another one and ask for the Pillar.

There's a clippie on the second bus, the first one I've ever seen; a wiry boss of a woman who keeps dinging the bell.

'Give us a minute, mate,' an old man shouts at her as he tries to wobble off into the night.

Ding-ding. She chews her gum; his entrails. I can't ask her for help.

179

The third bus drives into the blackness of Dartford Heath. After four anxious hours of travelling and waiting for buses in strange sounding places, I am here. Bexley Mental Hospital, a back-of-beyond place worse even than Mr Grogan's. I used to get the smell of its decaying hopelessness from Mam's letters home.

It's like a small town, spreading low across Dartford Heath, built for lunatics in Victorian times. It has its own farm, its own bakery, carpentry workshop and electrical department. Its own builders, plumbers and decorators. Church. Everything. And, of course, the laundry. It has wards in main blocks, locked wards and special buildings in the grounds for TB and things I couldn't mention. There's nearly 2500 patients and as many staff again to keep it all going. It's fine in the daytime when everyone is going about their business, or meeting in the canteen or staff sitting room, where we can watch television and have a chat. There's workers here from Africa, India, Italy, Spain, everywhere. It's full of Irish workers of every kind, especially nurses. There's six sisters here, the Clancy sisters, all nurses from Ireland and, would you believe, there's a beautiful girl from Persia. It's the nights that are difficult. Sometimes there's screaming out in the grounds. All there is beyond the gates is the heath, black as pitch, with a few little cottages straggling from the bus stop. There's a few shops further down towards the village and a few rows of houses, but sure

nobody would open their doors if they heard any
shouting . . .'

With all this in mind, I cross to the hospital gatehouse,
watching for mad people. Mam said they hide in the bushes
and creep up behind you. Nurses walk the grounds in pairs.
I stick out my chin and keep walking. Suppose the porter has
locked up and gone? Why wasn't Mam at the bus stop?
What have we done to be homeless, all three of us? What has
brought us to such a desolate place? Is it some sort of
punishment for all the pennies I took from the sugar bags in
the parlour? I thought we only pay for our sins when we die.
Poor Mam and Joan, they have to be here all the time and
they are not nearly as bad as I am. I can go back to Crawley.
Who'd have thought I'd ever like the idea of that!

I pray out loud, 'Oh, God and His Holy Mother, please
don't let anything happen to me. I'm sorry I don't go to Mass
or say my prayers, but I'm still wearing my miraculous
medal. I can't take it off like I did the St Christopher from
Kathleen. Help me, God. Help me.'

The gatehouse has all sorts of signs in the windows.
'Absolutely no admittance.' 'Ring bell at side window.'
'Knock before entering.' 'Have identity pass ready.' 'No
smoking.' 'Phone main switch board after 8 p.m.' What
should I do? I put my bag down and listen. People are
laughing inside. I knock on the door, but nobody hears me.
From the trees in the grounds, a man walks briskly towards
me. I concentrate on the notices intently. He keeps walking.
Dear Jesus. By a miracle, I keep breathing. There is no point

ignoring him. All the stories in Dunne's hallway have prepared me for this moment. He could change into a black dog and disappear through the railings. Dear God in heaven. Don't look into his eyes, I tell myself. They'll be as red as cinders from burning into souls. His teeth gleam as he smiles, all the better to eat me with.

He speaks and the expected flames of fire remain in his mouth. 'Are you Patty?' He is dark, Irish dark, and smiling. 'I'm Tom Kelly.' He shakes my hand firmly. 'Your mother and sister are waiting for you in the dining room. They're just finishing their supper and they're hanging it out so they can share it with you.' He winks at me. 'I'll just tell the porter I've met you, in case he's wondering.'

Ignoring all the notices, he puts his head round the door, shouts something through it, laughs heartily at a quip from the gatehouse guardians and picks up my bag. I follow him along ill-lit paths and long, tiled corridors, stopping now and then as he opens doors with a key; locking them firmly behind us. All the time, I am thinking I am in a dream. The kind of dream unrelated to anything you know, where you are endlessly walking, or going down steps, every step an effort made with legs that won't work properly. In the going-down-steps dream, especially if you float down, all light, then hit the bottom hard, you're dead. I've never hit the bottom. Of course. Corridors stretch like nerves ready to spring surprises from which you hold yourself back, ready to fly. I am doing this now and it is not a dream. There will be no waking up to familiarity. No hysterical laughter of relief in Dunne's hallway.

'Here we are, now,' says Tom at the final door, still locked, still needing a shuffle, 'in you go now, girl, and get your grub.'

Mam and Joan are the only ones in the dining room, eating sausages and chips. The lights are off at the serving counter.

Mam pushes her plate towards me. 'I've managed to get a second helping. It's still warm and it's all you'll be able to have for tonight. Try to eat it.'

She tuts at the revulsion on my face.

Joan hands me a small bag. 'Here, Patty, this might be better. I can't eat the food here either.'

I eat the shop-bought cake, and pad up the crumbs with my wet index finger. They watch me.

'Howaya,' I smile, my heart gripped with pity for them.

'Howaya,' Mam says. 'Wasn't it good of Tom to meet you? He's from Galway.'

Mam's tiny bedroom is like a cell. The iron bed is narrow and too small for two of us. Long after she has gone asleep, I lie watching shapes on the ceiling, marvelling that this is what Mam left Dublin for. This cell. This box. This box in this place of keys and darkness. This better life. Mam moans, disturbed by her dreams. I turn my face to the wall and lie until morning light speckles through the floating dust.

I'm introduced to all the girls and women along the landing. Most of them are Irish: three Kathleens, two Maureens and one Mary. All from country places, named like prayers on their painted lips: Lisdoonvarna, Ballina and Mallaranny, Newtownmountkennedy and Newbliss.

Blessington. 'And Dublin too,' I chant an Amen to their list. They laugh too loudly and hug too much, their hands constantly on each other's arms or distanced slightly by a hairbrush; running in and out of each other's rooms, reminding me of our childhood game, 'In and Out the Dusty Bluebells'. Each little room, in the daylight, has small badges of hope: a jug of wildflowers from the heath, scattered green cushions on an institution bed, posters of Elvis – three of those and one of the Pope. It reminds me of Sir Pope, with his long miserable face. And shoes. Shoes everywhere, in every room; all high with slingbacks and peep-toes, under beds and on them, but none on feet. I am fascinated by this collective extravagance. And achingly sad. I look at my feet in their schoolgirl pumps and want to cry. Why do I want to cry?

The corridors, empty last night, are full of shuffling people in awful clothes. I grab Mam's arm and hurry along, pretending not to see the madness and despair on every face.

'Keep looking ahead,' Mam whispers, 'and if anyone speaks to you, don't reply.'

'Oi!' a man shouts, making us look behind us.

He is extra tall and thin, in a shrunken grey suit. 'Oi!' he shouts again and starts to run at great speed towards us.

'Oh, Mam, Mam, what will we do? Let's run. Come on, Mam. Run.'

She doesn't move and he keeps running. 'Stand!' she commands, leaving me no choice.

Nurses and patients stand too, stepping aside to let him pass. His boots clatter loudly on the tiles. He will kill us. I know it.

184

He reaches us, dribbling and spitting, 'Oi! Oi! Oi!'

I close my eyes and wait to be struck, but he runs past us, on down the corridor in pursuit of horrors of his own.

We sit at the front of the Dartford bus. Mam is taking me into the Co-op to get a grey skirt for school. She tries to humour me out of my fright.

'How are you getting on at school? You've been there a couple of months. I don't know where the time goes to. You must be settling in by now.'

'Yes, Mam. It's great. I'm settling in fine, so I am.'

I understand why Auntie May kept telling me not to give Mam anything to worry about. Mam and Joan's everyday difficulties make mine with Miserabletta, Sir Pope and the easily shocked Miss Brown seem like a holiday with Bud Abbott and Lou Costello. I can't wait to get back to the flat, safe streets of Crawley and its comfortable sameness.

They don't know where to place me for the best in the school. Not a lot of Irish people have emigrated to Crawley. Those who are here, like Auntie May, just sort of arrived by accident, mostly with the relocation of the London work-force after the war. An Irish education is not like an English one, except for basics, like one and one make two. Irish English is unlike English English, but the kids think their version of English superior in every way. They go into convulsions when I say 'tree times', meaning 'three times', because I don't pronounce the *th*, but *they* leave off the *h* at the beginning of words, like 'hospital' and 'house'. These become, 'ospe'il' and 'ouwse' and turnips are swedes and scallions are spring onions and sweeping brushes are brooms – in Ireland brooms are only for witches. And I am bewildered.

Mr O'Reilly has some sympathy for me. 'Now, I don't want you to think we are judging you in any way, my dear, but the fact is, it is most unusual for a pupil to start here in the middle of term instead of the beginning. We like to take time to make an assessment before a final streaming. There is also the difficulty of you returning to education after leaving it. Working and so forth, instead of being at school.'

He speaks slowly for a Cork man and waits between sentences, ensuring I have understood him. Does he think I'm thick? His window overlooks the lawns and he keeps swinging in his chair to watch the goings-on of the children below.

'Of course, we must also take into consideration the differences between the Irish educational system and the English one.'

Auntie May sits on the edge of her seat. 'Garry soon settled in, as you know, Mr O'Reilly, and you were concerned about him when he started.'

'That's true enough, Mrs O'Toole, but Garry went to a Christian Brothers' school and Sarah here went to a convent. It's bound to be strange for her. We have several male teachers. Indeed her form teacher is concerned she finds this a problem.'

I'll bet Miss Brown is too, I think, seeing her as she paced up and down her study like a lioness, lecturing me about my appalling language. I want to tell him it is Sir Pope and his constant belittling of me that I find a problem, but I keep my mouth shut. I bet Sir Pope never calls Mr O'Reilly Mick.

The tea tray does a little wobble before the prefect places it on the desk. She smiles politely at Auntie May, ignoring me. She doesn't ignore me when she wants me to pick the litter up in the playground or tidy the sports equipment. They are becoming my special tasks.

Mr O'Reilly pours the tea and continues. 'Of course, Garry was with you, his mother, Mrs O'Toole. Sarah's mother is not with her, which must make it doubly hard for her to settle into a new country, never mind a new school. Then, of course, she does not have the support of her father at this time.'

Auntie May is becoming annoyed. 'Well she's never had that, so what she's never had, she'll never miss.'

He stands, holding his hands across the desk. 'I think she'll be better off staying in 4C for now. It would be almost impossible for her to catch up with her peers in A and B, preparing for their O-level examinations next year.'

After school, I let myself into the flat and collect the list of messages for Auntie May. I tidy the breakfast things and wash up before going across to the shops on West Green. It's Bonfire Night and kids are letting off bangers and fireworks, leaving smoke trails everywhere.

Ann Rice is in the greengrocers buying a big bag of potatoes. 'Hello, Pat, do you want to come to our bonfire tonight?'

I'm not sure I do. I don't know what to expect and I like

staying in with Auntie May and Garry when we've had our tea. We listen to Radio Luxembourg and the play on the Home Service, as well as *The Goons*.

'I'll have to ask Auntie May,' I lie, because she is always encouraging me to go out and make friends.

'Try to come. We're having baked potatoes and sausages. Lots of kids from school will be there.'

I think I might, after all.

I've just peeled the potatoes when Auntie May and Garry come in.

'That's a gift. I don't know how I managed before you came over. It saves me so much time.'

I never cook anything, just prepare the vegetables. She can start cooking straight away then and we can begin our meal and our lovely evenings all the sooner. She went on an outing one Sunday and left pork chops, cauliflower and potatoes for me to cook for myself and Garry. I burnt the chops to cinders, boiled the cauliflower away to nothing and the mashed potatoes turned to milk. 'You're no Fanny Craddock,' she told me. 'You'll have to marry a rich man and employ a cook.'

'Do you mind if I go to Ann Rice's bonfire party? I won't stay for long. The kids will think I'm funny if I don't go. Standoffish like.'

She smiles, glad I'm going out.

We are not allowed in the garden until Ann's brothers have fixed the firework display and built up the bonfire.

'Go into the sitting room and watch the telly while you wait, it's freezing outside.' Mrs Rice smiles.

Apart from seeing Grace Kelly's wedding on a tiny screen in Harty Place, I have never watched a television programme. That's another reason they think I'm odd at school. I can't join in when they talk about what they watched last night.

I get so comfortable in the armchair in the red and grey room watching a woman having a nervous breakdown and a man slapping her across the face to calm her down, I don't want to go out to the garden. Until I see the sky lit up with flames and hear the screams of excitement after each loud bang. I stand at the fence by myself, thinking they've all gone mad, like the woman on telly.

The boy next door leans across. 'I'm Philip, who are you?'

Most evenings after that, Philip, Ann, Clifford, the boy across the road, and I go into Mario's Coffee Bar. Buddy Holly sings 'Peggy Sue' on the juke box and I have become a teenager with a ponytail. I am nearly as English as they are, except in my heart. Like a parrot captured in a cage, I am beginning to speak like them. I almost fit. I don't get bullied any more, just mocked. All I have left of myself now is what I have hidden. Hidden like the Swan River. Out of sight. Buried deep.

When Garry is at the pictures on Saturday nights, Auntie May and I have supper. This Saturday, after we've scrubbed and polished the flat to Auntie May's satisfaction, we spread the table with small jars of Epicure pickles and beetroot, placing the bone-handled knives on the edge of the plates for scraping the meat and juices from the pigs' feet. I love it when rain beats on the window like it is now and the wind moans in the trees. It is not the same when the window is flung open in summer. I'm just like Auntie May, preferring cosy. Her winter room is mystical. Firelight polishes the sideboard several shades of yellow along the mahogany. Everything gleams on the table drawn up to the fire.

'Isn't it grand altogether to be snug as a bug on such a wet night?'

I nod agreement.

We pick the trotters up in our fingers, digging and delving into bone and sinew with knife-tips. We lick our fingers and sit back on our chairs at the same time, laughing.

> Did you ever hear the music in the tripe shop?
> With the ham bones dancing on the plate
> The sausages trying to do the Cakewalk
> And the pigs' feet yelling out 'Thief!'

'Where did you learn to sing such a stupid song?' I ask her. She is laughing again. 'Whenever I eat pigs' feet, I have to sing it. We used to go to Granny Reynolds's house in Pimlico every Saturday and she'd put a big basin of pigs' feet on the table and another of cockles and Dublin Bay prawns. We'd eat them with bread and butter and salt and pepper and poor oul' Uncle John used to sing that for us. Without fail.'

From the flat below, sounds of canned laughter drown out our giggles. They are watching telly.

Crawley is new. Crawley is hope. It is life after decay. Hope after war. Optimism is inhaled with the clean air and the streets are paved with green grass edges. Every road you walk along is much like another, making it a great leveller. There are few big mansions at the end of tree-lined drives, no art galleries or museums or buildings with stories hidden in the bricks, apart from the garage where Haigh carried out his acid bath killings and I can't blame Crawley for forgetting to mention that. No, what you see is what you get and at least everyone gets something. Jobs are plentiful and even the factories know their place, out at Manor Royal, away from the grassy centre. It is like living in the pages of a comic, with lines drawn simply inside each square box. I try to imagine Bang-Bang jumping on the buses to kiss the women, or shooting the men with his finger, and it just doesn't work. The women would be screaming and the men would beat him up. I look for things that just aren't there. I want to find something, anything, that will make this place special, but try as I might, all it is, is nice.

School is also like living in a comic too. Lord Snooty could easily walk down the grand staircase and Billy Bunter could slide down the banister. I could pass for Lettuce Leaf, the Greenest Girl in School. The masters and mistresses wear gowns and mortar boards a lot of the time, including Mr O'Reilly and him an Irishman.

Nothing really matters, I keep telling myself. Nothing really matters at all.

I am learning typing and shorthand and trying to learn history. It's hard to grasp the great span of British history and which king did what and when. In St Louis's we only learnt Irish history and as I had missed a few years one way and another, I am not too clear about that, either, though one or two names ring a bell on both counts, like Cromwell and Elizabeth I.

Mrs Stegas wrote in my report, 'Sarah knows little or nothing of the country she resides in.' On that basis, she decides not to teach me anything at all.

'Sarah should improve her private reading,' wrote the English mistress.

So should she, I think. All she offers us is *The Prisoner of Zenda*. I wonder if she's ever read *The Manxman* by Hall Caine. 'What shall it profit a man if he gain the whole world and lose his soul?' I don't understand quite what that means yet, but I connect it to the abundance of shoes on Mam's landing. It is the message at the beginning of the book, the very first I own. I bought it in an old musty shop instead of my comics. I keep looking at it on the chair by my bed. 'It is a work of genius,' the *Scotsman* says on the back cover, whoever he is.

How can she know what I read privately if she never asks me?

Auntie May understands. '"Knows little or nothing about the country she resides in"? I ask you! Well, she knows little or nothing about you, so you're even. "Improve your private reading"? If it's bloody private, how the hell can she comment on it?'

'Maybe it's just for the sake of a sentence. If they don't know it, they make it up.'

'Do you know what I think, love?' Auntie May asks. 'I think it's all they expect of a girl who's been working instead of being at school.'

'It's all they expect of an Irish girl too,' I reply.

'Aye. Maybe. They think school is the only place you learn anything, because they have never been anywhere else.'

From then on, I don't even try, which is just as well, because Mam has decided my fate once more. She wants me to go and live with her and Joan. I want to stay with Auntie May. My typing exam, until now a waste of time, seems the only thing worth bothering with. It is important I take it. I can smell the hospital.

'I can't go now,' I wail, feeling like Bunty, 'what about my exams?'

'It's for the best, love. It's only right and proper you are with your mother.'

If it is for the best, it is not my best. Mam has taken on a large flat in Crayford and she's needs me to work to help pay the rent:

Dear May,

I have decided to take a flat in Crayford. It is convenient for the Hospital as we will only have to walk across Dartford Heath. I cannot expect Joan to live-in any longer. She has been at me for ages to get a place of our own and my mind was made up for me when a patient attacked her. She was so badly shaken she had to go into the Infirmary. She has moved out to stay with a friend in Dartford. I have to get out of that place, May. You have no idea what it is like. Anyway,

May, the flat is the whole top half of a large house. Fully furnished, with a large kitchen and two bedrooms. The rent is more than we can manage, but with Patty working too, it will be a new start for all of us . . .

Auntie May and Garry see me to the bus and I close the comic on St Wilfrid's, just when I was getting to the good bit.

I want to be a window-dresser, I decide. In London. I want to travel on the train and walk from Charing Cross through the crowds to Oxford Street and move dummies around in glitzy frocks against backgrounds of mirrors and wafting gossamer.

'You can put that idea right out of your head,' Mam says. 'I'm not having you travelling to London at your age, meeting with God knows who. I'm getting you a job in David Greig's grocers in Dartford and that's the end of it. A window-dresser? I ask you!'

I become Mam's bed-warmer again, sleeping with her in the double bed while Joan has the single room to herself. The more things change, the more they remain the same.

The shop is new. A market with serving assistants behind counters for special things and long shelves of tins and packages of all descriptions. I'm placed on the Continental counter, an oval boat of exotic produce from France and Italy and I am the ship's captain. Carole is on the cooked meats counter and Pauline sells fresh chickens. In the lunch hour we walk arm in arm around the town, window-shopping and spraying ourselves with scent in the Co-op.

The shop floor is a stage for our dramas and while we prepare our counters before opening or clean them in the late afternoons, we sing all the latest songs until the manager storms through and shouts at us to shut up and get on with our work. Each evening, I float up the Station Road hill, a girl in a bubble, going home to Mam and Joan instead of Auntie May.

And what a home! It is like Mr Grogan's left-hand parlour with added extras, like more rooms and a bathroom just for us.

'For Christmas,' Joan plans, 'we will have a Christmas tree with lights.'

'A real tree?' I ask, unsure of the cost of such a luxury.

'A real tree. Six foot tall, and we'll stand it in the window and leave the lights on all night long.'

'And paper chains?' I ask, with a mixture of sadness for another time, as well as excitement.

On a crisp Sunday morning we walk to Dartford and order the tree.

'You'll have to have a high ceiling to fit this monster in,' the assistant says.

We smile at each other. Smug.

'Oh that's not a problem,' Joan answers. 'Our sitting room is enormous.'

'Lucky you,' he nods and scribbles sold on the label.

We are lucky. The flat can only be described as gracious, spread across the top floor of a detached Victorian villa, with a view for miles. Even the lav is gracious.

'Good gracious!' Mam said when she first saw the ornate, blue-patterned bowl in its polished wood surround.

'It beats the one out in the yard by the coal-hole at home,' I said, delighted.

While Joan arranges the lights on the tree, I spray 'Seasons Greetings' on the gilt mirror over the marble fireplace.

'Will we have a turkey?' I ask Joan.

'A feckin' turkey?' Joan mimics Mam, and we giggle with happiness.

I am able to get a big chicken and a Christmas cake at reduced prices in the shop, as well as tinned fruit and cream. On Christmas morning the flat smells of oranges and nutmeg and Joan's boyfriend comes to dinner. Mam sets the table in the big kitchen and between the three of us, we manage to produce a fairly decent spread.

'Have some more,' Mam says, her face glowing with pride and she passes vegetables around the table. 'Here,' she says to me, 'make a wish, but don't tell us what it is.'

There is only one wish possible. Please, please, whatever happens, let us all be here together in this beautiful flat next year. Don't let my bubble burst.

Being in the flat is wrong. It is nothing to do with paying the rent. We manage that. It is the feeling that is wrong, as though we have ideas above our station. The people underneath think so.

'Excuse me, dear,' the woman says, while her terrier yaps at me and jumps up, pawing marks onto my skirt. 'I don't like you putting washing on the line in the afternoons. I like to relax in the garden then.'

'I only do it on Wednesdays. It's my half-day,' I say, standing with wet washing dripping onto my feet.

'Even so, I feel it is inconsiderate to hang it on the line when I have to look at it,' she insists, taking lessons from her dog. Walking all over me. 'We have been here for twenty-five years, dear, and I'm afraid we are set in our ways . . .' She smiles. 'Though I understand that our ways are different.'

I'm not sure what she is getting at, but I have an inkling.

'I thought the clothesline was for washing . . .'

'Yes, it is. But washing should only be hung out early in the mornings. We have routines. We like to stick to them.'

My feet are soaking. I put the heavy washing basket on the grass.

'We have routines too. Called work. We're not here in the mornings, but if we were, we'd have to look at your washing.'

She stops smiling. 'You really must understand our ways if you are to continue living here.' She is red in the face.

Does she mean here in the house or here in the country? I think she means the latter, but won't say it to my face.

Without apology or victory, I peg the washing on the line.

Thirteen

Joan is waiting for me by the gates of Bexley Hospital after work. She beams, waving to me to hurry up.

'What are you doing here? Have you been round to see Mam?'

'No. No, I want to see you. I have something lovely to tell you, but I can't tell you in front of Mam. Where can we go?'

I link her arm. 'Let's walk across the heath. I need to get the smell of that bloody laundry out of my nostrils.'

Joan shudders. 'Don't mention it! I never thought Mam would make you work there after all the trouble I had in it. I'm glad to be out of it. It was like having to enter hell every day, with the smell of filth everywhere.'

'Don't I know it. It's in the very walls.'

We walk together in the late sunshine across the heath, past the little terrace of houses, into the dip. I throw myself on the ground, resting my back against the earth bank.

'So what is it you've come out on a bus from Dartford to tell me? No bad news, mind. You can get back on the bus and tell it to your husband if it's trouble. That's what he's there for.'

198

She sits beside me, smiling: 'It's strange when you say that, Patty.'

'Yes, strange. And stupid. A housewife at nineteen. Still, it beats slaving in the laundry in all that shite and steam.'

Upturning my hand, she places a tiny box in my palm. 'Open it, Patty. It's yours.'

'Mine? What is it?'

I inspect the dark red box, thinking she is playing a joke, expecting a beetle to jump out. On a raised velvet cushion a delicate gold crucifix lies on a chain, so fine it is woven like strands of flaxen hair.

'Where did you find it? It can't be mine.'

Sunshine catches the crucifix, shiny at her throat. She leans forward, her face shining brighter.

'They're from our Granny O'Brien. She sent them. Aren't they beautiful?'

I am speechless. I have never owned a piece of jewellery in my life. Granny O'Brien knows we exist. I can't believe it.

'I wrote when Mam was in hospital. I heard her telling someone that Dad came from Fair Green. As soon as I got home, I wrote.' Joan hands me a letter. 'It's from Eileen, one of Dad's sisters. She had to write to us. Granny O'Brien is blind now. Eileen said she was overwhelmed with joy to hear from us. It made her so happy to know we are OK. She didn't know Dad had left us. She thought he must have died, because she never heard from him since he left Limerick, except through Mam. Mam wrote to her for a few years, then nothing.'

Limerick is another name for heaven, suddenly.

'Maybe we can go and see her, Joan. Wouldn't that be great?'

Joan hugs me tight. 'Don't get your hopes up too much. Mam won't be that easy to pretend to. You'll have to let on someone else gave you the crucifix or she'll go mad. Besides, we could never afford the fare.'

In dreams I am walking up the path to Granny O'Brien's cottage. When she opens the door, she is smiling. She shows me to my bedroom. It is not unlike Moll's, with feather pillows and a goose-down quilt. There is another one for Joan across the hall and one for Dad, all aired and ready for him. 'I was expecting you,' she tells me. 'I've waited for such a long time.'

The crucifix links me to her and to Limerick, like an arm through an arm. It is proof of my connections to her and the half of myself Mam is often in conflict with. Maybe if I save up enough money, I can go and live with Granny O'Brien.

Since Joan got married last Christmas, we have moved out of the large flat in Crayford. We have been living in two rooms opposite the hospital. The living room is by the front door. All it had in it when we moved was a table and two hard chairs. The bedroom is two floors up in the rafters. To use the outside lavatory, we have to go through the land-lady's only living room and the communal kitchen, which serves as a bathroom. The bath is the kitchen sink. I went to a junk shop with Mam to buy furniture.

'I'm never going to get into debt for anything again as long as I live,' Mam said.

She sorted out a couple of armchairs and a wardrobe. She

haggled over a double bed, wondering how we'd get it up the narrow stairs to the attic. I sorted out a single bed.

Mam shook her head. 'This'll do for the two of us. There's no need to go spending money we haven't got on the luxury of separate beds, is there?'

I became an immovable mountain. 'If I can't have a bed of my own, Mam, I'll sleep on the bloody floor!'

I got the bed. It was placed where the eaves were lowest, near a lower door closing off the mysteries of a spreading dark space. When Mam was taken into hospital, I put off going upstairs to bed until the early hours. Mrs B was strict about turning lights out. If she saw a glimmer, she crept upstairs and sneaked her wizened arm through the door to switch the light out. Auntie May used to do this too, but only after I had read myself to sleep. Morning after morning, I was late for work in the shop, because I would lie in the dark, breathless with fear, closing my eyes at dawn.

Mrs Pryor, the manageress in the laundry, had what she considered a perfect solution.

'You can come and work for me, Patty. It's only across the road and since your mother won't be able to work there any more, I will be able to make your money up to the adult rate. Which will be exceptional for a girl of sixteen, so you'll have to keep quiet about it.'

'I can't work there, Mam. Please don't make me. Joan had to leave because it is so awful. Tell Mrs Pryor you won't let me work there. Please.'

Mam was sitting with her feet up. She had to have her feet up because of her heart. I was so pleased she was home, I wanted to agree with her about everything. She must not on any account be upset. Doctor's orders. I was so disgustingly healthy, I had no excuses to save me from the horrors of Bexley Hospital. But Mam had already sealed my fate with Mrs Pryor. Made all the arrangements. A week's notice, then start in the laundry the Monday after.

'You heard what the doctor said. I'm not up to heavy work any more. I won't even be able to think of work for another two or three months and what you earn in the shop won't go anywhere near keeping us. You should be thankful to Mrs Pryor, so you should, and not so bloody selfish. We can't all do what we want in this life. And don't I know it!'

An eerie grey light washed the hospital buildings that first morning. Staff of all types were coming and going through the gates, some on bikes, most on foot. Like robots, they each followed their own path to their respective workplaces or wards, walking in silence, not yet fully awake. I followed a group of women through the maze of paths and corridors to the laundry, compelling myself along, battling my instinct to run for my life.

I reported to Doris, the assistant manageress, in the office.

'You know the ropes on account of your mother and sister,' she said, then handed me two pink overalls. 'Wear one now and have the other for a change. You'll be working in the check-in room with Sheila Gray. Sheila will explain everything. She's just a couple of years older than you, so you should get on well together. The hours are from seven-thirty to four-thirty, with a half-hour dinner break.'

The smell was making me feel sick.

'That's the only time you are allowed to leave the laundry,' she continued, 'except when you're sent to the wards on laundry business. Then you'll go in pairs until you are eighteen. It's for your own safety. We can't give you a master key until then either.'

She smiled, promising the key to heaven.

'Be careful,' Joan warned. 'The patients are unpredictable. One minute they are laughing and joking with you, the next, they go berserk. I'll never forget the time those two women had a fight. Worse than tigers, trying to tear each other limb from limb, smashing each other with poles and chairs. No one could part them. They had to get a gang of male nurses down from the wards. They were taken out in straitjackets. I passed out with fear. Some of the women were crying with the shock.' Joan whispers, as if saying it aloud will revive her horror.

Sheila Gray had the check-in room under control. 'These are the shelves for Beckenham and Sydenham Hospitals' staff. We do all the doctors' and nurses' uniforms. Our nurses' and doctors' uniforms are checked in and out round the corner. We have to help out there too, although Lily MacKinley runs that. We also have to help with checking in the patients' laundry from the wards. That's done in the wash-house. With our own work, we make sure it's all washed, ironed and packed for Cyril the van-man at the end of the week. Frilled caps and sleeve cuffs, we have to do by hand: starching, then crimping with a crimping iron. We iron shirts for the top doctors.' She paused, smiling. 'What do you think?'

I winked at her, pleased with her friendly manner. 'I'll let you know if I last the first week. Who knows, maybe it's the caps I'll iron the frills out of and crimp the shirts.'

'I tried that, but it didn't wash in here,' Sheila said. 'They just stand over you and make sure you get it right.'

Shuffling throngs of male patients entered the grey-walled wash-house.

'What are they doing?' I asked Sheila. 'They don't look able for work.'

I was shocked at the herd of emaciated men, like prisoners of Belsen instead of a hospital.

'A lot of them came back from the war like that.' Sheila was matter-of-fact.

'You mean, this is the freedom they fought for?' I asked in Grandilla's voice. I asked for Grandilla.

'Mostly they shake,' she said, and together we watched them sitting on benches, changing into heavy clogs.

'Who?' I asked, upset by their hopelessness.

'The ones with war troubles, like him.'

She pointed to a man so thin he was hardly there at all, eyes wide and fear-filled, his rubber apron all a-rippling from his chest to his clogs like a second skin, trembling, along with his bones and sinews.

'Oh my God, Sheila, surely that poor man is not fit to work in here?'

'If they can stand up, they're fit. Don't let Jim hear you saying something like that.'

'Who's Jim?'

'There he is, the foreman.'

A small man with blue dungarees and Wellington boots strode with a purpose up through the wash-house. 'Come on, you lot, get your arses into gear,' he shouted at the patients, pulling an arm here, pushing a shoulder there as he passed.

Some of the men leapt off the bench, terrified, and began trundling trolleys stacked with heaps of stinking, shit-covered bedding to the huge washing machines. The noise from the machines, the trolleys and the clatter of clogs echoed into the pitched cathedral roof, startling pigeons perching on the rafters. Flapping wildly, they flew about, shitting with abandon onto encrusted window ledges and light fittings. We ducked.

Avoiding the waste water gurgling obscenely along gullies in the concrete floor before draining away, we shoved our deep trolley towards the machine Jim was pointing us to. Large pools of waste, watery and human, flooded over the clogged feet of the patients and spread darkly. In the laundry room, the wireless blasted out *Housewives' Choice* above the steam and din.

'This is the new girl, Patty,' Sheila shouted to the women feeding wet sheets into two enormous rollers.

They stopped singing a moment and waved, unable to shake my hand in case the sheets caught in the rollers, keeping the momentum going for the women peeling them off the other side and folding them. A fog of steam hung everywhere. Under a run of high windows, women ironed and patients folded. All the women were singing, the outside workers in pink overalls, the patients in ill-fitting clothes from another time.

'Hello, Granny Price,' Sheila shouted at a tiny old woman in a black Victorian dress and laced boots, screaming herself hoarse through one of the windows at an invisible stalker from her past.

Centrally placed tables were piled with clean sheets and towels and small pieces of fluff rose and fell like snowflakes on bent shoulders. In a glass-windowed office dome, isolated and pristine, Mrs Pryor sat, a painted doll, in her crisp white coat.

'Come in, Patty. I am so pleased you are coming to join us. You see, it's not as bad as people think, is it?'

'No, not so bad,' I said, deliberate in my words. 'It's not as bad as even I imagined. It's worse than anything I could ever imagine.'

To agree with her, in this place, not of my choosing, was more than I could do.

Her eyes pierced into me, warning me to watch myself. 'I hope we are going to get along, Patty, for your mother's sake.'

She dismissed me then, bending to read papers on her desk.

Every worker is expected to work with a patient. I have Ava. She is thirty-three; twice my age and more than twice my size.

'Mind this trolley, Ava,' I tell her, but she waddles behind me, following me into the ward.

I take her back, clutching the sheets I am delivering and

tell her firmly, 'Stay here, Ava, I won't be a minute and I don't want any patient running off with it while I'm gone. We'll get into trouble if we lose it.'

'All right, Patty,' she promises, 'then can we go to the canteen?'

'If you're good,' I tell her and hurry into the ward to check the sheets in with a nurse in case Ava herself runs off with it.

And so it is all down the corridors until the trolley is empty, except for one stray sheet without a laundry mark.

'Here,' I tell Ava, 'lie down.'

I cover her with the sheet and push the trolley into the grounds. Ava chuckles from her big belly as I try to steer it with the weight of her, pretending I'm taking her to the mortuary.

'Oh, Patty, Patty, Patty,' she screams with delight as we wobble over bumps. She shrieks at my mock surprise when we hit a wall.

I buy her an orange ice-lolly. I have to buy her one whenever we go into the canteen after our deliveries or she sulks all afternoon. Licking her lolly is serious work, interrupted with a wide grin, an unsuitable advertisement for toothpaste.

'There,' she says when she's finished, running her fingers through her pudding-bowl haircut, 'I'm a happy girl now.'

'Now, Ava?' I frown.

'Now I am. Not like the time I was knocked down by a bus in the old Kent Road. I wasn't one bit happy then, Patty.'

'I'm not surprised. I wouldn't be a bit happy if I got knocked down by a bus.'

Her broad flat face contorts, telling me she is working hard to think of what she wants to say. Her pain and memories have become will-o'-the-wisps, coshed from her brain with pills and confusion, chased away by shame.

'Me mum was by me bed when I woke up. She told me I'd 'ad a baby boy, but they took 'im away. "You're a bad girl," she told me. "And you can't come home again."'

I remain silent. What can I say?

'They sent me here, Patty, all them years ago.'

'When was that, Ava?'

She screws her eyes up to think and counts the years on her little fat fingers. 'Seventeen years ago,' she says, 'just before my seventeenth birthday.'

'Just about my age now, Ava,' I tell her, wishing I could tell her something better. 'Come on, we'll be told off if we don't get back.'

She holds the trolley with me as we walk along the corridor. 'I can't go home, Patty,' she says, repeating it again and again. 'Do you know I can't go home any more?'

'Nor can I, Ava,' I tell her. 'I can't go home either and I was never run over by a bus.'

Now and then, during lunch breaks, I take her across to our rented rooms. The landlady doesn't like it one bit. In all her years living opposite the hospital, she's never had a single one of 'them' in her house. I tell her Ava is my friend. I leave unsaid the bit about paying the rent and having the right to invite who I like into the place.

'She doesn't like me, Patty,' Ava says.

'Well, that makes it quits then, because I don't like her.'

Ava is sitting at the table, eating a sandwich when Mam comes in.

'What's she doing here?'

I know it isn't Ava she is angry about. She's used to me bringing her home.

'We'll be gone soon.' I keep my tone even.

Ava is terrified of raised voices. Even rain lashing the windows makes her cry.

'I've just left Joan in Dartford,' Mam clears a space to sit down. 'She tells me she's been in touch with her grandmother in Limerick.'

I blush. 'Was she?'

Mam stands up and bangs the table. Ava starts crying.

'Don't, Mam. Don't upset her. It's not her fault.'

Mam is raging. 'What about upsetting me? Did either of you worry for one minute about my feelings? Did you?'

'That's all we've ever done. Worry about your feelings. Well, we have feelings too, you know. And we have the right to get in touch with whoever we like.'

I don't know where the determination comes from, but it is there, under my top layer of skin. Flesh of my flesh. But for Ava, I might have banged my fist on the table too.

Out of control of the O'Brien saga for the first time, Mam struggles to harness it again. I should have known better than to expect her to concede any ground. One of us has to give way. I can't bear silences.

'I'm sorry, Mam, I didn't mean to upset you. I'm sorry.'

'Oh, are you now? How many times have I heard that

one? I suppose you didn't think I'd be upset if you lied to me about that crucifix around your neck either?'

I grasp it under my blouse. How does she know? Since Joan gave it to me, I have worn high-collared blouses or hidden it in the toe of a shoe under my bed.

'Joan told me. I had to force it out of her. I knew it was too expensive for her to buy, or her husband. I can't believe she'd go behind my back after all we've been through. And you! I knew you were hiding something.'

She stands over me. Ava has disappeared into the hall.

'It's only a crucifix, Mam. An oul' piece of jewellery. That's all.'

'I'll give you an oul' piece of jewellery!' She tears it from my neck and throws it into the fireplace, dashing the hopes of Granny O'Brien as well as mine.

I stand, wanting to lash out too, to throw something at the wall. To bang my fist against it, again and again, as if it is my father's face.

'All the time you live on my floor, you will not mention the O'Briens. Do you hear me?'

I hear her.

Honour thy father and thy mother.

When I come home again, the crucifix is gone from the hearth. Soon, I vow, I will be gone too.

Fourteen

Sheila sits on the table in the sorting room, running her finger down the checklist, calling out to me. 'Two starched caps, two aprons, four frilled cuffs, one starched belt.'

I check for the right laundry marks and stack them in the rack.

'Right. That's it. All done. Finished for another week.'

We clock off in the rest room and banter with the other laundry workers. All anxious to run out into the air, desperate to smell the world beyond the hospital gates, covering their need with familiar jokes and well-meant insults.

'How are you now, Patty?' Sheila asks as we hurry along the main corridor. We always hurry after four-thirty.

'I'm all right, Sheila. I can't do very much about it. Mrs Pryor and Doris were knocking at the door this morning before eight. Mam must have sent a note over to them when I wouldn't get up. She could see I was sick with fear, but she was determined to make me go to work no matter what I said.'

We walk through the grounds towards the gate, slowing our pace in the fresh air.

Sheila links my arm. 'So what happened when they knocked on the door?'

'It was awful, Sheila. The landlady was standing in the bedroom watching. She was delighted to see me in trouble.'

'Get up out of that bed before I drag you out,' Mam had shouted. 'Mrs Pryor and Doris are downstairs. They're disgusted with you altogether, taking to your bed because a patient has a turn. Suppose everyone did the same. Then where would we be?'

'I'll help you get her out, Sally,' Mrs B said. She moved to the foot of the bed.

'Don't let her touch me, Mam. I'll get up if you make her go away.'

'They can't make you go to work, even if you're not ill.' Sheila is able to put herself in my shoes. 'They can sack you, but they have no right to drag you out of bed.' We wait for Sheila's bus to Bexleyheath. 'Go on,' she urges, anxious to hear the end before her bus comes.

'It didn't matter what I said, Sheila, they had all made their minds up that I was going to work.' I laugh. 'Can you imagine it if I'd run away? The four of them chasing me down the dip like in a Charlie Chaplin film? Doris in her high heels and Mrs Pryor holding her hair in place. Mam clutching her heart and her hanky and the oul' landlady screeching at everyone to stop that bitch.'

When Sheila stops laughing, she says, 'I was frightened too when Helen had that terrible fit. I never saw anything like it, her running around making that terrible noise and foaming at the mouth, bashing into machinery, but I never let on to Helen that it upset me. She knows you are frightened of her and she enjoys tormenting you. You'll have to ignore her from now on. If you do, she'll find some other mischief.'

'I know,' I say, too ashamed to tell her that my nightmares are even worse than the day-to-day ordeal with Helen, when she comes up behind me, whispering terrible things. 'Help me,' she says, goading me.

Even the fun I have with Sheila no longer helps me through the days. Like the time we dressed up as doctors, pinning our ponytails into buns and wearing white coats from Beckenham's laundry boxes. In the staff teashop, full of importance, we went to the top of the queue and ordered our tea and cakes without objection.

'See the way they're looking at us behind the counter,' I said to Sheila. 'They think they know us, but they don't know where from. We could go up to the wards and do a lobotomy without being stopped. It's not who we are, it's who they think we are. These white coats open doors.'

Delighted with our hoax, we were up to all sorts of charades for a few weeks afterwards. It made a difference, laughing, while all around us, broken people staggered through another broken day. One Beckenham box belonged to a very large nursing sister. Sheila said it could be carried up a mountain and used as a tent. We put it on, Sheila's arm in one sleeve, mine in another and there was room for two more, maybe three, so we bundled as much as we could down our fronts, until our chests looked like the mountain ledges a tent such as we wore could be pitched on. We lashed ourselves together with the ever-expanding elastic belt, winding it about our middles, unable to stand upright we were laughing so much. With a crimped and starched frilled bonnet on each of our heads, we walked first into the wash-house, magnificent and stately, smiling indulgently at the patients, terrifying some into statues and scattering others, who probably thought we were their own special hallucination: a two-headed giantess, a Siamese sister, looking left and right at the same time.

The women in the laundry room stopped working, leaving their machines and irons, following us out, as two heads swivelled in every direction. Some women patients screamed until those who could saw the joke. The women in pink overalls had all the benefits of a fortnight's holiday in ten minutes. Even Mrs Pryor and Doris joined in with the giggles of a long weekend.

Now I have to force the fun, dreading the nights. And so, this morning, I couldn't get out of bed. I had spent the night waiting for Helen to come out of the darkness under the eaves. Every creak was the low door opening. I prayed, asking God to help me. I prayed to Granny, certain she must be a saint by now for all her sacrifices and suffering. Then I couldn't stop thinking of her moving below us on the night of her funeral. The room was full of imagined ghosts. Crowding around my bed.

'How will we pay the rent if you decide to rot in bed all day?' Mam cried.

I think Mam was as terrified as me. She had lost two

homes in Ireland because of poverty. Then our elegant Crayford flat. What will be become of us if we lose these miserable rooms?

'Mrs Pryor and Doris were disgusted with me, Sheila.'

'How can you put your poor mother through this worry, Patty? I expected a bit more from you when I gave you the job. I had more experienced girls ready to bite my hand off for it, and this is all the thanks I get.' Mrs Pryor's voice was clipped, her teeth clenched after each rapid delivery to stop the plums falling out.

Doris the Disciple was an echo. 'Poor mother . . . A bit more . . . Hand off . . . Thanks . . .'

Mam stood at the door, arms folded, nodding her agreement. I knew it was useless trying to speak. I walked across to the laundry between Mrs Pryor and Doris like a recaptured escapee. They thought they had won, but poverty was the winner. Fear of it again. Poor Mam, no wonder she would not let me lie in bed.

'Don't worry too much, Patty,' Sheila says. 'It'll be all right. Helen will find someone else to torment.'

She kisses my cheek before boarding her bus, leaving me smiling and waving. Feeling better. Glad I did the right thing.

When the bus disappears down the dip, I walk across the heath, needing the sun's warmth, glad I'm going to meet Ken outside the Granada in Dartford tonight. With Carole, my friend from Greig's, I kept bumping into him and his mates in the coffee bar on East Hill.

Carole had her eye on him. 'I think he's lovely. Just like Cliff Richard with his quiff and dimples.'

But he had his eye on me. 'Do you want to come to the pictures with me, then?' he'd asked casually.

We were all squashed round a glass-topped table on red leather seats, promises frothing in glass Espresso cups; shillings jingling in our pockets for the chromium juke box. Ready to rock.

'Yeah, OK, then,' I'd said, feeling glad all over.

Mam has spread a tablecloth and cooked a dinner of bacon and cabbage. It's her way of apologising – a treat for special occasions.

'Who's coming?' I ask.

'Only you,' she says, smiling.

I sit and eat, though I am not the slightest bit hungry, relieved she has forgiven me.

'Read it.' She passes me a letter. 'It's from Jane and John. They want to take over the tenancy of the house.'

'Oh, Mam, they can't, can they?'

She sighs and shrugs. 'I suppose it's for the best. I have to send home the difference in their rent every week. If circumstances were different, we could manage it. We'll have to let it go. I'll scrape the fare together somehow and go home with May to sell everything up.'

I can see how defeated she feels. I get up and put my arm around her shoulder. 'Don't worry, Mam. We'll get another little house at home one day. I won't always be stuck in the laundry and you'll be able to work soon. We can save hard and go home before we know where we are.'

Mam takes my hand, embarrassing me. 'It's a lovely thought, Patty, but what is there to go home to now? There's only Moll left and her life is secure. She picked the right man when she picked Alec. We're better off here now, love. We can never go back.'

'How, Mam? How are we better off?'

I don't want to upset her after the terrible morning and then the letter, but I need her to see our plight.

She runs her hand across the table. 'That's how we're better off. We eat every day and we have shoes on our feet. It's a start. I'll never go back to the worry I had before I came here.'

I look around the room, crammed with junk furniture and rules.

'We'd have ended up in the Union, or worse,' she says. 'I'll never go back.'

She needs to hear something nice. I search for something, willing to give her all my dreams. My future house by the Swan River. But I mustn't raise her hopes yet.

'One day, Mam, something good will happen. I know it. One day, we'll go to Dublin, all of us, and have our own little house again.'

She smiles, indicating that I eat my dinner. 'Poor Patty,' she grips my hand, 'you always were a dreamer.'

After dinner, I go through to the scullery to have a wash, disturbing Mrs B's telly-watching.

'I hope you're not going to be coming in and out here all night,' she says, irritated with me.

'I'm off to the pictures, Mrs B,' I say, thinking of Ken's smile, knowing I have hours of pleasure ahead before the terrors of the night.

I've never had a date before. I used to hold hands with Paddy Dooner and walk through the shrubbery with him in the grounds of St Wilfrid's. And Chris Cassella walked home from school with me a few times. There's a trainee doctor over on one of the wards called John. He keeps asking me out, but he's too old. He must be at least twenty-four. There was Jimmy Redmond of course. How is he? I wonder. Courting Baba Reid, no doubt.

'Nine brothers and sisters!' I whisper.

Ken whispers back, 'Yeah, and we're not even Catholics.'

For some reason, we both find this hysterical and the usherette keeps shining her torch at us.

'What about you?' he asks and I am forced once again to reveal my inadequacy.

'Oh, there's not much to tell, really. I have one sister. She's married. And I live with my mother.'

'What about your dad?'

I have a desire to tell him my dad is dead. I can't face any more explanations or questions.

'I never talk about my dad.' I say it with such finality that he concentrates all his attention on the screen.

That'll be the end of him, I think, telling myself I don't care.

At the bus stop, he asks if I'll be in the coffee bar again on Sunday.

'I might be. I'm not sure,' I answer, knowing I would crawl over hot coals to get there.

Later, I lie awake in the darkness, focusing on the future, instead of what is hidden in the far recesses of the eaves. I will have to settle down in this country and try to make my own life. Ireland is becoming a dream, an imagined place. Was I ever really there at all? Sometimes I try to work out why it is that so many Irish people had to leave. I can't make sense of it. I had to leave because Mam brought me over here. Would she have come, I wonder, if she had known how things would work out? I doubt it. She is nearly fifty, and she has nowhere to call home. She can't bear to think of Dublin, yet she does again and again. If it's sunny, she'll say, 'Just imagine, we'd be walking out to Sandymount now to have a paddle.' All the things she misses don't cost money. She even misses the Buildings. That looming Honourable Estate of Riches seamed in poverty's gloom. So do I.

Ken leaves his bike outside, under the living-room window. Mam is worried it will upset Mrs B. He sits on the arm of my chair and the room seems crowded. On his face, his surprise at the shabbiness flits, but when Mam offers him a sandwich, he tucks in. Mam looks at me. He has passed some sort of test. So have I. I realise have a boyfriend. An Englishman. Like Joan's husband. Not an Irishman, like Dad or Grandilla.

'And are you working yourself?' Mam asks him.

'Yes. I'm an apprentice in an engineering firm.' He blushes to the roots of his crew cut.

'That's grand,' Mam says. 'Grand altogether.'

Not for long is it grand.

'What about Mr O'Brien. What does he do?' Ken asks her.

I wish I had not dismissed his question the other night. Mam's lips disappear.

'Mr O'Brien does whatever he likes. He goes wherever he likes. He forgets he has a family. Daughters. Girls who need protecting and a roof over their head.'

Ken mumbles something about being sorry. I want to run, to hide my humiliation. How will he respect a girl whose own father forgets about her? Why should he care about someone so unimportant? I am so ashamed.

'Mam, Ken doesn't want to know about all that. He was just being polite, weren't you, Ken?'

Ken is too polite to admit that he was being polite. 'Oh, no, Mrs O'Brien, I didn't realise he didn't live here. Pat didn't tell me. It must be hard.'

It is. For the next two hours, Ken hears just how hard it really is. With each incident related, I grow smaller and smaller until I retreat into the dust in the right-hand parlour. I hate her, I decide. I really do.

'Your mother is very kind,' Ken whispers when she goes to make a cup of tea, gasping for a drink after all her talking. 'It must be very hard for her being on her own.'

I am now invisible. My work in the laundry is nothing: Mam is on her own.

On a cheap train excursion to Margate, Ken asks me to marry him. I am ashamed again. I haven't got a dad to pay for my wedding, but I will be as good as anybody else, I vow. I will have a white dress with bridesmaids and a three-tier cake. And we will have rooms of our own with furniture bought in a real shop. People will no longer pity me because I have no dad. They will respect me because I have a husband. One will cancel out the other.

'Yes,' I say, 'but you'll have to wait until I am eighteen. And we'll need to save up to pay for everything ourselves.'

I walk up the aisle on Paddy's arm, awed by the number of people in the church, most of them Ken's relatives. In the bridal car driving here, Paddy asked me if I was certain I was doing the right thing.

'It's a bit late now if I'm not,' I laughed, thinking of Mam's words last week.

I had felt overwhelmed by the speed of things. When the date was set last year, the wedding day was so far in the future it didn't seem possible. Picking the dress and planning everything had been exciting and I had worked overtime for the past six months to pay for it, so I hadn't had much time for reflection. Until last week.

'Can I talk to you, Mam?' I asked when she came in from work in the old people's home.

She had started working there nine months after I began my job in the laundry. We lived like flat-sharers instead of mother and daughter, splitting everything down the middle. We had a sort of independence, but were beginning to rely on each other. With a little more money in my pocket instead of being the main breadwinner, I felt rich, not just financially, but in so many other ways. There were small freedoms: going to London and down to the Kent coast and telling Mam I might be home or then again, I might not. I went regularly to see Auntie May, who said she was mesmerised altogether at the way I'd grown up. I even went to Dublin to see Auntie Moll. Everything was the same, which was a bit upsetting, because it was clear our going had not caused the slightest stir. Every blade of grass in Palmerston Park lay in the same direction. The locks at Portobello still opened and closed for the Limerick barges. Auntie Moll still left for work in Guinness's before the streets were aired, and Terry still called for his dinner. 'I wish you could stay a bit longer, Patty,' Auntie Moll had said. I knew she meant it and I knew it was impossible.

'Can I talk to you, Mam?' I repeated, after she'd had a half-hour with a cup of tea and her feet up.

'Of course you can, if something is worrying you.'

She seemed easier in herself these last months, especially since the old house was gone and all her debts in Dublin had been cleared.

'It's just that I don't think I'm ready for marriage yet, Mam. I'm getting really nervous now it's only next week. It's too soon.'

She put some more coal on the fire, raking it thoroughly.

'I know you're still only eighteen, love, but in many ways you're a lot older. You've been very good keeping everything going while I was ill, but I'm all right now. I have a great little job and I've me name down for a council flat.'

'That's not what I meant, Mam. I know you'll manage now with your job and everything. It's me. I can't see myself as a married woman. I wish I'd said I'd wait a bit.'

Sparks flew when Mam raked the fire again.

'Well, it's a bit late to think of that now, isn't it? You've your rooms in Welling ready to move into and your wedding dress above in the bedroom. It's a pity you didn't think of that when you were squandering money on it.' Her voice was trembling, preparing to cry.

'I'm sorry, Mam, I don't mean to upset you, it's just that I don't know what to do.'

Tears rolled down her cheeks and mine burned. I waited until she could speak again.

'Patty, love, what will become of you if anything happens to me? My heart is not what it should be. It was a great relief to me when you said you were getting married. I know you'll be looked after.'

I understood what she said, but I didn't see how I needed looking after. I did most of the housework and all the cooking. If anything, I looked after Mam. I realised there was no point in further discussion. Too many people would be let down if I changed my mind. Especially Ken.

I hugged her. 'Silly oul' me. I just wanted to stay here with you a little longer, Mam. That's all. I feel a lot better now.'

'That's the girl. Last-minute nerves. All brides-to-be suffer with them. And just think, you'll never have to set foot in the laundry again.'

'Will you take this man to be your lawful wedded husband?'

'I will,' I say, becoming Mrs Winchester.

And for the next twenty years, we do as best we can, for ourselves and our three fine sons.

Part II

Major Catastrophe

Fifteen

Hull, 1989

From the hotel, I walk alone across Pearson Park. Trees drip on undergrowth and twilight mystifies the houses strung around the old coach road. In the morning, I will find my father's house. I want to see it in the cold light of day. Now, all I need to do is savour my relief at journey's end. I am here, where my father lived. And died. He walked here, beneath these trees, across these paths. In winter, he hurried home, anxious to sit in the warm. In summer, he sat there on the bench near the duck pond. Did he think of Joan feeding the ducks with him on the canal? On grey winter evenings did he look across the park and see the tennis gardens of Mountpleasant? Did he miss us at all while he was living his reconstructed life in this northern English town? I need the walk to calm myself down after the journey from Kent; from St Stephen's Green. Since then, all the roads I travelled have been leading me here. No longer feeling a compulsion to search him out in crowds, I still need to place him somewhere.

I retrace my steps to the hotel, walking slowly over old

ground, pulling memories from the past, tugging them from their roots, glad of the darkness now descended.

Six years ago, as soon as I answered the phone to Joan, his death became a possibility. Only now is it reality. Then, Joan had sobbed that he was dead. I knew who she meant.

'When?' I asked.

'December 1981. Eighteen months ago.'

'Where?'

'I don't know. He wouldn't say.'

'Who wouldn't say? Who told you?'

'The man from the Salvation Army. Remember I told you I was writing to them? They trace missing persons.'

'And they managed to trace him?'

She began to read: 'We very much regret . . . our enquiries for your father have revealed . . . he is now deceased. We have not attempted to contact his second family since they are unknown to you . . . may cause distress to them . . . closing our files and returning your letter . . .'

Another family? He was married to *Mam*. In 1962, when she was sick, the Department for Health and Social Security got money out of him. I had gone with her. The clerk had his life folded into fact, filed in a metal cabinet. The first proof we had that he was alive. We should have tried to trace him then, but we were not strong enough to stand up to Mam, Joan and me, still strapped to her side since the goodbyes in the Green. Too late for might-have-beens. Too late now for hope.

'I phoned the Salvation Army when I'd read the letter,' Joan said. 'Though I asked the adviser for more information

– where had he died? what about his other family? – he would not tell me. But he never got divorced, I told him. We are his legal family.' She sobbed and I waited, crying quietly with her, but inside myself. 'He kept repeating it. "I'm sorry." *I'm sorry* was all he could manage to say.'

'I'm sorry too, Joan.'

Once, on a train, Joan met a psychic. An ordinary woman. Middle-aged. 'Excuse me, dear,' she said when the carriage emptied, 'I'm being given a message for you. Will you take it?'

Joan thought she was going to take something out of her bag. People came through the carriage and the woman stared out of the window. Joan thought she was mad. Only when they drew into the station, did the woman mention the message again.

'He will visit you in your own home. He will knock on your door and step across your threshold.'

'Who?' Joan asked, knowing exactly who she meant.

'Your father,' the woman said and turned abruptly away.

For twenty years, Joan had waited.

Now, here in Hull, I lean against a tree, still reluctant to leave the park for the comfort of the hotel. Standing in the shadows, just a short distance from the people in their rooms getting ready for dinner and the people in the bar where Gordon, my second husband, waits; allowing me my solitude while he has his. I recall my fool's errand then to another windswept northern town, south of here, on the coast.

'I might be related to your late father,' I had shouted as

229

wind whipped open the door of the phone box. I fed more money into the slot and yelled my name.

'Come out to the house,' Tom O'Brien had said calmly, 'and we can discuss it.'

I drove along the seafront, marvelling that my dad might have lived and died here . . . of all the towns in all the world.

Before going to Tom's, I went to the address given on the death certificate. The house he died in; a wendy house for the elderly with a hanky garden behind a wall built low enough for youngsters to sit on. Poor old sod, I thought, I hope they didn't torment him.

Tom was small and dark, with sharper features than I expected. Great, though, like his wife, who couldn't get over the possibility that her late father-in-law might have been a philanderer. We tried to make the pieces fit the dates: Patrick Francis O'Brien, born Limerick, Ireland, 1910. Died in England. One and the same? Or two different people? Tom's Patrick drove a lorry. I didn't think my Patrick would.

The next day, I met them at the cemetery. I stood and wept where they scattered his ashes.

'I can't imagine what it must have been like, not knowing about your dad,' Tom said.

'You're lovely, Tom. If you are my brother, I'm very fortunate.' I thanked him for the photographs and his kindness.

'He has similar features, though he looks smaller altogether. It seems like him.' Joan looked at the bride on his arm, his daughter. 'I don't think I can forgive him walking her up the aisle.' She holds the photograph closer, shaking her head.

In the end, Joan and I decided that Tom's father is not ours, and I write to tell him so.

Dear Tom,

After great consideration, we have come to the conclusion that your father is not the Patrick we are looking for . . . Too many pieces cannot be made to fit . . . I hope you are not too disturbed by my intrusion into your family . . . I will never forget your warmth and generosity to me . . .

'Christ, Joan, it's hilarious. I even picked up a handful of soil in the cemetery and sprinkled it in my garden.'

'You could earn a living doing that. Professional mourner. Burials, burnings and scatterings. Willing to travel.'

'Discreet dress. Black veil if desired. Portfolio available on request,' I added.

Full of black humour, smiling at the comedy of errors, I catch my reflection now in a glass as I enter the hotel. 'Like a feckin' demented Yeti,' Auntie May would have said, 'after being pulled through a hedge backwards.'

Gordon is in agreement. 'Look at the state of you, soaked to the skin! Here, let me take your coat.'

He drapes it on the back of a chair while I make some sort of shape to my straggling hair, aware that I have the undivided attention of the entire lounge bar.

'They'll all be checking out in the morning,' I say, picking up my glass of wine.

'How did it go, love?' Gordon asks. 'Did you find his house?'

'It's on the far side of the park. I couldn't make out the house numbers in the dark. Anyway, I didn't really want to knock on my own.'

I need to prepare myself for the possibility of meeting the woman who described herself as his widow on his death certificate. I don't want to barge in and upset her if, of course, she still lives there. Widow or not, she is the one who mattered most to him for thirty years. But it has taken me a lifetime to get here.

'There is no turning back now, Gordon. But what will I say?'

'She might actually be his widow,' Gordon had said as soon as he found the correct certificate in Catherine House. He had offered to carry out just one more search while he was in London. 'Mrs Hull,' he'd said when he phoned with the news, 'I've found it. Of all places, he lived in Hull! Imagine that!'

Gordon Hull's imagination had been captivated by my background since we met on a picket line. Though we were both trade unionists working for the same Inner London Authority, Gordon in Parks, me in Housing, it took five years and a strike before we could wave our banner together. Our first outing was to Croydon, as speakers and fund-raisers for the cause. I drove. It was rush hour. We could see the town hall, but could not get near it, so round and round the one-way system we went, chatting each other up until I said: 'For Christ's sake, will you find a parking place? It's not a feckin' magic roundabout we're on. The meeting will be finished before we get there.'

'There's a place,' he shouted. 'Quick, stop! Reverse back before someone else nabs it.'

I stopped instantly in the heavy traffic and took the tooting and expletives of other drivers as compliments, while I tried to locate the parking space.

'Where is it?' I yelled above the din, knowing I couldn't get a doll's pram in the only spot on the road.

'There. There behind you, you'll manage that,' he indicated, misplacing his confidence.

With a swerve, a reverse and a left swing on the driving wheel, I parked perfectly, just off the road in a spot I hadn't noticed.

'Now,' I said as if I parked as efficiently every time.

'What?' Gordon asked, amazed.

It took a moment. I waited for him to praise me. So did he. He waited patiently, until I realised I had parked in a small front garden, not much bigger than my car. And the traffic still sped past.

'I like your initiative, Pat O'Brien,' he said, grinning, 'but I think we'd better get back on the magic roundabout, don't you? That's some poor sod's garden, not a magic parking bay.'

We drove off, laughing. And we still raised money at the meeting.

I warm up, glad he is with me now, Mr and Mrs Hull in Hull. Glad he will be with me tomorrow too. Like he was in Limerick the year after we met.

'I want to go to Ireland in the spring,' Gordon had said in his rich Geordie accent.

'Really? I asked, astounded, recognising my map reader. I had been considering a trip to Limerick for some time; an unspecified urge to walk on forbidden ground. I wanted to stand where the waters of the Grand Canal and the Shannon dance. I wanted to sit in a Limerick bar and listen to the locals singing up the ghost of my father's voice.

I sigh now, sad it has all come to this.

'What's the matter?' Gordon asks, glowing from the wine and the meal.

'I was thinking about Limerick and Nora and her husband, Sean. When we sat in the Pike Bar with them, finding out about the missing years.'

'Just as well Sean Ryan is not here now, me drinking red wine.' Gordon smiles, remembering too.

Joan had kept our Aunt Nora's address since Granny O'Brien sent the crucifixes. I wrote, asking if we could call to meet her. Over a meal of smoked salmon, Sean and Nora told me about my grandmother.

Sean was very fond of her. 'Bookish, she was, and very frail for her last few years,' he said. 'There was a terrible sadness. She sat for hours at the window watching for your father, waiting for him to come home. "When Paddy O'Brien walks up the Pike, what a day we'll have," she'd say. It was heartbreaking to watch her. "We'll dance in the streets," she'd say.'

I could not bear to think of her suffering.

'Don't cry, Pat. We can change nothing,' Nora said, 'especially not old grieving or regret.'

Long into the night, we spoke about the mystery that was

my dad. And Nora's brother. I told Nora about the letter from the Salvation Army four years earlier. She listened. I watched her registering the news with a slight drop of her head and a down-sweep of her eyelids, just a flickering shielding of her eyes. A barrier of steel.

'Oh,' she said. Then after a silence: 'Oh, dear God.'

'We couldn't tell it was him for sure,' I said, telling her about my trip to the northeast coast. 'It was such a relief to think they had identified the wrong man. The wrong body.'

'So you think he's still alive then?' Sean asked.

'Well, I know he couldn't have been the only Patrick Francis O'Brien of his age living in England. All I know is, it is just not possible he was Tom's dad too.'

Nora did not know what to think. 'My mother never recovered from the loss of him. She couldn't bear to think of going to her grave without seeing him again.'

As a distraction, Nora began rummaging in a drawer, looking for something. A photograph. She clutched it to herself, then held it out. 'Your mother sent this to mine when she first met your father. It was very precious. She had it in a frame for years. I want you to have it.'

Mam and Dad are standing together in a garden; a beautiful couple. I had never seen a picture of them together. The only other picture I have is of Dad in military uniform walking in Dublin. Down O'Connell Street.

Gordon breaks my reverie, reclaiming me for the present. 'One last drink before bedtime, eh? It's going to be a big day tomorrow. You must be pleased with all you've achieved? Seen Limerick. Put flowers on your grandparents' grave.

Now you're here. Tomorrow you'll knock on your father's door. That must warrant a toast. To us,' he says.

'To searchers everywhere,' I salute, tipping glasses with him.

The rain is steady and set in for the day. We delay breakfast, delay packing, delay leaving the hotel. Daylight transforms Pearson Park. December mists do not detract from its charm, especially where the barren trees allow glimpses of once important houses, many now divided into flats, others of sterner stuff, still stately, defying the ravages of time.

My heart pounds in my ears as we near my father's house. Although I have been rehearsing what I will say to Mary Irene all night long, I have lost my opening lines in the confusion of my senses. Was I going to introduce myself as my father's niece, or as a daughter of his friend? Or will I lose my courage just when I need it most?

Nearer now, we count down the numbers to the gate. I stand to prepare for what will come next, surrounded by trees and old houses, pavements and park; textures of my father's existence. His life without us.

'What will I say to her, Gordon?' I am trembling, unreal.

'Whatever you want to say. Hello might be a good start. Here we are, love.' He grips my elbow.

We have finally arrived.

'It must have been grand once,' I say, shocked by the sign telling us it is now an old people's home, licensed by

Humberside County Council for the care of seventeen residents. 'Oh no, Gordon. The poor old sod, he must have been a resident. His widow won't be here after all. What will we do now?'

'Now we're here, we may as well knock and ask. They might remember him.'

A young woman opens the door.

'I'm sorry to intrude, but I'm trying to find out about my late father. His name was Patrick Francis O'Brien. He died in this house in 1981.'

'Step in for a minute. I'm new here myself. I'll ask the matron.'

The hallway is impersonal. I find it hard to imagine my dad going in and out. I want this to be his house. I want to imagine him walking down those stairs to pick his newspaper up from the tiled floor, going through that door into the kitchen to sit and catch up with the world before his day begins. I cannot. I never considered a council-run home. Although the years insist otherwise, my dad did not grow old. He stayed always in his late thirties prime, strong and smart. I have leap-frogged him somewhere along the way and grown older than him. And now? What can I make of this? An old people's home. Maybe he just sat, semi-comatose, all day. A deserved end? Not able to run any more. Hemmed in by zimmer frames.

The matron smiles and offers us her hand. 'Sorry to keep you. This hour after breakfast is our busiest time. I've looked up the name. Your father wasn't a resident here. At least not since it's been a nursing home. He actually lived here. My boss bought it from a Mr Taylor in 1985. I think Mr Taylor bought it from Mrs O'Brien about 1983 or 1984.'

I try to register this properly. Mary Irene sold the house. Did she own it with Dad? It is a mansion.

Gordon thanks the matron. She is glad to be of help.

'Do you have a forwarding address for Mr Taylor or Mrs O'Brien? One for redirected mail, perhaps?'

'I'm sorry, I don't have information like that here. I have no idea where either of them went.'

'It's very nice of you to tell me that he did at least live here. You'll never know what that means to me.'

Outside, we stand, trying to take it all in.

'Imagine him living in a house like that, Gordon! And Mam living in a tiny council flat. I can't believe it.'

Gordon is more circumspect. 'Let's not jump to conclusions. He could have been a gigolo. A kept man,' he chuckles. 'Let's knock next door. They might remember him there.'

On the wall next door, a blue plaque proclaims it to have been the home of the poet Philip Larkin. I wonder if he knew my dad. Did they stroll around the park together on fine afternoons to discuss ideas, like he did with Mr Grogan? If they met on the path, did they exchange nods?

I find myself explaining again to the man standing on the doorstep. He remembers Mr O'Brien next door. I am ecstatic. This is the first person I've encountered who can tell me anything definite, apart from Malachy, in the Pike Bar.

Nora had introduced me to Malachy that time in Limerick. He was an old school friend of the young Patrick.

'A wild one. Always full of devilment. He'd have your eyelashes and come back for the eyeballs. If there was a card school, he'd think nothing of diving in the middle of it to run away with the pot of stake money. Mind, he was educated. The youngest postmaster ever in Limerick. Yet he gives it all up to join the army. Never came home again.'

'Do you know why he never came home, Malachy?' I asked, when I'd bought him another drink.

'I don't think he could face it and that's the truth. He left his poor mother, a widow with three young daughters to bring up, and that was that.'

'Do you think there was anyone else? A girlfriend? Did he have to get away?'

'Oh, he had to get away all right. He never said goodbye to anyone. Just up and left. I met him in London, you know, in the early fifties. It was on one of the bridges. Chiswick, I think. I recognised his walk after all those years. He used to walk around Limerick like he owned the place. "Is it Major?" I asked him. That was his nickname from a young boy. Major. Because he was aloof, even then though, he could be a divil. Always testing people. "Is it Major?" I asked, and of course it was.'

I remember laughing when Malachy called him Major. Sean Ryan bred racing greyhounds. They were all called Major. Major I, Major II, Major III. When I asked him why, he'd said, 'Because you can't see their heels for dust!'

Major Catastrophe had more appeal for me as a suitable nickname for my errant father.

Malachy was perplexed by Dad's odd behaviour on

Chiswick Bridge. He shook his head, disbelieving. 'We stood on the Bridge for half an hour, just talking. He never asked after his mother. Not once. And I didn't raise the topic. It wasn't my place. "Come and have a pint with me, Major, for old time's sake," said I, and hailed a cab. I jumped in, expecting him to follow, but he just ran off, back the way he'd come from, like his life depended on getting away from me.'

The man in Philip Larkin's house is happy to tell me what he knows. 'A very quiet man. A bit aloof actually. His wife was friendly, though. A schoolteacher, I think. They lived there for years with the owner. A retired lady. I'm not sure, but I think she left it to them when she died. Or they bought it.'

'He was an antique dealer, wasn't he?' I ask, desperate for confirmation of any truth at all. 'That's what it said on his death certificate.'

'He may have been, but I think I'd have known it. I don't recall him being involved in anything like that. There was a well-known dealer, Titmus Jerome. Had a place with a big cannon outside. Cannon Antiques, in fact. He was an Irishman. Perhaps he knew your father. I can't recall Mr O'Brien dabbling in antiques. Unless, of course, he was in imports and exports or something like that.'

'Did they have any children?' I wait, not knowing what my reaction is going to be.

'Yes. They had a son called Sean. A clever fellow, according to the neighbours. He went to the university. I think his parents gave him his own flat in the house.'

I keep smiling, my mouth fixed. He called him Sean, Irish for John, after my dead brother. His dead son. The baby with the spiky hair. Mam's shadow child. I want to scream, but I keep smiling, thanking the man in Philip Larkin's house, thinking how mams and dads can truly fuck you up.

Malachy said he was aloof too. Very quiet, the man in Philip Larkin's house said. A devil, Malachy said. Great gas, Joan said.

We sit by the duck pond.

'Will the real Patrick O'Brien stand up?' Gordon shouts at the ducks.

The trees don't move. The real Patrick O'Brien will not materialise.

'Perhaps a visit to Hull library will give us more information,' Gordon says. 'We might look up the obituaries. Mary Irene might have put a notice in about the funeral. We can find out where he's buried.'

Upstairs in the reference section, a librarian listens.

'Best to start with the *Hull and Beverley Independent*.' She indicates a row of ledgers.

In no time, we find his death notice. It requests no flowers at the service and records that he was a dearest husband and devoted father. It confirms that his wife is called Mary (Irene) and his son is Sean.

So there it is. His secret life. Except we were his secret life, the hidden shame. For years Major Catastrophe had lived with Mary Irene, who asked in Latin that he might rest in peace!

I think of that enormous house in that beautiful park and I conjure up an image of them at breakfast, preparing for the coming day. Surely every day was a challenge for him. If someone like Malachy could bump into him on a London bridge and the Department of Health and Social Security could knock on his door for money for his legal wife, a wife now living in England, not safely impoverished in Dublin, then wouldn't he have to raise his drawbridge of lies as high as he could around Catastrophe Castle? Did he patrol the boundaries, ready with slings and arrows of deception to ward off accidental ramblers who might stumble into his secret garden? Was Mary Irene oblivious to the ghosts in the castle dungeons?

What of their son, Sean, to whom he had been a devoted father? Was that true? Or just a customary declaration made for death? Did Major Catastrophe fall off his pony as he galloped from Chiswick Bridge to Hull and have an epiphany moment? Was that why the divil from Limerick became the quiet man of Hull? I laugh hysterically. Everyone looks at me. I don't care. I slam the heavy record book on the table.

'Hypocritical bastard. Bastard. Bastard,' I shout.

People look terrified. So does Gordon.

'Come on, Pat, let's get out of here.'

He grabs me and we run to the stairs as the librarian begins to walk towards us. Outside, we try to cross through unrelenting traffic. I step into the road. As I do, an elderly driver accelerates, anxious to maintain his millisecond of advantage.

I bang hard on the car bonnet. 'Bastard. Bastard!' I scream.

In the nearest pub, after a brandy, we sit and laugh. It's either that, or cry.

'Pat O'Brien, Mrs Hull, what are we going to do with you? You can't go screaming at every man who crosses your path. I'll be terrified to be left alone with you.'

'I'm sorry, Gordon. I never knew I could feel so angry. If he wasn't already dead, I think I might have killed him. I must have released years of anger in those few minutes. I thought I was angry when we went to Limerick, walking like a stranger, when his sisters' children, my cousins, no different to me, all belong there. They walk around the city without questioning it. I should have grown up bored with the familiarity of it, instead of finding novelty at every corner.'

'Shock takes hold at times like this. Go steady, love.' Gordon holds my hand, unable to say more.

The clerk in Chanterlands Crematorium says there is no memorial to him, just a corner where his ashes were scattered. 'I can tell you where it is,' she says.

I don't want to go there. I can't face the Man in the Box Train blowing in small particles of ground-down bone and sinew across a wasteland of the dead.

Sean Ryan had taken me across from their house in Limerick to my grandparents' grave. They lie with their daughter Christina, surrounded by monuments and crosses.

Their cross weighs them down; bolts them securely in forever. Was that place of the dead the place my father really ran from? When he passed it every day growing up, knowing his father lay there, was it a constant reminder of his own final hour? Maybe he saw the long line of O'Briens spreading like a magic carpet. No beginning, no end. Him, the aloof Major of Limerick, a small swirl of artistry woven into the larger design. Maybe he just had to break the pattern.

Sean had pointed out the headstone of Michael Keyes, a Labour minister in the Irish Free State parliament.

'Michael was your grandmother's first cousin and her best friend. Aw, yes,' Sean said, as we picked our way through the graves to the gates. 'You came from good stock. The best Limerick has to offer.'

'I know,' I said, wondering if anything on earth could be better than Granny and Grandilla and Swan River.

'Thank you,' I tell the clerk at the crematorium, 'I don't really need to see where his ashes were scattered, but the name of the undertaker might help. It is possible he might know a little more about the family.'

Brown's, the undertakers, have no recollection of Mrs O'Brien arranging a funeral. They have records, though, including the name of the priest officiating at the service, Father White. We find the presbytery on Queen's Road. The parish priest invites us in.

'I only visited him in the weeks before his death. I used to go along to the house and give him Holy Communion. I gave him the last rites too. He rarely spoke to me at all. He was very frail. He had been ill for many years. Very reserved, though. You had the feeling he had put a barrier there. His wife was pleasant. English. She could have been from Hull.'

Driving once more around Pearson Park, past the nursing home, the lights are on, the curtains drawn, obscuring all the lives experienced behind them, including Dad's, Mary Irene's, the wife who was not, and Sean's.

'I'd like to meet Sean one day, Gordon. He knew Patrick O'Brien better than I did. Longer and better. He will know what it was like to have him as a dad. No matter how many scraps of him I've gathered, Sean will be the only one able to tell me what I missed, good or bad.'

'It will be like looking for a needle in a haystack, looking for Sean. We have no idea where he was born or when.'

Gordon is exhausted from the search.

'I don't think I will try to find him. If I am meant to meet him, I will. For now, I have to let it all go. I never thought I would ever know what became of my dad . . . Now I do. But I want to know what sort of man he really was. It will come to me. I know it will, but by degrees.'

When we left Limerick that time, we drove to Dublin. From the city centre, we walked out to Ranelagh, over Charlemont Bridge. I stood outside Grandilla's house, marvelling that ten of us once lived there.

So did Gordon. 'How did you all fit in?' he asked.

'Very simply. We needed very little then and we had it all. We should have stayed.'

'You didn't have your dad in that little house, though, did you?' Gordon asked.

'No. He never belonged in it. Maybe he was a person who never belonged anywhere, but everywhere he went, he left an indelible mark.'

Sixteen

I have to know if Mam is a widow or a divorcée. If she is divorced, I will not be able to tell her. She married for life, made her bed and there she vowed to stay, even though she married a fakir who provided her with a bed of nails. When I divorced Ken, my first husband, she was ashamed, contaminated with what she considered my sin.

'We never had anything like that in our family,' she said, not making a connection between her marriage and mine. She wondered at my second marriage in a register office and said she would pray for me. 'As far back as I can remember – my father, his father and his father before him – there was never such a thing in our family. The same with me mother's side. Only you have managed to bring us to this.' It didn't count that she liked both my husbands. Though it helped redeem them, for me there was no redemption. 'I must take after my father, then,' I'd said, 'since your side's arses rest on halos.'

Somerset House is crowded with amateur detectives checking up on their erring relatives. Some are investigating their last wills and testaments. I sign a ticket and search these first. It makes sense, because it might clarify my father's marital status, or introduce me to even more mystery. A long search proves fruitless.

'How do I search for divorce papers?' I ask, when I eventually reach the top of the queue.

'There's a small office down that corridor. They don't hold any papers. You register your interest and they look up the records.'

The office is too small to hold more than three or four people at once. When I am able to fit in, I have to sign for a time-limited search and pay a fee. Since I don't know when a divorce, if it occurred, might have happened, I find it difficult to put a date on it. It must have been after 1962, I reason, since he had to pay some money to Mam then, when she was sick. If there had been a divorce, he would not have been obligated. It had to be before his death in 1981, but if Sean went to university before his mother sold the house in 1983, he had to be at least twenty-four or twenty-five then. He just might have committed bigamy some time in the 1950s. I laugh. It is too preposterous to contemplate. The woman behind the counter is busy and I am flustered. In the end, I select years in the 1960s. There is no trace of a divorce in these years.

I park the car near Mam's council flat and shout to Joan beside me, trying to be heard above the whirring from the traffic going through Dartford Tunnel. 'It will be hard to tell her about Dad, but I am sick of secrets.'

Joan has agreed to come with me for moral support. It is hard to predict exactly how she will react. We steel ourselves and climb the stairs, walking in single file along the narrow landing. I hate this place. It is bleak, but Mam loves it, the first real home she can call her own. 'I'll go out in a box,' she says, warning us in advance of her decline.

Mam senses we are on a mission. 'There now,' she puts a tray on the table, 'you're not here for the benefit of your health. I hope it's not bad news.'

Joan pours the tea, nodding me to speak.

'It might be bad news, Mam, but we think you have a right to know.'

The clock on the mantelpiece has a dirty face with silver hands. I never noticed them before. It used to chime in another life. With a bit of attention, it might again, but it has remained silent, except for its tick. Tick-tock, tick-tock, Mam's only constant companion since she bought it in that junk shop to furnish the rooms near the hospital thirty years ago.

'Go on, then,' she sits back in her armchair and turns the radio off. 'It's him, isn't it, Paddy O'Brien?'

'Yes, Mam. I'm sorry to have to tell you like this, but he really is dead.'

Joan helps. 'When I told you about the letter from the Salvation Army in 1983, we were never able to prove conclusively that they meant him.'

We wait, giving her time to let it sink in.

'When?' she asks, without emotion.

'Nineteen eighty-one. December 1981. From pancreatic cancer.'

The clock has a maker's name on its chin. I'll have to see if I can make it out before I go.

'There's a little drop of sherry in the cabinet,' she says.

I get up and pour three glasses, waiting until she has taken a sip.

'There was another woman, Mam. A wife.'

'Huh,' she shrugs. 'He had no other wife. We got married in the sight of God in Rathmines church. How could he have another wife any more than I could have another husband?'

'That's how she described herself on his death certificate. It's a legal document, Mam.'

'How come I was given maintenance from him in 1962 if he had another wife? Tell me that.'

'It must be that he divorced you after that. I carried out a search for the 1960s. There is no record of a divorce then.'

Joan begins to clear the teacups, stacking them up. 'Listen, Mam, Patty is trying to be helpful to you. It's not for her to prove or disprove anything. You can do it if you want to and we can help. If there was no divorce, you are his widow.'

'Widow or wife, it won't make a bit of difference to my life, past, present or future.'

She is bent with regret, like Granny was, her head forever hanging forward, a weight she can no longer lift.

'It might make a difference, Mam, if you are entitled to his widow's pension. Instead of living on a pittance of a pension from your own contributions. It's worth a try, God knows. A bit of effort might ease things for you. One thing's for sure – you won't get it if you aren't entitled to it.'

She struggles with the thought of any relief from her poverty. It has become a habit, putting small amounts of money in envelopes to meet her bills when she gets them.

Her rent is paid by housing benefit. She is proud that she manages. It would be really nice if she didn't have to.

'It's your decision, Mam. If you want to make enquiries, we'll help you.'

She surprises me. 'When the Salvation Army wrote to say he was dead, I went to the Pensions to see if I was entitled to a widow's pension. They didn't seem to think I was.'

'Why didn't you tell us, Mam? We could have helped you. We could have insisted that they make proper enquiries. They could make enquiries when you applied for a few quid sickness benefit. They had a responsibility to do it for your pension too. More of a responsibility in fact.'

'Unless of course, someone else had already claimed it. It would not have taken much to find that out. Maybe that's why they told you not to bother,' Joan says.

'I never thought of that. I thought they meant that the amount extra I'd get wasn't worth the effort. I never thought for a minute someone else was claiming it.'

'We don't know that, Mam, but it's a possibility.'

We wait again while she takes it all in, aware that there is more to tell.

'It'd help if I knew how this woman is fixed. She might be ignorant altogether of the louser he was. Surely she wouldn't be claiming his pension if she didn't think she was entitled to it? That'd be against the law.'

'So is bigamy.' Joan picks up the stacked tray to take to the kitchen.

I follow her out, squeezing myself between the door and the kitchen sink, bracing myself.

'We're going to have to tell her about Sean,' I say. 'If we start a claim on Dad's pension, his mother will have to tell him. He might already know all about his father. He might know he has half-sisters, but once people like Dad deny who they are, lie by omission, they have to go on lying. On and on until they have invented a myth that is written down as their true story.'

I wonder how these stories, once invented, can ever be unwritten. Joan is practical. She fills the kettle in the stone sink and waters the pot plants above it, opening the window to let out her cigarette smoke while the kettle boils.

'First, we have to assume that since Mam is unaware of any divorce, she is his widow. As his widow, she is entitled to his pension. Complications beyond that will have to be overcome and put right. If they are paying it to someone else, it will be up to them to sort it out. At least we'll know the truth.'

'You're right, Joan. Apart from the pension, we have a right to the truth.'

She stubs out her cigarette. 'Come on then, let's face the facts, whatever they are.'

I wipe the worktop and follow her back in to Mam.

'There was a son, Mam,' I say bluntly, because there is no easier way.

The clock slowly ticks a minute.

I repeat, 'He had a son. Sean, they called him. Do you hear me, Mam?'

Her lips are moving. I know she is communicating wordlessly to her shadow child.

'I thought he might,' she says. 'A son? He always wanted a son.' Placing her cup on the saucer, she turns the handle, carefully matching up the decoration, pale rose to paler rose. 'And how is this son? Is he well?'

'I think so. Yes. I'd say he is. Clever too, I think. He went to university.'

'I'm sure he would have done,' is all she says.

No mention of the name. Where are her emotions? Lost in another life like the chimes of her clock. Tick-tock, she goes. Tick-tock.

I hug her. 'It's OK, Mam. You still have us.'

'It's getting a bit chilly now the sun's gone in.' She turns on the gas fire to its lowest setting.

This is our wake for him, I think, and pour another glass of sherry, becoming sorrowful. 'Mam, you won't like hearing this, but I have to say it anyway. I cried when I knew for certain he was dead. All the grief I had locked away came out. It was such a release. At last I could say with certainty what had happened to him.'

Joan affirms. 'Yes, Mam, sad as it is, it helps to heal us.'

I go on, unable to stop the words, so long forbidden. 'If only you had let us talk about him, Mam. That's all we wanted to do. We wanted to ask questions that other people never have to consider, because they know the answers. You never had to ask our questions, Mam. You buried your father when you were forty-two. You had no right to stop us talking about him.'

'Or knowing him,' Joan says.

We wait for her tears, but they don't come.

'Don't you think I know that now? Don't you think I've paid dearly for what I did, watching you both pining for him, knowing he was no good. I can't change the decisions I took, but whatever I did, I did the best I could.'

Leaving, Joan reminds her to put the chain on the door.

'I'll sort out a few papers when you're gone,' Mam says, holding Dad's death certificate in her hand, 'to go with this. Maybe you can take me down to the Pensions on Monday, Patty, though I'm still worried about the other woman's situation.'

'It's better than yours, Mam, that's for sure.'

I root in my handbag and find the photograph of Dad's house – its many mansions – as well as the one of the duck pond in the park. She can't see them in the twilight and turns back to catch the light in the hall, sucking in her breath.

'Well, whoever chased him out of Ireland would never think of looking there,' she says. 'It looks like a proper gentleman's house. It's a long way he travelled from Limerick and the streets of Dublin, stomping around, cock o' the walk in his military policeman's uniform and that's a fact. I wonder what uniform he donned for his stomping in Hull.'

I wonder too.

Monday comes, and we're at the Pensions.

'Did you see the face on that one when I insisted on claiming his pension?' Mam whispers, telling the whole waiting room. 'Her lips puckerin' like she's sucked a lemon.'

'Shh, Mam, she'll hear you.'

We slide along the seats until we are next. Sourpuss is replaced by a smiling young woman who listens to Mam without interrupting, writing out the nature of her claim: an increased pension based on Dad's contributions up to his retirement; an increased pension due to his death in 1981 and arrears of both benefits from the date of entitlement.

'It may take some time to sort out, Mrs O'Brien, and we usually only backdate any claim one year prior to it being made.'

'There's rules and right action,' I tell her. 'Let's establish the validity of the claim first. We can sort out the rest once it is established that my mother is his legal widow.'

'Wasn't that easy, Patty?' Mam reclines back in the car. 'Wasn't that girl very helpful all the same?'

'She was, Mam, but don't get too carried away. They'll have to check and cross- reference, not just within their own departments, but with courts and maybe with Ireland too, especially as we're claiming a pension from there as well. It might take more time than you think.'

'I have a feeling about this, you know. I'm positive they'll find I'm entitled to his pension. Can you imagine me getting some sort of justice after all these years? I won't know what to do with meself, will I?'

I park the car near her flat. My stomach does its usual drop at the greyness of the block, built like packing cases, one flat on top of the other.

'We'll still have to do our own bit of detective work, Mam. They might miss something, like they have already.

255

When you asked for his pension before, they should have investigated then, even if we weren't certain it was him. If they think we'll just accept what they tell us, it's possible they'll try to cover up any mistakes they might have made back then. We can continue our own search for a divorce to prove conclusively that there wasn't one.'

On the stairs she impulsively grips my hand, 'Come in for a cup of tea, Patty, I have something I want to tell you. You've been very good to me, going to all this trouble. I couldn't manage any of it on my own.'

I follow her in, wondering what it is she has to tell me.

When we are finally settled in her front room, coats behind the door, fire glowing, tea on the tray, she sits back against the cushion and folds her hands in her lap, the way she does when she is nervous.

'Do you ever remember me telling you about him and that Father Sylvester?'

'Do you mean the priest who was baby John's godfather?'

I can see she is having a struggle, whether with her conscience or her memory, I don't know.

'Him. He was in Adam and Eve's on the quays. I never liked him. There was a time him and your father were like shadows, one following the other. Your father was always going off to see him. If he wasn't out parading the streets in his army greatcoat, he was with the Holy Orders on the quays. Writing feckin' poetry they were, the pair of them, while John was dying. Me going backwards and forwards to the hospital, you only a baby yourself and Joan just beginning to feel her feet. Mrs Purcell and Bella used to have her down in the basement with them nearly all day at the end and Mr Grogan let me push you in your pram into his room so he'd keep an eye on you.'

'Go on, Mam. Go on, let it all out now.'

'And him, the big I am, and his poetry. If he was home, he'd sit at the table, staring into space like he was demented, thinking of a feckin' rhyme.'

She stops to catch her breath.

'Why are you telling me this, Mam? Why now?'

'Because I know you love to write. You were always scribbling at the kitchen table and it used to put me in mind of him. You'd rest your arm in the way he would and bend your head low, hiding the words. Just like him.'

I see it clearly, head down, trying to write before she caught me and threw the paper in the fire, saying, 'It'd answer you better to go out and play and give me a bit of peace instead of wasting your time on that nonsense.'

'I remember, Mam. Go on.'

'Well, maybe I should have given you a bit of encouragement, but there we are, if we'd all done what we should have done, there'd be no fools and no mistakes.'

I can't help smiling. This is the nearest I'll get to an apology.

'Is there anything else before I go, Mam? I have a lot to do at home. I told Gordon I would only be an hour or so.' I feel a need to be on my own.

'I haven't finished telling you yet. If you don't have patience, I won't be able to.'

'Go on then.' I put my bag on the floor, staying.

'They had a magazine down in Adam and Eve's, *Assisi*, I think they called it. They were Franciscans. Apart from religious things, they published all sorts in it. They published poetry too. That's how a lot of Irish writers got started, in church magazines. Anyway, they published some of your father's poems. That's what I wanted to tell you.'

She waits for my response as if she has done me the greatest favour.

'They published his poems?'

'Yes.'

'How many?'

'I have no idea. Thousands I'd say from the time he spent there with the Holy Orders, but maybe no more than a dozen or so.'

'A dozen, Mam? Are you serious? Dad's poems there all these years and you never thought to say anything until now.'

'I didn't think they were that important. He did, though. Thought he was a cut above the best of them.'

I can't believe she didn't understand how important these poems could be for me and Joan. I know any censure will silence her for good. I swallow.

'What were they about, Mam? Do you know?'

'High-falutin they were, the ones I saw. There was one about the Mass. Another about 1916. He was stuck like an old record on that. He'd have been in his element in the Post Office with Pearse and Plunkett if he'd been old enough. That's what most of the rows were about with me da. "What good has it done, with the country divided and people still in the gutter?" Your father used to bang his fist on the table: "We can govern ourselves. We're no longer in the chains of Britain." I remember once after he'd said something like that, me da laughed at him. He couldn't bear to be laughed at. "Sure, will you get sense!" me da said. "As long as Britain occupies one town, never mind six counties, we're still chained. And if you think De Valera and his Free State will offer anything better to the flea-ridden population in their tenements, then God help you. No doubt you think he will, since you're never out of the church." I have an idea he was thick with Father Sylvester before either of them set foot in Dublin. If it wasn't poetry, it was politics. I couldn't make head nor tale of what they were talking about most of the time.'

She has said enough by the look of her. Her head seems less heavy on her chest.

'Gordon, as true as I stand here, she as much as said that there are things in his past that forced him out of Ireland.' I try not to shout in the crowded supermarket, picking up vegetables, weighing them without checking, standing in the aisles every time I think of our conversation, stunned.

'She used to say he was no good, but I thought it was his personal behaviour, beating her, going with other women, keeping us short of money. Arrogance. And the way he was feared in the army. Bowsie O'Brien, they called him. He was an army boxing champion. They used to say he got his practice rounding the men out of the pubs of a Saturday night.'

Gordon is queuing for his favourite custard tart, trying to listen and keep his place. 'Apart from Cassius Clay,' he says. 'I never heard of a boxer who was also a poet.'

I want to find his poems. Since Mam told me, I can't stop thinking of them. I don't remember his voice, try as I might. If I read his words, he might talk to me, adult to adult. If what Mam said is true, I don't expect to like him. All I want to do is understand him a little and myself a little better. To think I could have gone into Adam and Eve's when I lived with Moll and felt so lost! I passed it constantly in my walks around the city. I could have picked up an outdated copy of *Assisi*, published a dozen years before, and seen his name on a page. Old publications hang about for years before being archived.

But for Gordon finding his death certificate and our going to Hull, I might never have known that my dad's words lie waiting for me along the Dublin quays. Would Mam have told us, Joan and me, some time before she dies? Did it trouble her at all keeping it from us? I don't think it did. The less we knew about him the better, was her belief. She has never once told us anything good about him. Only John, Auntie May's son, had a good word, when we talked about old times at his mother's wake.

'He used to walk into the Villas to meet your mam and people stopped to look at him. He had an air about him. Not just his looks. I don't know what it was, but it was compelling. I've never come across it since. I was only a young fella then, but he always had time to talk to me. "The only way out of this place is education," he said. "If they don't educate you, you have to educate yourself." I was wild, like a lot of the lads then, always out at Booterstown swimming. Or up the park, swingin' from the trees like feckin' Tarzan. He used to lend me books. He lent me one about Marco Polo. It was his favourite book, but he trusted me with it. Someone like me. I'll never forget that.'

And I'll never forget Joe Courtney, surrounded by his stone angels and headstones, telling me about Grandilla, before I left home for England. People stopped to look at him too as he passed them in the streets. Maybe Dad and Grandilla were mirror images. Maybe his poems, if I can find them, will reveal their similarities.

Seventeen

Poor men wander around the gates. In the sanctified richness of Adam and Eve's, a lost beggars' army lie quietly on back pews, resting after the cold night. Nearer God's altar, manicured people tip manicured fingers in prayer. Somehow, they have managed to squeeze through the eye of the needle. A man asks if he can help, concerned that we are wandering, lost souls too. He directs us to the bookshop facing the Liffey.

The shop assistant is run off her feet, serving customers with medals and beads on top of the books.

'You'll have to go to the offices to access the records. If they have the time, they might be able to help you.' She directs us to the right and up a bit.

The heavy door is locked. We speak through a grille, waiting several seconds before the door is released. A flustered man sits behind a desk not too happy at having his work disrupted, keeping his eye on a flickering screen, observing the shufflers in the church and the yard by the Cork Street entrance. Minutes ago, he had been watching us, no doubt wondering why we were rambling about instead of praying. He tidies his desk.

'Excuse me disturbing you, but I'm trying to trace information about my father. He had some poems published in your magazine in the 1940s. If it's at all possible, I'd like to have copies of them.'

Frowning, his eye on the screen, he answers his keyboard. 'I can't help you with that. I wouldn't know where to look at all. I can make an appointment for you to see someone who can.'

Gordon intervenes, anxious to keep me calm, remembering the library in Hull. 'That would be difficult. You see, we've come over from England to find them and we're only in Dublin for today. If there's any way you can help us, we'd appreciate it.'

He sighs, and telephones someone, turning his back on us while he speaks.

'Father John will be free in ten minutes.'

We follow him across the hall, just as I imagine Dad following the Holy Orders.

'There now,' he says, showing us into a deceptively simple room, ordained a special place.

My heart flips, my hands sweat. This is the room they wrote in, my father and Father Sylvester. The room is furnished with a wide table and well-upholstered chairs. We sit quietly, the three of us, Gordon, my imagination and me, because it is a room for hushed voices and reverence. Please God, let them find his poems. Please God. A porter puts his head around the door. Father John is busy. I explain all over again to him and he disappears to see what he can do himself, promising nothing.

'It's not the poems in themselves that are important,' I whisper to Gordon. 'It's just that his own words will connect me to him more than any recollections from other people will. Do you understand what I mean?'

'I think so,' he answers, glancing around uneasily, waiting for the door to open. Waiting for something to break the tension.

It all seems so melodramatic, waiting for words from my childhood. I see Dad hanging his uniform on the front of the wardrobe, then easing his feet from his highly polished army boots; easing them into worn brogues, getting ready to go out. Mam is clearing the table, making her frock rustle every time she moves. Otherwise, all is silence. I sit on the floor watching their feet move here and move there. Joan bends down to me, then runs away on fat little legs, chasing a cat. Mam picks me up and sits me in the middle of the bed in the corner. I watch them. He has a rough wool jacket on, with a row of pens in the top pocket. His magic pocket. Throwing a black scarf around his neck, he picks up a sheaf of papers and rolls them in his palm. 'I'm off,' he says and goes through the door in a gust of wind and darkness.

My imagination lets me follow him down the steps, through the Square onto Mountpleasant Avenue and over Portobello Bridge; swaggering, money in his pocket for a pint in one of the pubs along the quays to whet his creative urges. He rings the doorbell, the one we rang thirty minutes ago, and steps in, joking with Father Sylvester, quoting a line of poetry as he enters the room.

'Have you been busy, Paddy?' Father Sylvester asks,

anxious to fill a couple of pages of his magazine. 'Or has life got in the way?'

'There,' Dad says, 'will that be doing you?' And he places his papers on the table, smoothing them out; reading his cherry-picked words. Soft and juicy, they flow from his lips. I watch him. So full of himself is he that he doesn't notice me. Or perhaps he is trying to ignore me, unnerved by an outline from the future. He doesn't see the porter coming back. He is limiting his sights to his pages.

Smiling, pleased with himself, the porter places six thick volumes of *Assisi* in front of me. 'I hope you find what you're looking for. I had a terrible job sorting them out, but if they help at all, I'm a happy man.'

Immediately, I find a poem called 'The Moon', by Pat O'Brien. Could this be his? Mam never called him Pat. Only Paddy. I find two more poems also by Pat O'Brien: 'The Sun' and 'The School Bell'. They are surely his? 'High-falutin,' Mam said. These are simple observations.

Gordon is flicking through the pages of another volume. 'What was that poem your mother said he wrote?' he says.

'The Mass. He wrote one about the Mass, but I don't know what he called it.'

'Here it is.' He shoves the bound collection across the table. 'Page twenty-seven, the August edition for 1943. "The Mass" by Patrick O'Brien.'

My father moves to sit beside me and we read his poem together, chanting the words, him in ghostly syllables of the dead, me pulsating. Free.

265

A Church's busiest, quietest hour
Flocked whispering barely reach
    The beggar's chair
Presence of Unseen Power
Is evident
As scented breezes
    Waft by candle-flare
Make holiness all prevalent.
Tyrants who have ruled by poverty.
    The fear
Take ear
As conscience, grinning with reflected
    Leer
Calls sanity from its blood-celled
    Dungeons.
Fool!
Why dost thou miss
This hour of bliss
Where goodness shows abundance.

I can see him clearly, the window behind him, his elbow resting on the table, his hand with the cigarette supporting his handsome dark head. His words resound in the room, filling it with pious reverence. Father Sylvester bows his head, and the Poet waits for accolades. The Priest, eager to publish, gives them in excessive measure. I say nothing, though he beseeches my praise. I watch him under the window, bathed in immortal light. I read the poem again, then again, shocked by its religious zeal. His words deny the truth of him. He must have stood in that church with his umbrella up, when goodness showed abundance. I suppose he wrote prayers too while he was at it.

'Hypocrite,' I say, feeling sick.

I have to get out into the fresh air. I am overwhelmed with the smell of death and decaying flowers. I am feeling faint. Beads of sweat are on my forehead.

'Are you all right, love?' Gordon's voice is far off.

He pours me a glass of water. I am still trembling, but less so.

'I'm fine now, thanks. It's just so weird to think these poems have been lying here for fifty years. Waiting for today. Waiting to be read. I used to pass this church when I lived with Moll. I came in once or twice out of curiosity. I knew Father Sylvester was his friend. I thought I might see him. He was an O'Brien as well, you know.'

'There might be more of his poems in the archives. Do you want me to see the porter?'

'No. I think we'll stick with the ones we have here.' I count ten in all. 'Let's go and see the man at the desk and ask him to photocopy them.'

He does, without a word, uninterested, unaware that we have been listening to a voice from beyond the grave.

For several weeks, I can't bear to look at the poems, much less read them. I wish I could share them with Joan, but we have not spoken for some time. Misunderstandings and our haunted past have cast a shadow on our friendship. I know she will see them one day, but I cannot make any more effort until I gain back some strength for myself. I cannot show

Mam the poems either. She did not want to read them the first time.

Though they disturb me deeply, I do, eventually, read them again. I accept them as his only gift to me, my only inheritance from my father. Joan had gifts from his magic pocket and rides on the crossbar of his bike around Mountpleasant Square. Sean had him all to himself, with the benefit of undivided attention. These poems are Mam's to give and she gave them to me, provided I could find them.

Now that I feel able, I begin with his nationalist poems.

'The Border'

Eire
My tragedy!
Thy kisses are as wine to me
Hair of rippling diamond fall
From noble mien
Rose-tipped lips
A song between
Where'er thou be
Is day to me
My dreaming soul awakes
To realisation
It cannot be
Thine eyes like dancing moonbeams
    Darkened by cloud
Appeal to me.
What do they say?
'Still unfree.'

'The Eternal Flame'
(Easter 1916)

Our Lamp of Manhood was but a dim spark
– Feast of Lily's dawn-and-hark!
A Nation stirs from dormancy
Resuscitated by patient patriotism
And small nations' foolish fallacies
The flame fed by such impersonal ethics,
Wherein lies no thought for own sweet life
Or bloodless critics,
Acts blood-father to fostered ignorance of youth
Singes the beard of age
And vellum of ill-bred sage.
Militarists may vouch this sacrifice a puny effort
What matter! It served its purpose:
We read of Horatius, but breed costumes.

I have to accept that my father was a complicated man. I will never be able to fathom him. I make a coffee and ramble about the house reading aloud. I laugh when I read the moon poem, published in 1945, the year he made his getaway from whatever demons were chasing him.

> 'The Moon'
>
> Cascading Luminals
>   Fall from thy radiant bower,
> Oh Cynic!
> Who dost count the hour

Of happiness
Dwell with us
E'en thou lower.
   'The world's a stage' is truly true
Whilst thou linger,
And hearts will sue.

Was he seeing his own face reflected in the face of the cynical moon? Was that written as his presence waned in Dublin? Did his light go out? Did he run away from accusing fingers to wax on an English shore? There is still so much I have to know about him. The more I know, the more I need to know. So far, every ending has proven to be another crossroads. I put the poems at the back of a drawer and await my direction.

Mam phones.

'I've finally heard from the Pensions, after all this time. Four years it is. Would you believe it? They are satisfied that I am the legal widow. I had to phone someone and they told me it took so long because someone else was claiming it. They had to carry out an investigation before they could stop it and give it to the rightful claimant.'

I sit down, shocked with the news.

'That's marvellous, Mam. I'm so pleased for you. I hope you'll get at least a little more money than you're getting now.'

'You'll be amazed at how much I'm entitled to,' she says,

amazed herself. 'He worked until just before he died. He paid enhanced contributions. I'll have enough pension to pay my own rent and a fair bit left over for extras. No more benefit or forms to fill in.' She is crying. Gut-wrenching sobs. I wait until she is able to continue. 'For the first time in my life since I married your father, I won't be living in poverty. I'll be able to pay my way without benefits or handouts. I'll be under no obligation to anyone, so I won't. I'll be able to hold my head up!'

'Now, Mam, you know you won't be able to that. Not with your neck!'

We laugh together, then she cries again.

'I'm so lucky, Patty. It's like winning the pools. I had to sit down I was trembling so much when I opened the letter.'

'Listen, Mam, it's anything but luck. It's a disgrace that you've had to wait so long. You've earned every penny of that pension and more. Just think how hard you had to work to bring us up. Every penny he deprived us of when we were in Ireland is not even accounted for in that pension. It's a pittance compared to the cost to you over your lifetime. Never forget that. You paid for it in much more than money.'

'I know what you mean, Patty, but it's hard for me to see it like that. I'm so used to disappointment that now I've won the claim, I just feel lucky, I suppose.'

I wish she would stop being so bloody humble.

'Mam, all along the line, the Pensions, Housing Benefit, Supplementary Benefit, all of them – they failed you. Had they cross-checked sufficiently, they would have discovered for themselves that you were his beneficiary and taken steps to ensure you received your dues. Instead, they paid it to someone else and to add insult to injury, told you it would be too much trouble to correct their mistakes. You have enough material to ask for an inquiry yourself.'

She is agitated at the prospect. 'I don't want to have any more worry, Patty. I'd rather let it go. It'd be too much for me altogether.'

I know. She is eighty-two, lucky to have lived to get her meagre justice.

'Mam, the last thing I want to do is put you through more stress. I just want you to live out the years ahead of you with a bit of comfort. That's all.'

Later I help Gordon in the garden, weaving old bricks around a pond to make a new path. I float a basket of irises over to the water lilies and stick the remainder in the sand between the pond and the path edge.

'It was all worthwhile, fighting to get the pension. I never really thought it would happen, since we never had anything at all from him while he was alive, but I had to try.'

'Give me that hammer, love,' he asks, listening. He gently taps the last few bricks into the sand, then asks, 'What next?'

I begin collecting the tools, placing them in the wheelbarrow.

'Nothing. Mam knows she is entitled to whatever else he left, but she has been through enough.'

Gordon can see the point, but does not agree. 'Getting that pension is only the half of it. What about any private pensions? What about his estate? If he made no will, whatever he left legally and morally belongs to your mam. And eventually to you and Joan. Will you contest it?'

I am aware that so very much hinges on this decision. The absence of a will obscures all his assets. Perhaps he didn't make a will because he had nothing to leave. Or he signed his estate over to others. I have to ask myself the question, what do I really want?

We lock the potting shed and take our usual evening walk down the back drive, past the pig pens and the sheep making eyes at us on the other side of the fence.

'All I want is for Mam to have peace of mind now. It's the least we can offer her. She's been worrying terribly about the woman who called herself his wife. He must have lied to her. I can't see that any woman would agree to a bigamous marriage. Time and again, Mam was tempted to stop the lot, give in, but the dye was cast. It was cast long before she claimed his pension.'

We turn and skirt in single file along the side of the country lane, silent as we concentrate on keeping out of the ditch. I know I will have to come to some decision soon. No doubt Joan is considering hers, able to discuss it fully with Mam, who lives nearby.

'I think, Gordon, we have to be grateful Mam won the case.' We begin to stroll slowly along the avenue of limes towards the big house standing like a fairy palace behind its ornate gates. 'Perhaps it's time to let the rest go.'

Gordon is responsible for managing this fairy kingdom of trees and ponds, vegetable and fruit gardens and greenhouses. It has an echo of the garden in St Anthony's without sea breezes. He places a fallen branch by the fence and we continue our stroll.

'It might not let you go. Have you thought of that?' he says. 'If they took his pension from the bigamous wife, she might try to trace your mam – or you, since you made the claim on her behalf.'

By the log barn, we stand listening for the white owl, though the evening is still too light. I am unnerved by Gordon's suggestion.

'Why would she want to have anything to do with us, especially now she's lost her pension?'

The lights are on in Gardener's Cottage and the porch light beckons in ours, Dove Cottage, like Wordsworth's.

'Because,' Gordon is getting impatient with my lack of focus on the matter, 'she might want to find out about his early life. Think about it. If he deceived her and kept her in ignorance throughout their life together, it's natural she'd want to find out about his past. I imagine Sean would too. She's bound to have told him. He might want to find out about his own background. I know I would.'

Sean. Real. Like Tom in that other northern town, with a life of his own. Suddenly, I want to meet him.

Just as I contemplate such an event, Gordon adds: 'It might also occur to her that your mam is entitled to any other pension and assets too. She might want to negotiate a settlement suitable to all of you. After all, if he misled her, she's a victim too.'

'I'll sleep on it,' I tell him, preparing dinner.

Morning starts early in the countryside. Tractors roll up

the back drive and the birds are chirping. Gun dogs bark across the fields. We sit in the garden to drink our coffee, though it is really too chilly. Shivering, I tell Gordon what I have decided.

'The ball is in the court of the family in Hull now. Let's see what they do. They are better placed than us to know all that is involved. Knowing about Mam now, if they didn't before, must surely mean they have decisions to make too. No doubt they'll be contemplating the rights and wrongs of it all, just as we are. Let's wait and see what conclusions they arrive at. Time will tell.'

Big splats of rain fall on our breakfast remains, hurrying us up.

'Come on, love,' Gordon says, 'it's too cold to sit here any longer. I think you're right. Leave them to it.'

I follow Gordon all over the place. Nomadic, delighted with days as they dawn, unfolding on adventure and closing on discovery, like a wandering gypsy, Gordon stays long enough to landscape other people's places, creating magical vistas for them in woodlands and vales of green. Once the plants – named by him in Latin on his designs – take root, he becomes rootless. He has a need to sow, not reap; to plant, not keep. I am his apprentice and he is the sorcerer, weaving dreams. Behind the cottage door, when the day is done, I sit and write.

'That's great.' Gordon picks up a page, annoying me. 'You should do something with it.'

'Don't be silly. It's just for me. You know that.'

'When I plant out a garden,' he says, 'I want people to see

it. To smell the fragrance. I can't imagine locking it away behind walls. Keeping it secret.'

'We did that when we were kids. Made secret gardens. Chanie beds, we called them.'

Gordon listens, sitting on the window ledge, still in his old jumper, never wanting to miss the smallest thing.

'They weren't real gardens. We were city kids. They were pieces of broken china and delft. Colours. Edges of rainbows. I collected mine in a seaside bucket and hid them in a corner of the kitchen. We'd scrape out a piece of earth in the back lane, placing the pieces in a pattern, arranging them, then covering them with a sliver of a glass, a milk bottle shoulder or a shatter of windowpane. When we were satisfied with our creations, mesmerised by their beauty, we'd spread the earth across them, concealing them. We'd return to look, marvelling at the kaleidoscopic visions, hurrying to cover them quickly before other city gardeners robbed them to make chanie beds of their own. Little Burkes and Hares lurked everywhere. There was a chanie bed season, same as for skates and skipping. Summer, I think it was. As soon as we saw the blooms in Palmerston Park.'

'What's the Latin for chanie bed?' Gordon asks. 'I might win a gold medal at Chelsea if I design one of them.'

He picks up my story again and waves it at me. 'Don't hide it, Pat. Don't leave it until the Burkes and Hares have to steal it from your grave. Send it off. That's all I'm saying.'

Eighteen

I wander about the garden, waiting, dead-heading old blooms and smelling buds, laughing at my rituals. I still tie sweet peas the way the old nun taught me in St Anthony's and I never water plants when the sun is on them. 'It burns the edges of the leaves and petals as the water evaporates,' Gordon instructed, guiding me.

I fill the watering-can and quench the plants, enjoying the shade, listing other guides: Mr Grogan, Grandilla, Auntie May, the tramp at Portobello.

Auntie May believed our paths are crossed by guides for some of our distance. 'We don't always know we need them when we meet them, but they walk with us a bit of the way, guiding our steps. Our real guardian angels.'

Though I knew she meant living people, I used to shiver whenever she mentioned these life guides.

'How do they know we need them?' I asked her.

'Because we are at a place too steep to climb,' she said, 'and we grasp their hand. Or follow where they lead. We'll only know them when we look over our shoulder and see them walking away.'

That is how I recognised Gordon as a guide, from the back

and from a distance. Walking away. Sherpa Hull, the man who reunited me with my past. Perhaps when that was done, his purpose in my life had been served.

'Perhaps,' I say aloud, drawing a rake across the gravel, smoothing the path.

Parting from Gordon took several rehearsals. When his work ended at the fairy palace, he agreed to come and live in Kent with me, by the sea. He would put down roots, he said, believing it, and become an oak. I would become a writer. In earnest. Apply myself and send stuff off. Believe in myself.

The removal van had barely driven away from our tall house before Gordon began wondering where to go next.

'I'm not going to find many gardens by the sea,' he said. 'Most of the houses have balconies or yards. And it's too far to drive to London.'

'I know there's a recession, Gordon, but the kind of gardens you design and build never seem to have an owner short of a bob or two. Give it a chance. Since I met you, we've lived in so many places: the Pennines, Durham, Leeds, Herefordshire. I like Kent. My family is here. I like the sea.'

'I like hills – high places and open spaces; I can't be an oak near the sea,' was all he said, but it was enough to warn me.

When he went to Jersey to build a canal through a hillside garden, I was too weary of change to follow him. I liked the tall house, the space, the rickety back stairs down to the old kitchen. At night, though I rattled around the house, I never felt lonely. For the first time in my life, I was living alone and liking it.

'I need to follow my own dreams,' I told him when he returned.

Though he understood, he could not stay for long.

'A job's come up in Scotland,' he said. 'Aberdeen. What do you think?'

'I think you'll love it. Mountaineering, spectacular scenery, nearer your roots. You always told me that Geordies are Scots with their heads bashed in.'

'How'way the lads,' he said, packing his bags.

I swapped the tall house for a cottage with a garden just for me. And that was that.

It is looking good, I think now, and sit, lingering longer than I should on this special morning, feeling unreal, excited, delighted; anticipating the life-changing experience I am about to undergo. I have always felt like this when things are about to change; a weather barometer, predicting pressures unseen. Like a Russian doll, all the girls I was and all the women, sit inside me, waiting with me, ensuring I do not betray them when my visitors arrive. The most demanding of my trust is the first small girl, wandering through empty rooms, endlessly searching.

When I scanned faces for my father's, people said, 'Let it go,' not understanding. 'Get over it.' They were people fortunate enough to have nothing to get over at all, it seemed to me. I learned to smile for them, not accepting the advice. And the small girl from Swan River was left in a house of dust and cats, a tiny Miss Havisham, waiting.

Every separation after that first one was a division. Every separation from the people in the small house in the shadows of Mountpleasant Buildings was another division of myself into many selves, a process started by the man in Pearson Park, slinking to the duck pond, ducking beneath the trees.

'It's OK,' Gordon used to say. 'He was your father. You must rid yourself of guilt about him. About searching. Never let anyone tell you different. He was your dad. That's all that really matters.'

That was then, this is now. The enormity of what I am about to face is almost too much to bear. I want to go into the cottage and lock the door against the day, but I cannot fight fate. His son, my father's son, Sean O'Brien, will come walking through my garden to my door in just a few hours. I will welcome him in. He is coming to lunch.

After the break-up with Gordon, I had taken to spending Sunday mornings in a seafront hotel with coffee, the papers and new friends. Several months back, Barry had passed me the Culture section of the *Sunday Times*, while he did the crossword. I flicked idly through the pages, seeking a head-line to catch my eye. 'Sean O'Brien', it said on the Poetry page. I almost missed it.

'Anything interesting?' Barry had asked.

'Nothing really, except this name. Sean O'Brien. My half-brother's name is Sean,' I told him, more for the sake of conversation than anything else.

'Common old name that, O'Brien. Like Smith or Jones. I bet if you look in the phone book, there'll be hundreds of them.'

'Hmm,' I said, 'it's just that my father was a poet, that's all.'

He laughed. 'My father was a teetotaller, but I'm not.'

And now, Sean will be here at one o'clock. I check my watch. Not yet ten. All I have to do is go shopping – keep it simple, fresh salads, meats, cheeses and old wines – then a bath. There are no books of etiquette for such a meeting. In their absence, I have to make my own rules. Easy does it, seems the best and only one to follow.

I pick up the photographs Sean sent. To prove my identity, I had sent him birth and marriage certificates and some family photographs, including the only two I owned of Dad. In return, he sent photographs too. I study one, unable to believe that I am looking at my father's aged face. He looks like Einstein, wise and mellow. He was still smart in a snappy panama hat to protect him from the sun. I compare it to the one of him striding through Dublin in his uniform. I trace my fingers slowly on his two faces and wonder how he ever transformed himself into this elegant old man who looks as though he could not hurt a fly.

Weeks ago now it was, that I began to draw the curtain back. The hotel was quiet in the early morning. The coffee was fresh. The papers untouched. I opened the one I wanted.

'There's that poet again,' I said to Barry. 'Sean O'Brien.'

'Do you seriously think he's your brother?'

'It's possible. It's the words too, not just the name.'

Barry was sketching a boat bobbing far out beyond the hotel window, across the green sea. He kept his head down. 'What words? Words are words. That's what poets and reviewers do. Use words. The tools of the trade.'

'I can't explain. It's the order of them. I know it sounds fanciful, but I really think it might be him.'

'You've lost me, Pat. You're going to drive us both mad if you don't do something about it. For months now, every Sunday, even if he hasn't written a review, that's all you can talk about.'

And now, on the day I am finally to meet Sean, I meander through the shop, selecting the freshest food. I buy newly baked bread, then browse along the wine shelves, wishing I knew their taste. Gerry, Sean's partner, is coming too. I hope we get on. When we speak on the phone, Sean and me, we are easy with each other. At first we were reticent, but after a couple of calls from Sean – I left the calling to him, giving him time to come to terms with events – we relaxed. Most of the time. He asked questions and I answered as honestly as I could, telling him nothing of the low opinion my father was held in; how he left us with nothing. I kept reminding myself that none of it was Sean's fault any more than it was mine.

I had a lifetime of questions I wanted to ask him when we spoke, but I held back, scared to go too fast. I felt I might be able to ask him some of what I need to know over lunch.

On the way back from the shop, I pick Barry up. He can sit sketching in the garden while I have a bath.

'If he's bringing Gerry, you might like a bit of moral support too. I'll come along if you like,' he'd suggested. He felt involved with it. He had been since I first saw the name in his Sunday paper. I was glad I would not be alone.

A strange car is parked near the garages when we pull into the road. I feel hot and clammy; a little faint.

'Oh, no, don't tell me they're early. It's only eleven thirty. They're not due until one o'clock.'

Barry wanders across the road. 'I'll check if there's a trace of a poet,' he says.

'How would you be able to tell?'

'Easy. There's bound to be clues, like a notebook and pencil, or a pipe.'

I sit laughing, losing some of the tension, while he looks in the car windows.

'Yes,' he says. 'It's him all right. I told you he'd leave a clue.'

'A notebook?'

'No, a copy of your map and instructions on the dashboard.'

He helps me carry the shopping.

'Look at the state of me, still in my old skirt and shoes. What sort of first impression will that make? I thought I'd have plenty of time to have a bath and smarten up. I haven't even prepared the lunch.'

We walk the length of the garden wall. I have to brace myself before we turn in through the gate. Mercifully, they are not waiting, wondering where I am. A note on the door tells us they have arrived early, gone to find a coffee.

'You're all right as you are. Go on in and I'll find them. I bet they've gone to the nearest pub. No self-respecting poet would drink coffee.'

He gives me no time to suggest something else. Perhaps to wait until they wander back themselves. It is as though not only Barry, but life itself is arranging a timetable on my behalf.

In a bookshop, months ago, I was browsing through the shelves, a pleasure I enjoy alone, free-floating to see where I will land, always hoping to arrive in an old familiar place. There was a book by Sean O'Brien, the one I had read about in the Sunday review. My summer sandals were like diver's leaden boots on my feet. My neck began to tingle at my hairline. I picked it up and held it, too nervous to turn the pages, telling myself I was being fanciful and ridiculous, yet compelled to go with my deeper instincts. Instantly I was in that simple room in Adam and Eve's again. Or so it felt. I had an urge to open the book, yet I wanted more than anything to put it back and run. I wanted to nudge the elderly woman at my elbow and tell her my predicament. Or engage the man behind the counter as an aide to this extraordinary moment. Instead, I opened the book a few pages in and read the first words.

Invisible, yet sure, as sure as the book in my hand, my father was beside me, reading in my ear. He knew the words. I knew the words. I could not go on. I turned the book over and held my breath. The photograph of the author was a collage of faces I already knew so well. The poet, Sean O'Brien, was no stranger.

'Write to him, care of the *Sunday Times*,' Barry said, putting the pen in my hand. 'If you don't, I never want to hear you mention it again. If he is your half-brother, he won't be able to resist answering. If he isn't, he'll think you're a crank and throw it in the bin.'

And so I wrote to Sean, telling him that I thought we had the same father, giving him the relevant facts. I expressed the hope that he understood about the pension, and apologised for any distress it had caused his mother.

A few weeks passed before he phoned. His voice registered low and sure. It was full of curiosity. He apologised for the delay in responding to my letter. And I apologised again for any upset the transfer of the pension may have caused. At first he did not understand what I was talking about. He had not known about the pension; his mother had kept silent about it for the past five years.

'I'm sorry,' I said.

God only knows how he managed to deal with the shock, but to his credit, he accepted for the moment what I had told him. He said it sounded as if my father and his were the same man, but he had to be certain. I mentioned Dad's poetry. His father had never told him about any poetry published in Dublin. I quoted a couple of poems: one about the sea; one about a river. The line went silent. I asked Sean if he was OK. He told me then that his father had recited the same poems to him at bedtime when he was small. Beyond a shadow of a doubt, he agreed, he was indeed my father's son.

Now I put the white wine in the fridge and uncork the red, letting it breathe, while my own breath comes in short supply. I am glad I set the table first thing this morning. I give it a quick glance, everything in the right place on the blue painted wood. 'Set the table,' Moll used to say as she prepared for Terry's nightly visits, 'and you've set a welcome.' Unlike her, though, I decided against a crisp tablecloth. Too formal.

My hands are sweating. I hurry to the bathroom to wash

them, then rinse my shiny face. The mirror is steamy and I see myself through a mist, wondering how I came to this place, this point in my life. The doorbell rings. I look a mess. Of all times to be so unprepared! Take a deep breath, I tell myself, and don't.

I wipe my hands on my skirt and go to the door. I have a sense of something operating beyond the moment. Almost as if we are acting out unrehearsed scenes from an ancient script. When I open the door, my world will change forever. For just this brief moment, I do not know the man on the other side; my half-brother. My father's son. Once we meet on the threshold, I will know him. And he will know me.

Sean fills the doorframe. No dust dancing or floating, only me. He looks like a poet. He looks like anyone would want a newly discovered brother to look – large, handsome and smiling. We lock eyes. His crinkle at the corners. Is that because he is always smiling? I wonder. Then he puts his arm around me and kisses my cheek and I am in the Green again. I am in Dad's arms looking in Roddy's toy shop window.

'It's amazing to meet you at last, Sean, truly amazing. Come in,' I say, standing aside. 'Oh, please, come in.' I hold out my hand to Sean's partner and add, 'You too, Gerry.' She smiles and I relax a little.

We have such a lot to talk about. We begin with trivia, talking about their journey and whether my directions were easy to follow or not. About the glorious June day. My garden. Anything except the purpose of their visit.

'I told you they'd be in a pub,' Barry says, pleased he found them so easily.

'But we were only drinking coffee.' Gerry disproves his theory on the drinking habits of poets.

'If it wasn't for Barry, I'd never have written the letter to you at all,' I say.

Even though they are here in my sitting room with the sun streaking the walls and dust adorning the mirrors and the pictures, even as I recount the experience in the bookshop; even though I know it is true, it is unbelievable. Yet there he is, Sean, sitting opposite me on the sofa. I want to mark the moment with profundity; a sentence that will reverberate in our hearts and minds and in the room and outside it in the world beyond, a galaxy of words for all time.

When I open my mouth, I say instead, 'I always wanted to find my dad. Over the years, bit by bit, Joan and I managed to gather small scraps of information about him, but we could do very little beyond that. It was only when I remarried in 1988 that the serious search began.'

Sean is surprised that Gordon and I stood outside the house in Pearson Park. So much of what I have to say surprises him. He knows nothing of his father's life in Ireland; he only knows he was born there. This is a terrible shock for him, I think. He probably feels as unreal as I do, sitting in a strange room with a half-sister he has only just met. And because I exist, his life, as he believed it to be, does not. It was underpinned with deception. I will have to go at his pace. Give him a chance to come to terms with it.

I am not sure if Sean is more intrigued that his dad had poems published in the 1940s than that he had been a military policeman. I tell him all I know, except the really bad bits. I tell him about Limerick and Nora and scribble her address.

'I wish he'd gone home to see his mother. Even if he couldn't come back to see us. Just imagine her torment, every single day, waiting for him. Wondering what happened to him. It must have broken her heart. Nora said her mother adored him, her eldest child and only son. Whatever happened in his life, she would have loved him still.'

He is nodding as I talk. The woman I am speaking of is our grandmother.

Over lunch, we digest the morsels we have of our father's early life with the meats and salads. I am disappointed that they refuse wine – lack of it and the absence of clinking glasses cancel the mood of celebration.

'We never drink in the day time,' Gerry explains, as Barry pours for just him and me.

I want to ask Sean what sort of man my father was in England, the father he knew, but feel unable to. Instead, I revert to my usual method of information-gathering about him, painstakingly piecing together suggestions of him from small clues. Even these are elusive.

Sean speaks of how Dad suffered in the end and of how his mother was so protective of him. I recall her arms draped around his shoulders in the photograph he sent. I had felt resentful, seeing ownership, not protectiveness. The other images they sent, scanned on their computer, had upset me too. On a page headed SEAN PATRICK and PATRICK FRANCIS O'BRIEN there were comparative studies of Sean and Dad: 'Sean in Corfu, August 1984, aged 31' and 'Patrick (in Dublin), April 1938, aged 27'. Then 'Sean in Corfu, 1984, 31', beside 'Patrick in Dublin, c. 1942, aged 31–32'.

To make the comparison, the only image I had of my parents together, the one Nora had given me, had been cropped to show just the head of my father. The other image was cropped from the photograph of him in uniform strolling through Dublin. To get the first photograph I had travelled to Limerick and waited forty years. The other one was begged from Mam, like blood from a stone. Until I found his poems, they were all I had of him. Now, even these had been tampered with, diminished, leaving me bereft of my father once more. Though I am sure the act had been innocent of any intended hurt, I pondered on the studies for weeks, grieving for my loss. I still had the originals, of course, but nevertheless I felt a wrench on seeing the copies treated so casually.

But making allowances for his apparent need to identify with his father, and wanting to share whatever I had with Sean, I had sent him copies of Dad's poems.

'What do you think of his poetry?' I ask, expecting a detailed critique.

Sean says he was surprised by them. Especially the ones he used to say to him.

'Do you think he was any good?' I ask.

'He could have been,' is his reply.

Could have been? What stopped him? What was he doing all the times he was not writing? French-polishing old furniture? Buying and selling rare paintings? Or hiding? Hiding from the truth of his deception. Was he was hiding behind the cut-glass life he was forever acting out, waiting for someone to denounce him?

Our lives were so different, I realise, looking at Sean. He doesn't appear to have suffered for his father's deceptions, though appearances count for nothing. Perhaps there are clues in Sean's poetry. Certainly, he is hailed as a poet of the left. I wonder, though, if commentary alone defines political persuasion. More than what we say we are, we are what we do. It will be great discussing politics and ideas with him, I think, watching him watching me.

'You had an incredibly close relationship with your father, didn't you, Sean?' Gerry says, prompting him.

He smiles his agreement. The death notice runs through my head: 'beloved and devoted father of Sean'. I give in, I want to say; I forgo any claim to him at all. I cannot compete in any way with this man's incredible closeness to my dad. For the first time since my search began, I wish I had never bothered at all. I still know very little, despite all my efforts. All I have done so far is add to the knowledge already held in a silent vault by Mam. Sean too seems to be locking his knowledge in a safe. Though ignorant of his father's past, he knew intimately the man he became, sharing an unbreakable bond, unintentionally weakening my thin threads, all but severed with my father's disembodied head.

To hide my tears of disappointment, I stand, proposing coffee. Barry, sensing my distress, offers to help.

'How do you feel?' he asks in the kitchen.

'Terrible. It's as if we never existed at all for my dad. I feel like I count for nothing.'

He makes the coffee, allowing me to pull myself together.

'It's an emotional experience for both of you, meeting for the first time like this. Don't expect too much from today.'

'It's not them, Barry. It's me. They're OK, but I'm just so nervous. I want to do the right thing. I want the day to go well. I know we are all just feeling our way with this. It seems an impertinence to ask him questions about Dad. There might be things he has to learn to share. After all, until a few weeks ago, he was an only child.'

Barry steps into the back yard with his cigarette and I follow.

'It may be hard for them too,' he says, 'but this might be the only chance you get to ask questions.'

'I know.'

He waits, deeply inhaling the cigarette smoke, unhurried despite the kettle singing for attention.

'What should I do?'

Without hesitation, he winks. 'Go for it.'

Nineteen

S ean is inspecting my bookshelves.

'Greg Delanty! His *Southward* collection.'

At last we have a mutually safe topic. He reads the inscription, signed for me.

'Yes.' I take the poetry book from him, returning it to its rightful slot on my shelf. 'I met him at the Listowel Writers' Week in 1992. I really enjoyed his readings.'

Sean is still inspecting my books, telling me he meets Greg on the poetry circuit.

'It's a small world,' I say.

Barry pours more wine for him and me. 'Why don't you tell them you went to Listowel to collect an award?' he says.

The award was for historical journalism about emigrants, but I don't want to talk about it. I change the subject – not for one moment do I want him to think I am trying to impress him. I did my writing in secret, stuffing small observations into books and drawers, embarrassed by my pretensions. High-fallutin' ideas, Mam would say.

In Listowel, I saw a sign: *Teampaillín Bán – Famine Graveyard*. It pointed up a track seeming only to lead to fields. I had plenty of time before the prize-winners' lecture, so up the track I wandered, idling and dawdling, marvelling at the blueness of the sky against the yellowness of buttercups peeping through the dark green grasses. I came across a little white churchyard. On a white-washed wall sat a small white sculpture of the Last Supper and a white Celtic cross erected by P. Whelan in 1932 with the simple message: *In loving memory of God's poor. R.I.P.*

I read the notice at the gate: WHERE VERY MANY NAMELESS VICTIMS OF THE IRISH FAMINE OF 1845–47 ARE BURIED. ALSO BURIED HERE ARE OTHERS WHO DIED IN THE NEARBY WORKHOUSE BUILT 1840.

And then I turned, catching my breath at the fields spread wild. And the buttercups. And the main field. The Famine Field. I went to the library instead of the lecture. Instead of listening to other writers speak of their muse, I listened to my own. I remembered when I was one of Ireland's poor. Too poor to stay. Only words had brought me home.

One day, I will tell Sean where that track led me, and about the churchyard, but for now the moment is lost. Sean is still trying to make sense of his own newly discovered story. He is bewildered about his father's army career. 'It's so unlike him,' he keeps saying.

'I know. And a military policeman too. And a boxer.' I keep quiet about the beatings the boxer gave Mam. And the leather buckled belt.

'I was holding you at the time,' Mam had said, 'but that didn't stop him. Nothing stopped him when he was in one of his rages. The Bowsie O'Brien, that was your father. He wanted money for a pint on the quays before he met up with Father Sylvester for his poetry session. He emptied my purse on the table – the army always sent the money to the wife – and because there was nothing in it, he went berserk, dashing the dinner against the wall, smashing his fist on the table. He loved to use his belt. He'd wrap it round his fist like a boxing glove and punch the wall with it. He was using it then, swinging it and lashing the furniture with it. The buckle caught you on the spine and you screamed. You were only nine or ten months old. I was terrified he'd seriously injured you. Mr Grogan put him out of the house that night and Mrs Purcell sat up in the room with me until morning in case he came back. Joan and you were terrified. He was an animal. A bloody wild animal.'

I think of the man who scarred me, sitting in his garden in Pearson Park, refined, elegant, no belt wrapped around his blue-veined fist, and look across the table at his son, anxious to hear of his father's early life. It must be shocking for him to know his father had married his mother in a bigamous ceremony; was not the man he and his mother believed him to be. I seek the right words.

'He had to get out of Ireland quick. I do know that much, but I don't know why.'

The sun is filling the room in the heat of the afternoon. I know how Sean feels. It has been a long journey and a long day. He asks what barracks he was in.

'Portobello Barracks it was then. It's called Cathal Brugha now. He was also sent to McKee Barracks, though what they call that now, I don't know.'

I want to ask him if Dad was an antique dealer like it said on his death certificate, or if that title covered a multitude – I like antiques myself – but the question sticks in my throat. I have an impression he was a member of the Labour Party – I think that comes from one of Sean's poems – but again I can't bring myself to ask. It would be something else we had in common, my dad and me. Already, I am clutching at straws to weave the connection I need. I also have an idea that he painted, like Joan. She'd be delighted to know that he did too. But I can't ask and Sean can't say.

Connections? Are they wired in the blood? Written in the stars? Who made the connection between me and the man sitting opposite? By what route did he really arrive here? Where are coincidences rooted?

His eyelids are becoming heavy. Routinely at home, he says, he has a sleep in the afternoon, after a full morning writing. Refreshed, he is ready for another stint into the evening. I vow to follow his good example.

'Pat won't mind if you lie on the sofa in the other room,' Gerry says protectively.

I smile at Sean. 'I don't mind at all. You can go upstairs and lie on one of the beds if you like. You'll be much more comfortable.'

Routines apart, I know how stressful emotional upheaval can be and he is in the thick of it.

Sean excuses himself and goes upstairs, like any brother would in his sister's house. I can hear Barry and Gerry chatting in the kitchen. More coffee. More contemplation. I wonder at the significance of the day. I thought I had finished with revelations when I went to Hull ten years ago. I had not searched for Sean, I accidentally discovered him. He is up there now, resting. In ancient Ireland, poets sat at the right hand of the king, second only to royalty. Their arrival in a great house, with their family and followers, was met with feasting and entertainment for days. I think of all the cleaning and polishing I did to prepare for this visit and smile. Not everyone is lucky enough to find a poet as well as a brother at the same time. And it is finding the brother that pleases me most.

In this interlude while Sean rests, Gerry is telling us she is a schoolteacher, head of English, and I groan inwardly. Sean's mother was also a teacher, head of a girls' grammar school. I think of Mam and feel a stab of guilt. How would she feel if she knew I am entertaining her husband's secret son? I understand better her sharpness whenever she caught me with a pen in my hand and a faraway look in my eye. Poor Mam, with a life at just one remove from slavery because she didn't listen when her darlin' man recited his poems. She was too simple for him. Too ordinary. He wanted to move in intellectual circles and she paid the price. I wonder at the way life unfolds.

As we sit sipping coffee, my mind wanders off again. Barry and Gerry don't seem to mind; they have found some mutual topic. I leave them to it and stand on the inside of a rainy window with Mr Grogan, listening to his rich voice; straining to hear the trickle of the Swan River underground. Feeling my father's blood racing through my veins. Now there was a day that nudged my imagination. A Turning Day like the one in the Little White Churchyard. A Turning day like this.

I can hear Sean stirring above. Soon, he will be saying goodbye. I hope he has realised some of his expectations. It would be a shame if we were both disappointed. Too late, I wish I had been bolder, asked more questions. He might have answered them. Somehow, I have failed to make contact with the man he really is. I can hardly blame him for what seemed to be his secretiveness, defensiveness. Perhaps it is a family trait. Perhaps it is only with a pen that we can reveal ourselves.

The stairs creak, and he stands, smiling, in the room. I smile back, glad he came. We gather in the sitting room for the goodbyes.

Fresh as a daisy now and bright as a buttercup, Sean glances into a corner at a pen and ink drawing behind its unsuitable frame.

I take it down and hand it to him. 'It's Mountpleasant Square. The first few houses.' I point out the Purcell Rooms. 'I cut it out of an Irish newspaper years ago, so it's yellowed nicely now.'

Sean studies it intently. Is he thinking of his dad?

'Keep it,' I tell him impulsively.

He gracefully accepts, pleasing me.

Gerry takes a few more photographs as we go through the garden to complete their mementoes of the day and add to those taken at the table. We walk them to the car, promising to keep in touch. Then they are gone. Like that, in a finger snap, back to realities of their own.

Barry goes into the cottage and returns with two glasses and the remains of the bottle of wine. The garden is high-summer lush. We sit, listening to the hum of insects and bird calls, unwilling to voice unformed opinions until we know them. We sit until the sun dips behind a cloud.

'There was a boy,' I say, 'hidden behind the glass. I forgot about him until now.'

'What boy?' Barry is almost too lazy to form the words.

'In the picture I gave Sean. There was a boy standing on the first set of steps. The cutting was too big for the frame, so I folded him behind the glass. Out of sight.'

He doesn't answer, not seeing any significance at all in it.

'That way, the Purcell Rooms was more central in the frame.'

'So?' Barry might just drift off to sleep.

It would take too much explaining.

'So nothing,' I say. 'I just thought I'd mention it. That's all. No reason.' I begin to shiver. 'It's getting chilly.'

Going into the cottage to get a jacket, I marvel at the boy behind the glass. There, but not in the picture, just like Mam's shadow boy, behind the glass on Sean's wall. A shadow of Dad's first son, united with his second and much loved one. I will tell Sean about him next time we speak.

Twenty

'I think you'll have to come up to the hospital.' Joan is on the phone. 'Mam is very ill.'

'What's the matter with her? How ill do you mean?'

Joan struggles with her news. 'I don't think she'll get over this. The hospital calls it an intestinal blockage.'

Our conversation is stilted. I want to ask Joan so many questions, but I cannot.

'OK. I'll get there as soon as I can. Give me the details.'

Joan is sitting in the corridor, waiting to see the doctor. 'You can come in with me if you like,' she says, unaware that her invitation sounds like an exclusion order from my mother's life. It is not her fault that she has always been the favoured one. And God knows, her position has not always worked to her benefit. She never managed to escape as I have done. It occurs to me that Mam and Joan have each other, like Dad had Sean. Great double acts.

The doctor explains that Mam could not withstand an operation to remove the blockage. 'She is too old. Let me see.' He glances at her notes. 'She's eighty-nine. The best we can do is make her comfortable.'

We agree.

The old lady propped up on pillows is still in charge. 'You took your time getting here.' She is angry with me.

'I know, Mam, but I had to come a long way.'

She smiles a warm welcome for Joan and David, barely speaking to me at all.

A few years ago, I had let go of trying to please Mam. I woke up to the fact that no matter what I did, Mam was never going to have the same kind of relationship with me that she had with Joan. Joan was all she needed. And Joan's husband, David, who was very good to her.

We wait in the corridor while they transfer her to a side ward. Nurses and doctors walk past, smelling of death. It clings to their clothes like disinfectant; like their patients cling to life. Mam is clinging on, frightened of where she is going. She believes in heaven and hell and life ever after. Her fundamental Catholicism, such a comfort in her life, waits in the shadows as they grow darker.

'How long has she been ill?' I ask Joan.

'Well, she's been poorly for a long time, but this thing only developed a few days ago. I don't think she has long left. I know it will be hard for you when she goes, because of the way things were between you. I thought you ought to be here, though. She'll want to say goodbye to you.'

Although I sit with her, taking my turn to be there day and night, she never acknowledges me, preferring the attention of others.

She wakens early one morning and lies listening to rain pit-pitting on the window. 'I've always loved the sound of rain,' she says, and turns her head to gather up the insistent melody it is making on the glass.

I stare at her, doubting the clarity of her voice, wondering if speaking will ruin her pleasure. I go into the corridor, shaken with her revelation. I have always loved the sound of rain too. I wish I had known.

The hours are long and ripe with memories, some long-buried, as we sit while she decides when to go. I know her departure will be her decision. She seems to rally after a restless night. Exhausted, I race home to shower and grab some clean clothes to stuff in a bag. While I am doing these mundane things, she is playing the greatest scene of her life. Now, she says, I'll go now that I'm good and ready!

We never say goodbye.

The funeral is just before Christmas. 'The worst time of the year,' Mam used to say. It always reminded her of her mother and father. The irony strikes me. Here we are burying her on a day before Christmas Eve, just like them. Too many coincidences. Sean was born when Grandilla died in 1952. On the day of his funeral, the day before Christmas Eve, as I searched the headstones for my father's grave, he was holding his new son in his arms, his life renewed, not ended.

Paddy and Garry are already in the church with Joan as I arrive. It is packed to the back. I watch the white coffin containing her body at the altar.

'Mam had a dream,' Joan told me. 'She dreamt she was waiting at the doors of the church. All alone. All night and all morning and she was cold. She was wearing a flowing gown and she felt strange. She was waiting for people to arrive. Waiting for us.'

People are seating themselves at the back, behind us. The whisperings stop and a woman's voice, crystal, unaccompanied, soars with Mam's spirit, singing her song: 'I'll take you home again, Kathleen'.

There's a line in the song about a bonny bride. When Mam was Dad's bride, she was bonny. Beautiful. I used to look at her when she prepared to go out, not just to somewhere special, but to Mass, or down to Camden Street late on Saturday afternoon to buy the dinner for Sunday. Unlike Moll, who attracted the eye immediately, you had to let Mam's beauty dawn on you like a soft sunrise.

Where have the years gone? How did you get here, Mam? Where will you go now? The song ends. Maybe her spirit has gone home. We follow her hearse to the edge of town to lay her body in a Dartford graveyard. All alone.

'I have something to tell you, Joan,' I say afterwards. 'I think you might like to sit down.'

She sits on the sofa, balancing her teacup.

'You might need something a little stronger than that.' I am nervous, wondering where to start. 'I hope you'll understand why I didn't tell you while Mam was ill, or at the funeral.'

Her face is ashen.

'Don't worry. It's good news. Or at least I think it is.'

She urges me on.

'I've met Dad's son. Sean O'Brien. Do you remember when I found the house in Hull? His name was on the obituary.'

'Of course I remember. When did you meet him?' She is stunned by the news.

'Summer of 1999. He's a poet.'

She has not heard of him, but she is delighted. 'I'm not surprised by that at all, with Dad's love of poetry.'

'Not that it matters,' I say. 'He could have been a painter and decorator for all I care. It's just the coincidence of how I found him.' I tell her, recounting everything. 'I think I instinctively knew, but I couldn't accept it. I pondered on it for months. Strange, isn't it? Maybe some similarity of phrasing connected to a voice in my head. I don't know, but I recognised him by his words.'

Joan has let me ramble on, almost incoherently.

'It's unreal,' she says. 'Did you get on well with him?'

'I think so. At one level, we seemed to get on, but we were polite. Like strangers. And of course there were two other people there. His partner, Gerry, and my friend, Barry.'

'Perhaps you'd have been better had it been just the two of you.'

'Perhaps, but I was glad of the moral support. I suppose he was too.'

I realise I still have to tell her about finding Dad's poems. It is going to be a long day.

'Come on.' I lead her to the kitchen. 'Let's get another cup of tea, it's quite a story.'

We talk all afternoon. I sort out a collection of Dad's poems. They make her cry. I know she is with him by the canal. Having great gas.

'Why didn't Mam tell us? It might have made all the difference to us, having something of his when we were young.'

'She wasn't able to, Joan. The words would have choked her.'

We sit for hours, going over everything. And then going over it all again. After a while, she stands, exhausted. She has to get home. At the door, she kisses my cheek and I hug her, unusual for us.

'I thought when we buried Mam, it was the end of them,' Joan says. 'Mam and Dad. Both dead. The other Mrs O'Brien, by her silence, dead to us too.'

'I hoped at first, when Mam got the pension, that Sean's mother would try to find us. She never did. Fair enough, I thought, after a couple of years. That's it. At least we know a little of what happened to Dad. We should be thankful for that. Then I discovered Sean. Instead of ending, the story has opened out to another horizon.'

Joan agrees. 'I can't believe Dad lived with Sean and his mother and never ever spoke to them of his past. It's what people do. Talk about their lives. It's the way we make sense of things.'

When she has left, I feel relieved I have told her, but I wish it would all evaporate. Disappear. I feel heartily sick of wondering and wishing.

Moments later, the phone rings.

'Patty,' Joan says, surprising me, she must only have walked into her house. 'I can't get it all out of my mind. I'm going to read the book of Sean's poems, as well as the copies of Dad's, but I'd really like to meet Sean. Do you think he'd like to meet me too?'

'I'm sure he would. I gave him your name and address when he first phoned me. And your phone number. I know he never wrote to you. He told me when he came to see me. He said he wanted to take one step at a time, which is understandable. But let me write to him first and tell him I've told you about him.'

I am feeling uneasy about Sean. I have a sense that he would like to fade quietly away, distance himself. Keep Dad's secrets and any his mother might have. Since his visit eighteen months ago, he has phoned a few times. He asked about where we had lived in Dublin. He was going there for a poetry event. He thought he would like to see for himself. I gave him the addresses of Mountpleasant Square and Rugby Villas, thinking how easy it was for him, when I had to search so hard for all the missing pieces.

'You'll have to meet me when you come back and let me know what you make of it all,' I said. 'Maybe then you'll be able to tell me all about him, Sean?'

It has been dawning on me that he never will divulge anything unless he is openly asked – but how can I? Asking about Dad always ended in guilt. In tears. Doesn't Sean understand that our long search indicates a consuming need to know about Dad? Should he wish to revisit Dad's past, I've told him all he needs to know. He will be able to meander back over trodden paths at his leisure, not set out on a long and arduous trek over uncharted grounds as we have done. I wish he would reciprocate. Little things:

305

whether Dad smoked or drank, went fishing or preferred golf. Perhaps he loved Yeats? I long for a true sense of him. I am frustrated with Sean's hoarding of these small gems. I can never take what he has of Dad. Why is he being so closed? I wish I could help him to open up, find a way to communicate with him, get him to see things from my perspective.

I send him a Christmas card with a note about Mam's death. He sends one back, saying he is sorry. Later I write that Mam's death has brought Joan and I together again. 'She would love to speak with you,' I tell him, 'but appreciates the need for you to make the choice. I think we both realised that life is too short and too precious to bear resentments or grudges. It is also important to piece as much of the "jigsaw" together as possible.'

He does not reply, nor does he contact Joan. I feel now that I probably went about it all the wrong way, frightened him off, perhaps.

Joan decides to write herself. She agonises for hours on the wording. It has to convey her needs, while respecting his right to privacy. She does not seek a relationship. Just knowledge of Dad. It takes only a week to get a reply. Not from Sean, but from Gerry.

'Just listen without interruption.' Joan's voice is choking with emotion.

I listen in complete silence. Gerry's letter, though sympathetically worded, cannot be mistaken for anything other than a warding off. She appreciates our feelings, our need to know, but says that Sean has difficulty with meetings that have to be kept from his mother. She hopes that the little she is able to tell Joan will be of some consolation for the time being. The letter comes with a signed copy of Sean's latest book, which he has asked her to enclose.

We are both lost for words. Joan is upset, torn between hurt and anger.

Next morning, I too receive a copy of Sean's book, with a copy of the letter to Joan and one for me. Gerry tells me he enjoyed our meeting, but is finding it hard to adjust. He is scrupulously honest, and has always been completely open with his mother. He find all this very difficult. She goes on to say that I can keep in touch with her, if it helps, and she will let me know what is happening in his life.

I am wounded by these letters and fold them into the pages of the book. I will need time to recover my humour, as well as my enthusiasm to continue with my search for the truth of my father. But I know I will continue. If we cannot ask our father's son about him, we'll have to ask whoever will tell us.

Joan is just as determined as I am. 'He is our father too,' she says. 'Whether or not Sean wishes to speak to us about him, we have a right to act as we see fit. Mam was his legal next of kin. I am hers. The issue is not whether we should or shouldn't make further enquires, but how we go about it.'

'But where will we start, Joan? I don't think I can face any more journeys or disappointments.'

'I know you've done most of the digging and delving. If you like, I'll carry on with it. The Irish army seems as good a place as any for now. Who knows, we might finally learn why he really had to get out of Ireland.'

I let her take up the search, unable for the moment to face it myself.

Twenty-one

Joan's studio and art gallery pretends it is a home. Stepping into her cosy sitting room from the street keeps up the pretence. All is as it should be. Until she opens the other door into what she calls the dining room. On polished surfaces, she mixes her paints, spreading the tubes, pots and canvases everywhere. Her easel faces the window and the light. On the walls and stacked against them, her paintings pose, defying the homeliness around her, struggling with cushions and convention.

'If we knew where Dad ran his antique business, we might find people who remember him,' Joan says, dabbing the brush, squinting. 'Have a look at the local paper while I finish this. There's an interesting piece about a man who found sisters he never knew he had. In Canada, they were. I think there was one here too. He found her through the electoral roll. Says he wants to help others do the same.'

'Really?'

'He's had more luck than us. His sisters are ecstatic. He's flying out to Canada to meet them with the sister from here. They want to celebrate their good fortune.'

I read aloud: 'They want to keep in contact now they've found each other.'

'There's a phone number for that man. He'd like to hear from anyone who might need his help tracing their families. I thought maybe he might be able to trace Mary Irene.'

'Sean won't like that. I think he is finding it hard, coming to terms with the secrets of his father's past.'

'We are that past, Pat. Inevitably, we're always going to be associated with betrayal in his mind. Maybe he'd rather turn the clock back. Stay ignorant about it. Living with his father's lies might have been better.' Joan is torn between sympathy and frustration.

'No. I asked him once if he'd rather not have known about Dad. Without hesitation, he said he would rather know. Don't worry, Joan. One day he might have to face our refusal to share any more of what we have of our father with him.'

'We have nothing more to give.'

'Oh, yes, we do, Joan. We have our children.' I tap her shoulder and give her the thumbs-up. 'He may be in dire need of our generosity one day.'

'What could he possibly want?'

'He might need a kidney!'

We both laugh.

'Apart from Sean himself, his mother is the only one who can tell us about him. If we wait, we may never have our minds made easy. For far too long, we've been told to shut up, wait, put others first. I don't know about you, but I'm sick and tired of being the sacrificial lamb.'

Wiping her hands on a rag, she picks the phone up and dials the man in the paper. He is only too pleased to help. After taking the details, he promises to phone back as soon as he has any information.

'How long do you think it'll take, Joan?'

'He didn't say. He has to go on the Internet. We'll have to wait and see.'

Ten minutes later, he reads out Mary Irene's address. He also provides her phone number.

'I don't know how to thank you,' Joan says. 'We really wouldn't have known where to start. I'm not sure yet what we'll do, there are so many implications . . .'

'Shall I speak to her?' I say.

After two rings and a lifetime, Mary Irene O'Brien is saying hello. The woman who lived with my dad for thirty years is speaking to me.

'Hello?' she says again, in such a straightforward way.

'Hello,' I say, trying to sound ordinary too, 'are you the Mrs O'Brien who lived in Pearson Park, Hull?'

She answers that she is and waits for confirmation of who I am. What my reason is for phoning now.

'I am Patrick O'Brien's daughter and my sister Joan is sitting with me. It is not our intention to cause any upset.' I hope she can hear the truth in my voice.

She is shocked, telling me she knew of me. She wants to know how we found her.

'The electoral roll. A man on the Internet. We have been searching for our father a long time. I would not be phoning you at all . . . I hoped Sean . . . I mean, I hoped Sean would give us information. I've been waiting for something, anything, since we met two years ago. We have a need to know about our father.'

I wait. This must be overwhelming for her; actually speaking to her late husband's daughter. She tells me again she knew of us. It is still a shock. I let her recover, hoping she doesn't hang up. When she does speak, I am surprised by what she says. Even after two years, Sean has still not told her about the contact we've had.

'Perhaps he didn't want to upset you. He was protecting you, I imagine.'

Her restraint is remarkable. She sounds as if I might like her. I want to carry on with the conversation, aware that the least pressure on my part will end it.

'You say you knew about us?'

Someone, a social worker, visited and sat her down telling her she had no right to his pension. It belonged to his legal wife. Her voice is firm, yet there is a kindness in it.

'You and Sean are the only ones who can tell us about him.'

She asks me what it is I want to know.

'Everything. What he did for a living. Likes and dislikes. Mannerisms. Everything. We were never allowed to mention him. It was awful, not knowing where he was.'

Although she understands our need to know, she will have to think about it. I ask if she will discuss it with Sean. Possibly, but she never told him about losing her pension.

'We don't blame you for what our father did, but you could help us now,' I tell her. 'That's all we want.'

She wants time to think about it, though she does understand. She is shaky. She asks for my number. She will call me back.

'I will be leaving to go home to Ramsgate. You can call me there, or speak to Joan.'

She promises to call this evening.

'Goodbye for now. I appreciate you listening to me.'

I smile at Joan. We are both a bit tearful. Every other step forward took months and years of agonising before we could make a decision, yet the phone call had been so simple.

'She won't phone you,' Joan says, starting to work on her canvas once more.

'She said she would. Twice she said it. I think she will. I had to trust her, didn't I? I think she'll try to anticipate my questions when she recovers from the shock and prepare something before she calls.'

Joan is not sure. 'She might write instead. Or she might do nothing.'

'Let's wait and see. We're good at that.'

I watch the clock all evening, Doubts creep in. Maybe she wrote the number down incorrectly. But she repeated it back to me. Perhaps she is finding it too stressful, dealing with a voice from her partner's past. Did he ever speak of us? Where there times when he appeared to be somewhere else? What did he tell her about his mother? About his early life? Was everything an invention, or was truth woven through it? He could not have invented a completely false background, could he? It must be devastating for her, I think, if everything was a fabrication.

When he died, she made all the arrangements. Took control. Wrote the death notice. Had him cremated instead of buried. Requested no flowers. Called herself his widow. Wife of the deceased. His death notice did not mention his life beyond the one he shared with her and Sean. In it, he was nobody's son. Nobody's brother. Nobody else's father. Only part of them. Late only of Hull. Until this day when lives and truth converged. Unlike the earlier convergence with Sean, when a collision had been avoided by my application of the brakes, when I did not ask directly for what I wanted, we have collided head on, Mary Irene and me, though our mutual politeness cushioned the impact. I have asked. The question is, will I receive?

When the late news comes on at ten, I accept that she will not phone. Not tonight. Not on any night. Whatever she knows about my father she intends to keep. She will not relinquish the keys to his kingdom. I tidy away the papers and the clutter, dim the lights. Switch off the television. I imagine she is preparing for bed too. I wonder if it sits well with her, her decision not to phone. As my father's memory's keeper, is she aware that there are keys she will never own, including the keys to our rooms of dust?

Joan agrees with my decision not to phone her again. 'She knows who we are and where we are. If she wants to put things right, she knows what she has to do.'

'What if she doesn't want to do anything, like Sean?'

314

'Then that will have been a conscious choice. To tell us nothing. She will have to live with it. There are other routes to the truth of him.'

The other routes are dead ends, with the possibilities of other families in other parts of Ireland. I don't think I could cope with any more stepmothers or half-siblings. One of each is quite enough. The man in the records office in Dublin thinks different. Patrick Francis O'Brien had lived in Cork. As a soldier. After he left us in the Purcell Rooms.

'He may have lived in your house a long time ago, perhaps 1945 to 1950, maybe longer, possibly as late as 1977,' Joan writes to the address in Cork.

When the reply comes, the current residents say they have never heard of him. They have asked older neighbours who have no recollection of him either.

'Just think,' I tell Joan, 'we could have a string of brothers and sisters stretching from Limerick to Ranelagh, down to Cork and back again before he ever set foot in Hull.'

'Well if we find any, don't go playing Mother Teresa of the O'Briens and Bards, doling out your scraps of information like alms. Let them drop a penny or two in your poor box first.'

'Do you really think he had other wives and families?' I ask her.

She shrugs. 'Maybe he just needed an audience.'

In the middle of our fantasies, an army commandant phones from Dublin. Irate. He asks her where she got her information. She tells him. It was wrong. The man in Cork was an honourable man. He was not her father. The Commandant did not usually get involved in tracing ex-soldiers, but in the circumstances, because of his concerns about the false identification, he will investigate further himself. He will send her a copy of her father's service record when he writes.

'Back to the drawing board, then?' I say, wondering if we could get into *The Guinness Book of Records* for the longest search ever.

The letter arrives at last, confirming that he enrolled in the defence services in August 1935 and was discharged in October 1944. Nine years and fifty-two days service. Because of defective vision. In January 1941, he attained the rank of acting corporal, reverting to private in September 1944. The records show that he was 'over-enthusiastic' arresting a soldier, was confined to barracks after insub-ordination to an officer, then lost his stripes. The Commandant hoped that the material would be of use. He could not provide any more. Dismissed.

Mam was right. Bowsie O'Brien, liberal with his fists. It is clear that he was involved in a serious assault resulting in a charge. Shortly afterwards he was declared medically unfit, and he was discharged. What did he do between then and the date he left Ireland in 1945? How did he earn a living? Mam must have known he had left the army because his pay would have been stopped. No longer able to command respect, he must have felt a considerable loss of self-esteem. Jobs and money were scarce then. I cannot imagine him spending his days in the Purcell Rooms. Whatever the causes of his exodus, no doubt he will have rewritten the story over and over again. Will we ever know the real cause? What is it that Mam repeatedly hinted at? What final awful thing did he do?

Joan has some other documents to show me.

'While I was waiting for replies from Ireland, I managed to get hold of the bigamous marriage certificate in 1952. That took place in Ealing and he gave his profession then as "salesman (general merchandise)". He promoted his father to "sergeant major (Munster Fusiliers)".'

'Marvellous how he could levitate the dead,' I say. 'On his legal marriage certificate, when he married Mam, his father was a labourer. It was Grandilla who was a sergeant major, in the Royal Irish Fusiliers. They had their biggest rows about that. Him a Free Stater, and Grandilla taking the king's shilling. I suppose he transferred his father-in-law's rank to his own father so that when he was telling his tales, he wouldn't trip himself up. He could relate Grandilla's experiences with confidence. And when Malachy saw him on Chiswick Bridge, no wonder he sprinted like one of Sean Ryan's greyhounds. There goes the galloping Major!'

Joan implores with open hands, 'Ah, now, Patty, be fair. He could hardly invite Malachy back to meet the family, could he?'

Did Patrick Francis O'Brien know who he was himself? I wonder. Where did he call home? He must have had an amazing memory, every day another part to play. Did he masquerade as an antique dealer, the best the trade could offer?

'I can't imagine a man of his pretensions selling junk off an oul' pram, can you?'

'No,' Joan says, 'I can't, but life is full of surprises.'

It occurs to me that we are doing too much talking and not enough action.

'I think it's about time I took another trip to Hull. Either I find an oul' pram in the duck pond or I find his antique emporium. Whatever, I will leave him there, in his final resting place.'

Thirteen years after my first visit to Hull, I traipse in the rain, in and out of the 'antique district' around the corner from Pearson Park. Chances of finding someone who remembers him are slim, but I might be lucky to find someone ten or so years younger than him, still working. The only Irishman remembered is called Jerome. The man in Philip Larkin's house had told me that too. I leave my phone number in several shops, for elderly owners.

The man in this palace of varieties has a lived-in face. There is an air of permanence about him and the shop. I leave my umbrella at the door, and go drip-dripping towards the polished counter, waltzing between Victorian spoon-backs, jardinières, an Art Deco bureau, ebonised heads, tables with Limoges bowls and majolica pots, Meissen parrots, Staffordshire dogs. Over Turkish rugs, I trip the light fantastic, chin up and smiling, hoping to God the man eyeing me with suspicion knew my father.

'There was a man used to sit at the back of Jerome's shop,'

he says, polishing a silver candlestick. 'Never spoke though.'

'Can you remember his name?'

'I can't recall ever knowing it.'

Dejection is setting in. Nothing lifts this barrier to my father. My energies are flagging. Tired and cold, I turn to leave.

'You say he lived in Pearson Park?'

'In the house next to the one Philip Larkin lived in.' Everyone around here must know that house, surely?

'I know it. Near the duck pond,' the man concedes, still polishing.

'Yes. That's right. Near the duck pond.'

'No. I know of no O'Brien who lived near there. If your father was an antique dealer in the seventies, I'd definitely have known him.'

'He had a son, Sean. He went to Hull University one time.'

His stares blankly. 'Pity you didn't try to find him. He's the one to tell you all you want to know.'

I keep a civil tongue. 'We met three years ago. He didn't tell me anything. That's why I'm still searching.'

He puts down the candlestick. I wait. I always wait. He gets a pen and a scrap of paper. 'I wish I could help. Everyone has a right to know about their own parents. What's the point of learning anything if we don't learn our own history? Write your phone number. I'll ask around. If he was genuine, we'll find him. If he traded anywhere the length and breath of Yorkshire, someone will know of him.'

I scribble down my phone number for the umpteenth time. This time, it might be worth it. 'Sorry to trouble you,'

I say. 'I really do appreciate your offer to help. Thank you so much.'

The house is still a nursing home. Braver than I was the first time, I ring the bell, glancing at the building, an impersonal monument to the mystery of Dad. I step in when the assistant invites me. If his ghost is here, I don't sense it. The woman goes away to find someone who can help. I place my hand on the banister, shuddering inwardly, thinking of his hand gliding along it. Morning, noon and night; going upstairs or down, gliding through lies and deception.

'Dad,' I whisper, summoning him, 'if you hear me, help me. Help me find whatever it is I need so I can bury you and let go.'

'Did you say something?' the woman asks, returning.

'I was only talking to myself,' I tell her, 'trying to remember something I've misplaced. First sign, eh?' I manage a smile.

'What is it you want, dear? Only nobody here knows anything about the people who lived here years ago.' She is very polite, trying not to rush me.

'Do you mind if I look around? I'd like to get an impression of him living here.'

She hesitates. I could be a mad woman. Probably am. I lose things and talk to myself.

'If you don't mind doing it yourself, you're welcome, but not upstairs, there are some people very ill in bed.'

It is pointless trying to conjure up the rooms as they used to be. The elegance of the high ceilings and wide windows are just a backdrop to uniformity. Zimmer frames and trolleys bar my way through doors. There is nothing here that has my father's stamp on it.

'Bye, thank you,' I call out and stand in the porch, not knowing which way to turn.

Rain drizzles miserably on the trees. Still, I want to walk across the park once more. I want to sit and watch the ducks. From a window, the woman keeps her eye on me. Before I cross over to the duck pond, I walk along the side of the house. I want to see the back garden, where he sat with Sean and Mary Irene, playing the part of the refined old gentleman who has earned his golden days. The garden is small. I had hoped to see paths meandering through shrubbery to a potting shed. His refuge. I wanted him to be a gardener and grow trumpet lilies fluted at the fence. I wanted proof that he had been here. I cannot find it. There is an old terrace and stunted flower beds against a northern wall. No ethereal perfume fills the air, only the smell of fish steaming in the kitchen.

The ducks huddle on their muddy island. I huddle in my coat. He is gone from this place too. Sean spoke of him being full of melancholy, brooding and often withdrawn, as he neared the end of his life. Maybe he was thinking of his religious zeal; haunted by his own lines:

> Tyrants who have ruled by poverty.
> The fear
> Take ear
> As conscience, grinning with reflected

> Leer
> Calls sanity from its blood-celled
> Dungeons.
> Fool!

He must have been a fool, to have built up a lifetime of regrets. If he believed in the religious poetry he wrote, he must have dreaded his last breath. Did he lie in bed in the house waiting for his final moment, listening to rain tapping on the windowpane? Tapping out the secrets of his life, calling him to account. Did he like lingering in a Dublin garden with Sally. Did the memory make him smile?

Twenty-two

I know this will have to be goodbye. I have to let go of my hope that I will somehow discover for myself just what sort of man my father was. All I have are other people's opinions, nearly all damning. Despite the rain, falling fine and insistent, I am in no hurry to let these last moments go. I try to focus on what it is I would like to tell him, if I could speak to him, but a long ago memory invades, the day I brought Rita Mullen home after school. I lose myself in it. We were having the grand tour, the way kids did then, inquisitive, always poking and prying when the adults had their backs turned. I was letting her have a look, showing her upstairs, opening bedroom doors, letting her poke her head around them.

'This is my room,' I said, showing her the return room where Mam, Joan and I slept.

'Oh,' she said, 'do you sleep in that big bed all by yourself?'

'This is me sister's room,' I said, showing her the back bedroom with the big iron bed and the feather mattress where the boys slept.

'Oh,' she said, 'it must be lovely for her sleeping in that squashy bed all to herself.'

'Yes,' said I, 'she's like the princess and the feckin' pea when she's in it, calling Mam all night long to plump it up for her.'

I rolled my eyes and Rita rolled hers and we got hysterical, giggling, holding each other up in the room. I knew Grandilla would be mortified at a young-one like Rita making so free in his home. I kept going all the same.

'And this is Mam's room.' I flung open the door to Grandilla's room like an estate agent.

It was dark, because the blinds were down. I pulled them up and let her pick things up and put them down. She was turning on lamps and smelling books and stroking the fringes of the eiderdown. She picked up one of Grandilla's pipes and stuck it in her mouth.

'Goney,' she said, 'my mammy only smokes Woodbines.'

On the stairs, she asked where my daddy's room was. I'd run out of bedrooms. I was at the big wardrobe on the landing where Grandilla kept his books.

'Here,' said I, opening the door and looking in. She watched me, while I had half a conversation with the daddy in the wardrobe. 'He's lying down with a headache. We're to go out and play and stop tormenting him with our giggling and carrying on.'

Rita knew it was only a wardrobe, but she never said anything.

I sigh. It is easier to imagine him in the wardrobe than here.

It's all so extraordinary, poetry and poets. Words. Always there were words, I think, trying to find some to say to Dad.

Without a body or a ceremony, burying the dead seems impossible. I don't belong in this northern park. Did he have a sense of belonging? Or did he long for somewhere else? I ask him and when I finally speak to him, the words are easy.

'Do you remember Mountpleasant Square, Dad? And the house? So elegant. It lifted us up in all that poverty. The people were elegant, Mrs Purcell and Bella. And Mr Grogan. They spoke like poets too. I loved that house. And that Square. We used to visit them all until we too left Ireland. I used to think I'd find you there every time I returned. I'd stand on the step waiting for one of them to answer the door, and hold my breath in case exhaling would blow you away. Only Mr Grogan knew I watched for you in the Purcell Rooms. Only Mr Grogan made me feel important because I was your daughter. "Paddy O'Brien's girl from Swan River," he used to say, and my heart would swell to bursting. Things could have been so different if you had stayed. I think you might have liked me, Dad. I wanted to like you too.'

I have always made sense of events by working out connections between one and another, mapping beginnings and endings, building bridges in my mind to name the moments. Flagging up the junctions. I am doing it now, realising that my journey to Hull began the day he left us forever in St Stephen's Green. Watching him disappear in the going-home umbrellas has always been connected to the tramp at Portobello, planning to follow the Grand Canal all the way to where it meets the Shannon. To Limerick. I could have gone, too, but I had a journey of my own to make.

'When I get there,' the tramp said, 'I'll turn back and contemplate it all from the other direction.'

And now that is what I have to do. The duck pond in this place is my Shannon. There is nowhere else to go. I have torn away the umbrellas shielding him from my sight. It is time for me to listen to the tramp.

My hands are wet. The gloves I am wearing are itchy, letting the rain soak through, serving no good purpose. I take them off and ball them together, squeezing, contemplating the other direction. Turning back. The ones I wore in the Green were mittens. On a string that went up the sleeves of my coat and across my shoulders, keeping them attached in case they got lost. I couldn't bear the wetness on my hands. All I could think of was getting home to take them off.

When I came to Hull the first time and found his house and his secret life, it was raining then too. And people with umbrellas were walking through the park. After we found the death notice and learned about his beloved son, I wrote a poem. I just wrote it to remind me of the day Dad left. Making a connection. Building my bridge between Dublin and Hull with words. I sent it to Sean, including him in it. He never commented on it. Perhaps it was just as well. It was not written to impress. It was only a memory. And the voice of a girl a long time ago.

I stand up and throw the gloves right into the centre of the pond. Plop. The ducks flap, then settle down again. Then I say my poem, loudly and without hesitation. I say it for Dad, my epitaph for all that never came to pass:

'Mittens, 1989'

Mittens wrapped around cold fingers
Breezes blowing on spindle bark of naked trees
Buses breaking green striped through
The rails in ever-mourning black

He is standing too tall for me to look him in the eye
My seven years have not taught me
How best to say goodbye
So I say nothing

The Green surrounds the ribbon paths
That will transport him to a future with a son
Mere girl I am and so small it is no surprise
He cannot see me at all

My shoes are shining, buckles bright
I hear my mother cry, a strange noise
Like a bird trapped under a stone
Squashed. Her wings are broken.

In a minute he'll be gone forever
And we can go back to the warm kitchen
And I can hang my damp mittens
By the fire.

Acknowledgements

Many people have encouraged and supported me with writing this book and I am indebted to them all. Special thanks are due to: my sons, Stuart, Tony and Graham Winchester for their faith, over many years, that it would be written; my sister, Joan Martin, and Paddy and Garry O'Toole, who shared so much; my dear friends Terry MacKay and Barry Revell; and Lee Dunne and Robin Hardy for their generous advice.

Immeasurable gratitude must go to the publishers of *Assisi* in the 1940s, and to the staff and Franciscan Brothers of the Church of the Immaculate Conception, Adam & Eve's, Dublin, who preserved for me my father's voice.

Deserving also of my appreciation are the publishing staff and editors involved with bringing this book to life, especially Cassandra Campbell, Angela Herlihy, Deirdre O'Neill and Siobhan Parkinson. Finally, for everything, thanks to Treasa Coady who made it possible!